Persia Triumphant
in Greece

Persia Triumphant in Greece

Xerxes' Invasion:
Thermopylae, Artemisium and
the Destruction of Athens

Manousos E. Kambouris

Pen & Sword
MILITARY

First published in Great Britain in 2022 by
Pen & Sword Military
An imprint of
Pen & Sword Books Ltd
Yorkshire – Philadelphia

ISBN 978 1 39909 775 8

A CIP catalogue record for this book is
available from the British Library.

Typeset by Mac Style
Printed and bound in India by Replika Press Pvt. Ltd.

MIX
Paper from
responsible sources
FSC
www.fsc.org   FSC® C016779

Pen & Sword Books Limited incorporates the imprints of Atlas, Archaeology,
Aviation, Discovery, Family History, Fiction, History, Maritime, Military, Military
Classics, Politics, Select, Transport, True Crime, Air World, Frontline Publishing,
Leo Cooper, Remember When, Seaforth Publishing, The Praetorian Press,
Wharncliffe Local History, Wharncliffe Transport, Wharncliffe True Crime
and White Owl.

For a complete list of Pen & Sword titles please contact

PEN & SWORD BOOKS LIMITED
47 Church Street, Barnsley, South Yorkshire, S70 2AS, England
E-mail: enquiries@pen-and-sword.co.uk
Website: www.pen-and-sword.co.uk

Or

PEN AND SWORD BOOKS
1950 Lawrence Rd, Havertown, PA 19083, USA
E-mail: Uspen-and-sword@casematepublishers.com
Website: www.penandswordbooks.com

This book is dedicated:

To *Manitarita obnoxia*, the love of my life
and the Shadows of the Fallen in the line of Duty

Contents

Introduction

After Marathon

The Battle of Marathon (490 BC) was the first straight infantry clash the Persian Empire lost to the Greeks. All involved parties understood the moral impact; it was not just the defeat, which was a first but, much more importantly, it broke the perceived invincibility of the Achaemenids heralding the possibility of deliverance to their subjects, nor was it just the immense confidence gained by the Greeks. After all, Scythia had shown them of human proportions and not of divine mandate. But in the battlefield, in an open battle, it is possibly the first outright defeat of Darius' proxies.

The magnitude of the defeat was just as important; the hard core of the expedition was annihilated, elite Saka subjects and crack Persian troops. The latter may have been first-line assault infantry, or close-combat seasoned veterans, as the revelations of Xenophon on Persian mobilization patterns may indicate (Cyrop I.2,9 & 13) if combined with some interpretation by Herodotus (Her VI.112,2). Most definitely, the greater number of those killed in action were no expendable subjects, despite the fact that even this line of thought is fundamentally mistaken. Such levies, raised with care and from selected subjects, were and still are the building blocks of an empire, as the latter is always in short supply of enough warriors of the master race to expand continuously and, even more so, to garrison and guard the conquests and keep the subservient populations in check and competitors at bay. From a long line of such willing subjects came the Gurkhas and Maori units of the British Empire and the Roman *auxilia* who were to show some millennia later, whether the 'Allies' of the Athenian and the American Empires and the 'Comrades' of the Soviet Empire are considered any different in form, if not in function.

If Darius received a proper and honest debriefing (and this is a big 'If') on the campaign of Marathon, he would understand that the problem was not the event, nor the magnitude of the defeat, but that the Greeks used in the battle a novel approach, called Generalship. It was difficult to digest that these unruly simpletons planned and executed something unheard of, exercising control in the middle of the battle so as to manoeuvre during the different stages of a collision. Similarly, the way they conducted the campaign was flawless: it is true, they did not seek battle after having won it, but they did anything to increase their possibilities of success. And they showed that they knew very well both themselves and their enemy.

Of course, all these are the wisdom of Sun Tzu; Darius had never heard of the man who lived some years earlier and closer to the East; nor he had any reason not to think the whole mess as just some bad luck. But he may have felt that there was something amiss. He had the common sense to immediately embark upon a next round, hoping to reverse the psychology and right the damage suffered in terms of prestige, before such ideas sank into his own subjects and propagated, especially amongst prospective subjects.

It was the second failure in a row, as Mardonius had a disastrous experience and given the sub-stellar performance of his choices during the Ionian Revolt, things were not inspiring confidence. Darius thought that he should take the field himself one more time. He thought it prudent to prepare a major campaign, not an expedition. He also must have thought that the novelties such as amphibious campaigns should be aborted and more orthodox campaigning should be reverted to, to allow larger size and more comfort in supplies and support, that would permit exploration of more options without being affected by possible aggregation of hostiles and neutrals. But this is not a safe conclusion, as we know the strategic choice of Xerxes. Whether the northern route was Darius' or Xerxes' decision is not clear. The magnitude of the preparations indicate that Darius had opted for this, but a solid proof is missing. On the other hand, elite, small expeditionary forces were out of the picture. Competent Greek armies could annihilate them, and their fabled mobility in a country of many passes and a patchwork of political entities was to dilute and isolate them. A show of might could, on the other hand, once more, as in Thrace, lead to individual capitulations that would form a domino effect if not a tidal wave. And it would allow for further expansion in Europe.

If the Achaemenids were set on a rematch, Greeks were also. Not the victorious Athenians; they thought they had conquered the Persians. After sulking, trembling and some other phases of psychological fluctuations, they were feeling the bliss of deliverance but also the intoxication of triumph. True, their exploitation of their victory was nothing short of a fiasco in Paros, but they blamed the architect of Victory and that was the end of it. With one swift move they failed to learn and they got rid of the main architect of their victory. Their victory also made them much more aggressive against their neighbour, Aegina and perhaps Corinth; highly arrogant towards the whole of Greece and especially the Spartans (a feeling not altogether unwarranted, to be honest) and most un-vigilant. Not simply beating but crushing the enemy at his game after a decade of reverses was an excellent pretext to abort the programme of Themistocles for naval aggrandizement, as the Hoplites returned and reigned supreme (although their commander was rotting in prison) and also to forget about their ridiculous incompetence to seriously degrade the enemy fleet, caught vulnerable on the beach with broken spirits and no discipline and cohesion.

But there was one Athenian that did expect a rematch and was preparing for it: Themistocles. It took him many years to draw the teeth of the opposition and recast his naval programme, in the nick of time and thanks to a silver bonanza found in the mines of Laurium, at the southern tip of Attica. At least this allowed a resource to finance the construction of vessels and, just as importantly and seldom mentioned, to raise and train crews (a most expensive proposition), without vexing his well-to-do citizens. Giving a means of life to them or their brethren, so as not to fear for insurrections, coups and outright treason, as in Marathon, made the patriotic element of the Hoplite class accept the idea of the investment in a fleet. Timber must have come from Macedon, from King Alexander I, explaining his prestige in the city; shipwrights must have come from the West, from the Corcyraeans, the Sicilian and Italiot Greek cities, enticed by the spending spree of Athens and contacted by Themistocles during his western trade dealings.

And then, there were the Spartans. Their heavy-handed dealing with the Aeginitean Medizers somehow brought the island state squarely in line and it never flinched in its allegiance in the upcoming war; the Athenians were far less stable. It may have been to no small extent due to Aristides the Just, who was residing in their midst, a Hero of Marathon banned from Athens due to Themistocles, so as the latter could proceed with his shipbuilding programme.

The meticulousness the Spartans showed in Marathon, to study the field and the dead, was professional but also indicative of the fact that they were considering the event an opening act rather than a showdown. True, this was under their maverick King Cleomenes, who was probably deceased by the mid-480s if not earlier, but the whole staff and chain of command that supported him remained intact after his demise. All these, under his successor Leonidas had the blueprints and the expertise of the renegade and plainly ingenious king. And the blueprints were drafted to the tune of a war of manoeuvre, as coined in late 60s (Samuels 1997; Elliot-Bateman 1968).

The Persian forces were by definition manoeuvrable; without this quality an empire was not within their potential. Under Darius I, who became an exemplary city-taker as seen in Behistun inscriptions, this manoeuvrability was used for positional warfare purposes. Massive hosts with siege trains spell the Achaemenid supremacy in positional warfare and this rang true in the Ionian Revolt. Marathon, on the other hand, following the Scythian example, showed that although highly mobile, the Imperial forces were dependent on heavy support trains and thus mobile warfare was not their best, although in many cases they were still pursuing victory by subjugating an enemy army and not by occupying terrain features. But occupation, especially of cities, by assault, or siege, was their standard operating procedure (SOP) throughout the clash with the Greeks.

The Greeks were going to take it a step further; although they were following the set-piece battle approach (Her VII.9) – a feature of mobile warfare – they had no mobility advantage over the Imperials, nor the terrain of Scythia so as to manoeuvre with clear advantages. What is very impressive is that they made their country work for them, not by strengthening defensive positions so much as by giving them a manoeuvring advantage not seemingly possible by the comparison of the mobile elements of the two hosts. The Greek strategy, if taken as a whole, tried to disrupt the enemy, mess with its command and support, expose its units to the elements, and keep him uncertain by changing tactics and approaches and finally trying to beat the very few key enemy commanders (especially the *Karana*) instead of the troops and their leaders. This approach with armies of allied constitution that used similar or identical troop types but without having met, trained and operated together was a Herculean task, and its implementation *ad hoc* and with minimal pitfalls must be credited to the professionalism of the Spartans; after all, the moment the Athenians led a campaign, which happened after the staggering success of the Greek counter-attack at the Hellespont in 479 BC, conquest of cities (as with Sestos) and territories became automatically the order of the day.

Such allied, or confederate armies as the Greeks could assemble, although standardized in troop types, weapons and syllabus, could not face a cohesive, even if differentiated enemy host with many tactical and operational solutions and a robust command system. The Greeks solved this problem by facing, in the battlefield, enemy armies by single-contingent task forces (Her VII.212,2), or at least task forces consisting of as few allies as possible and these with a history of efficient co-operation (Her VI.111,1 &IX.28,6; Her IX.28,3), thus dividing a single action into multiple smaller ones, independently led, commanded and controlled, where their cohesion matched or even outdid that of the Imperials.

The events *ante* invasion

The loss of prestige in Marathon, building on previous reverses of the empire was now reaching a critical mass possibly because of the Imperial supremacy, including the Scythian campaign and the seven-year-long insurrection of Ionia, combined with heavy duties in supplies and work. Some intrigue and pharaonic projects were undertaken, such as the cutting of a canal between the Nile and the Red Sea, a massive event. Egypt erupted in revolt, and this became the No 1 priority in the middle of the preparations for the next campaign against Greece. Darius died before being able to deal with the situation (Her VII.4), and Egypt re-emerged partially, with a new native Pharaoh and a problem with the Persian administrative staff located there (Wijnsma 2019). Xerxes swiftly dealt with the situation, probably by dispatching the army prepared by Darius and not by leading it (Klotz 2015). When the army conquered, his brother Achaemenes was appointed Satrap and savage retribution was exacted (Her VII.7); its religious nature shows either the hand of the native clergy in the uprising, or the religious fanaticism and intolerance of Xerxes as described in the 'Daiva inscription' -XPh (Klotz 2015; Herzfeld 1932), and despite concerted efforts to interpret the latter in benign terms (Kuhrt 1997; Abdi 2007) – or both.

Most scholars agree that there were two rebellions in Babylon after Xerxes was enthroned and before his campaign in Greece (Ossendrijver 2018; Waerzeggers 2018). It is true that Xerxes ultimately struck the Babylonian titles from his royal etiquette (Waerzeggers 2018; Llewellyn-Jones 2017). This says little; it could be because he gave them to the viceroy of Babylon, as he had been himself. But Herodotus mentions a satrap, not a viceroy, later in Babylon (Her VII.62,2), which means Xerxes abolished the Trinity introduced by Cyrus and confirmed by Darius; he had not appointed one of his sons, the heir apparent, as viceroy but a nobleman; and he was satrap, not viceroy.

Moreover, in Xerxes' campaign Herodotus, and Diodorus, mention no Babylonian contributions. There were contributions from the area (Her VII.63), but not from Babylon, and Aeschylus' contrary testimony (Persai 52–4) in this case may well be due to poetic licence. This proves that before Xerxes invaded Greece there was at least one Babylonian uprising, and it was dealt with swiftly and savagely (Waerzeggers 2018; Llewellyn-Jones 2017). There is no need to assume a second one, and, even more important, we do not need to assume this first uprising taking place *after* his coronation in 486 BC, although some arguments do indeed corroborate it (Llewellyn-Jones 2017). It could have been during his years as a viceroy (Gertoux 2018), and one may dare to blame his religious zeal in a liberal city, at least in terms of morals. The second rebellion must have been during his sojourn in Greece (Mumford 2019; Waerzeggers 2018; Llewellyn-Jones 2017), probably after the battle of Salamis, a perfect reason to expedite his return (Her VIII.103) and to stay for quite some time in Sardis instead of returning to Susa (Her VIII.117,2). As in Egypt, he dispatched someone to do the job and in this case, we have a name: Megabyzus (Burn 1962; Green 1970), one of his six Marshals (Her VII.82). He was the son of Zopyrus, who had reconquered Babylon for Darius and he did it for Xerxes, most probably to quell the second rebellion which had claimed the life of his father Zopyrus, the Satrap (Gertoux 2016) installed after Xerxes had advanced to kingship.

In any case, the safe conclusion is that once the army of the Egyptian expedition was back and disbanded and Achaemenes firmly established at the satrapal seat (an indication that he had commanded the task force sent to crush the rebellion), Xerxes dwelt upon the Greek expedition. With two major revolts in ten years, if not three, he might have been sceptical. The wisdom of straining the resources for a massive European campaign, not only against Greece, could cause further dissatisfaction. On the other hand, success could well bring in a hefty profit, not only from spoils, slaves and from hammering the Imperial identity into dissatisfied subjects, but also from the increase of his own splendour, radiance and prestige as a warrior king. This was his prerogative: a warrior chosen by warriors (Fields 2007), as inscribed on Darius' grave (Dnb 9).

Once his mind had been made up, Xerxes hated half-measures and novelties to the tune of the campaign of Datis. He liked grandiose things; after all, he was to take the field himself this time. But it must be noted that the spirit of Datis was living and his house suffered no dishonour due to the defeat: his two sons were two of the three cavalry generals (Her VII.88,1) and, more important, the fleet would not move independently but would be augmented with a most powerful marine contingent (Her VII.184,2) which included masses of cavalry, with mounts loaded on horse transports (Her VII.97).

Part I

Preparation and Invasion

Chapter 1

Lore and Reality: the Host of Xerxes

Structure and nature of the Kingly host

There are intriguing details in the Herodotean account of the Imperial host, which testify to its accuracy and reliability. It reads like a knightly host (Delbrück 1920), with non-combatants and retainers aplenty (Her VII.55,1 & VII.83) that made it rather a horde than an army. The same happened to the once lean and mean army of Alexander the Great after Issus and the capture of a major Achaemenid war chest. But the army of Xerxes was also the army of the realm, raised from different geographic conscription areas, which do not coincide with the satrapies of any list; neither of Herodotus' own (Her III.90–96), nor of Behistun (BD 6). This arrangement probably resulted in mobilizing standard levies. It was a massive, Imperial army, neither professional nor standing, but with a professional core. Professionals, *sensu lato*, must have been the Immortals, the guard units and the knightly and infantry cavalry that were sustained by land grants of the crown.

Herodotus explicitly states that the King mobilized and took along his household and his elite warriors (Her VII.83). Any notion that the description of the army comes from any secondary source and does not correspond to the reality of the campaign is arbitrary. The differences between lists of satraps and commanders and between satrapies and recruiting grounds speak of an actual host, not any kind of administrative roster. The very high proportion of princely blood in the command of even the most exotic and geographically isolated units (**Table 1.1**) coincides with Achaemenid's martial ideology and martial practices (Burn 1962) and possibly points to the military, not civil element of the satrapies as the basic cell of recruitment. As seen during the Ionian revolt, such offices were preferentially assigned to scions of the ruling elite and most importantly, the royal family. This explains the diversion between satrapies and levies and points to a degree of standardization in the levies raised, as too numerous ones would be divided and too small or neighbouring ones would be aggregated, so as to fit a logistics master plan.

If the numbers of Xenophon (Cyrop I.2,4–15) apply to the days of Xerxes, then the national Persian host, mobilized at 50 per cent, would amount to 60,000, the very strength usually assumed for each contingent of the army of Xerxes (Her VII.61–80). It is possible that for this particular campaign exceptional

Table 1.1. Infantry contingents of Xerxes' host.

Marshals	National contingents	Commanders
Mardonius	Persians (M)	Otanes
Masistes	Medes (M)	Tigranes
Tritandaechmes	Cissians	Anaphes
Megabyzus	Hyrcanians	Megapanus
Gergis	(As)Syrians	Otaspes
Smerdomenes	Bactrians & Saka (M)	**Hystaspes**
	Indians & Eastern Ethiopians (M)	Pharnazathres
	Arians	Sisamnes
	Parthians & Chorasmians	Artabazus (M)
	Sogdians	Azanes
	Gandarians & Dadikae	**Artyphius**
	Caspians	**Ariomardus**
	Sarangae	Pherendates
	Pactyes	Artayntes
	Utians & Mycians	**Arsamenes**
	Paricanians	Siromitres
	Arabians & African Ethiopians	**Arsames**
	Libyans	Massages
	Paphlagonians & Matieni	Dotus
	Cappadocians & Ligyans	**Gobryas**
	Armenians & Phrygians	Artochmes
	Lydians & Mysians (M)	**Artaphrenes**
	Bithynians	Bassaces
	Pisidians, Meiones, Milyae	Badres
	Moschi & Tibareni	**Ariomardus**
	Macrones & Mossynoeci	Artayctes
	Mares & Colchians	Pharandates (M)
	Saspires & Alarodians	Masistius (M)
	Persian Gulf islanders	Mardontes

Bold names: Royal family members
M: Present in Mardonius army in 479 BC

measures were taken (Her VII.1,2), but in any case the human capital of the empire had not been mobilized to its full extent (Her VII.48). For these reasons, a 2/3 mobilization quota is plausible for the Imperials and the following estimates in this chapter shall use this ratio rather than the 50 per cent suggested by Xenophon.

All subjects had to partake of their master's quest for aggrandizement and for avenging the honour of the dynasty, the empire and their supreme deity. And they were armed with their own distinctive weaponry to which they were accustomed and had accumulated generations of know-how. In this, Xerxes did nothing innovative; Dionysius I of Syracuse almost a century later will implement the same approach and go to great expense to have his mercenaries outfitted with their customary hardware (Diod XIV.41,5); the Seleucids did the same.

Xerxes evidently recruited four types of infantry in terms of fighting methodology. The first type is the light javelineers, who were expendable and very useful for manoeuvering in mountainous country which, ironically, was fielding less flexible, shock heavy infantry. Such were the Mysians, the Thracians and the Lybians (Her VII.74,1 & 71 & 75) and many others, massively conscripted in Asia Minor. They were good skirmishers and excellent devastators, and the primitive look of some of them was a great psychological weapon, meant to instil terror (Burn 1962).

There were also some shock units, the second troop type, expected to perform well in close quarters and hand-to-hand combat, especially the Assyrians (Her VII.63) and the Lydians (Her VII.74,1), who had panoplies and weaponry for close quarters warfare. They were supposed to take over and absorb the shock of the Greek Hoplites, while the third type of infantry, engaging in hand-to-hand combat, but outfitted with a lighter kit, such as the Moschi and the Colchians (Her VII.78–79) were to flank or infiltrate among the heavy Hoplites to corrode the phalanx.

These three tactical elements imply that Xerxes might have taken heed of Mardonius' analysis (Her VII.9B) that the Greeks fight pitched battles on level ground instead of taking advantage of the features of their broken country by guarding passes and blocking straits (Burn 1962). This analysis was compatible with the events at Marathon, especially if the defeated and disenchanted Imperial leadership of that campaign related the facts with a pinch of salt. The same cognitive background must be understood for the raising of a massive cavalry arm to operate in a mountainous and relatively barren scorched landscape during the summer. The Imperial troop types eventually missed their mark, as the Greeks, possibly due to the Spartans who had taken supreme command, refused to oblige and did make use of such natural barriers and chokepoints, at Tempe and then at Thermopylae and Isthmus.

Last but not least, a considerable fraction of the Imperial infantry was armed with the bow as their main, secondary or only weapon. A total of at least 16 and possibly up to 19 land army contingents out of 29 were armed with the bow (Her VII.61–80), inclusively or exclusively. Archers, the fourth infantry troop type, were raised from – and possibly permitted only among – reliable and dependable ethnicities, especially Iranians (Her VII.61–62 & 64 &66–7) but others as well, including

Indians, Arabians and Ethiopians (Her VII.65 & 69–70). Assyrian infantry and Egyptian marines, both with brilliant archery traditions, were armed with hand-to-hand weaponry only (Her VII.63 & 89,3), beefing up the lines of close-contact shock troops as were the Lydian infantry (Her VII.74,1). This must have been a security precaution, to make them – at least the former two – less prone to mutiny against their fewer masters who, however, were able to decimate them from a distance should the need be.

In terms of tactics, the amassed archers would soften the Greeks with impunity, while the subjects would close to skirmish with javelins and, when disruption became critical, shock action would follow by the respective troops, to finish the job, so as the master race could implement their preferred function: pursuit and hunting, their national sport. At the same time the skirmishers and shock troops were well-suited to keeping the Greek Hoplites away from the Iranian archers should they launch violent charges to catch and butcher the invaluable but vulnerable archers in a concerted shock brawl, as happened in Marathon.

The structure of the Imperial host

The first detail of interest during the Great March is that the army is structured *de novo* at Doriscus (Burn 1962). Until then, it is an assembly of recruits, led by their provincial governors, recruiters or local military commanders, as is very clear in the detailed description (Her VII.61–80). These provincial commanders were – allegedly – to turn to corps commanders (Her VII.81–2), 29 of them. The knightly armies had no structured chain of command; the assembled aristocrats were appointed as commanders by their overlord and their betters, with some regard for their social status and position, not their military prowess. The good commanders, among their peers, were assigned the most demanding missions. Thus, the chain of command was introduced in Doriscus and was top-bottom, with the commanders selecting their subordinates. There was a one-rank tolerance; this means that to name a subordinate, an officer had to outrank the nominee by two ranks, not one, (Her VII.81).

As a result, one has to accept that the expeditionary army had all its echelons fully manned. It is probable that the Persians were using the 2/3 expeditionary fraction reported for the late fifth-century Peloponnesian alliance under Sparta (Thuc II.10,2) but probably applicable to the Persian Wars era as well. This may have been functioning at the recruitment level. Thus, the recruits led to Doriscus were the 2/3 of the available manpower resources of their provinces subject to recruitment and as they were divided to form standard units only when at Doriscus, the units formed should have been fully manned. The Persian host seems indeed not bereft of reserves, since Xerxes argues that he may draw larger forces if need be (Her VII.48). On this, Aeschylus (Persai 1024) is clearly poetic and exaggerating when saying that the King had no more men to command after the retreat; 'reliable men', though, is another issue. Even if the army was operating at 2/3 in terms of *units*, the Persian practice was (in stark contrast to the Spartan approach during Xenophon's time) to fully man the lower echelons (Sekunda & Chew 1992).

As an exercise of logic, if not at the raw manpower level, which was the level where the expeditionary fraction was implemented, another possibility would be that the 2/3 rule applied to the army level. The six armies of the Imperial host, one per Marshal (Her VII.82), may represent another implementation of the Persian decimal system: six were mobilized out of ten, which would have been the full tally of the Imperial grand army. That means that the lower echelons, such as corps, baivaraba, hazaraba, sataba and dathaba would have been fully manned. The concept of 'hollow force' as described for *peacetime* Cold War Soviet military, with 2/3 complement *per echelon* (Karber & Combs 1998), projected to Xerxes' invasion army *on full war footing* is unwarranted; the same holds for estimating the baivaraba at reduced strength, especially once this rule is applied indiscriminately to expeditionary and home defence instances (Ray 2009).

Still another top-bottom possibility is that the 2/3 rule was applicable to the 60,000-strong corps level, which may have had 100,000 nominal strength, under a total projection of the decimal system followed by the *Kara*, the Persian army. A full corps mobilized for home defence was 100,000, ten baivaraba; an expeditionary corps was six full baivaraba, 60,000 men and an expeditionary army was ten corps, 600,000 men. This figure is very near to the number of the invasion force of Darius against Scythia (Her IV.87,1) and double the strength of Mardonius in 479 BC (Her VIII.100,5). Within Imperial soil, for home defence, an army could be expanded to 1,000,000 full-levy. In this format, the army may be divided into two five-corps groups, between the commanding officer – CO – and the second-in-command, which agrees with novel concepts on the issue (Boteva 2011). The latter supposition allows for a full panel of six, not ten, Marshals under the King, in close parallel to the Seven Conspirators under Darius and to similar Zoroastrian symbolism, the six Amesha Spenta archangels assisting Ahura Mazda.

The cavalry is a prominent feature of the invasion (**Table 1.2**), mainly, but not exclusively, for the reasons mentioned above. It is divided amongst three commanders (Her VII.88,1) and its full tally is 80,000 mounted horse cavalry (Her VII.87), plus chariotry and mounted camel cavalry. Herodotus tries to use the strength of the two latter groups to round it up to 100,000. The number seems excessive, but some 150 years later Darius III was able to field 40,000 cavalry in Gaugamela after having already lost half his empire (Arr Anab III.8,6) and following some years,

Table 1.2. Cavalry contingents of Xerxes' host

Cavalry Commanders (Hipparchs)	Cavalry contingents	Present in Plataea
Armamithras Titheus Pharnuches (Masistius)	Persians	+
	Medians	+
	Cissians	
	Indians	+
	Bactrians-Saka	+
	Paricanians	
	Caspians	
	Lybians (Chariotry)	
	Arabians (Camels)	
	Sagarteans	

or decades, of decadence (Xen Cyrop VIII.8,20). The sum of Bactrian cavalry alone has been occasionally reported as 30,000 (Cur VII.4,30), the figure probably representing the total regional/national tally.

The main questions relate to the *distribution* of the cavalry. The existence of three commanders or Hipparchs (Her VII.88,1) implies three similar commands/groups; these are commanders, not recruiters. A handsome number, some 20,000 at the very least, serve with the navy since their horses are carried by 850 horse transports (Diod XI.3,9) the capacity of which is at least 30 mounts, as discussed previously, regarding Datis' such vessels in 490 bc (Kambouris 2020). This leaves 60,000 horse-mounted cavalry, 20,000 for each of the three Hipparchs, one such assigned, along with two infantry armies, to each invasion route: north, middle, south (Her VII.121). Thus, each route was followed by an army group formed of a 20,000-strong cavalry formation and two infantry armies with a nominal strength of 300,000 each. It would have been much easier to suppose, in this function, three, not six, armies, each with a commander, a vice commander and a Hipparch/Master of Horse, as proposed by Boteva (2011), assigned to each invasion route (Her VII.121) instead of army groups; such a disposition would also corroborate the above mentioned structure of ten corps of 60,000 men per army.

Expanding the original proposition, these three armies could have been conscripted at the Eastern, Central and Western parts of the Empire, possibly each overseen by one member of the regal Trinity. Incidentally, Xerxes presided over the central group (Her VII.121,3), being the head of the Trinity, Masistes was in the eastern group (Her VII.121.2–3), being a member of the trinity as Head of Bactria (Her IX.113). Each army was divisible into two theatres, as was standard in Achaemenid army echelons, which would take over different geographical areas;

like the army of Mardonius and Masistes in 479 BC. This line of thought could be interpreted differently so as to ultimately bring the sum of the Imperial army to 900,000 infantry: three armies of 300,000 each, the strength of the command of Mardonius in 479 BC (Her VIII.100,5) and 100,000 *total* cavalry (Her VII.184,4), an enticing 10:1 ratio and a good, round million for the entire host.

Indeed, the assignment of three cavalry commanders/*Hipparchs* for six separate armies implies a somewhat strange command structure, with three 20,000-strong cavalry formations – instead of the much more compliant six 10,000 (cavalry baivaraba) – one for each invasion route and army group. How this massive and unitary cavalry formation may have been divided and delegated to the two nearby but separate armies, remains unfathomable but could, in principle, follow the commander/vice-commander scheme for a cavalry group. One baivarabam was assigned, with the Hipparch, to one army and the other to the 'vice-hipparch' with the other army.

Still, once citing and examining the above arguments is over, the armies must have been six, as implied by Herodotus, by Zoroastrian tradition; and by conventional wisdom. With the possible exception of the campaign of 490 BC (Her VI.94,2), culminating in Marathon, Persian dual commands as proposed by Boteva (2011) are a rarity. In Marathon, Artaphrenes may have been the commander of the cavalry, not a fellow commander of Datis (**Table 1.3**) or the local contribution in a mixed Satrapal-Imperial expedition (Kambouris 2022); the latter case is inapplicable in

Table 1.3. Commanders of Achaemenid expeditionary forces.

Commanders	Chronology (BC)	Campaign
Otanes	518	Samos
Megabazus *	513	Thrace
Otanes	512	NW Asia Minor, Bosporus, Lemnos, Imbros
Megabates and Aristagoras**	500	Naxos
Artybius	498	Cyprus
Daurices	498	W AsiaMinor/Troad Caria
Hymaes	498	W Asia Minor/Troad-Propontis
Artaphrenes and Otanes	498	W Asia Minor/Ionia
Datis ? *	494–3	Ionia-Karia-Straits
Mardonius *	492	Thrace
Datis and Artaphrenes**	490	Marathon
Mardonius *	479	Plataea

Single asterisks (*) denote Imperial expeditions; double asterisks (**) denote satrapal projects with Imperial endorsement and support.

the army of Xerxes. Thus, the idea of Boteva (2011), brilliant as it may be, and a perfect fit with the three hipparchs and the three itineraries of the invasion force, probably is not correct. After the Persian ebb, in 479 BC, with Xerxes residing at Sardis (Her IX.3,1), there is *one* army of special structure under Mardonius in Europe (Her VIII.133 & 126 & 114,1) and most probably another under Masistes in western Asia Minor (Her IX.107,1). It is an arrangement that provides for two separate armies, each operating independently and with wildly different objectives; not two divisions of the same army. Important as it seems that the two COs are the Marshals who were operating at the southernmost itinerary the previous year, it means nothing for the greater problem of the Persian higher-echelon force structure.

Hammering recruits into an army

A nobleman's commission could be very different and perhaps totally irrelevant to his status within the Imperial administrative system and to the troops he originally raised and led (Sekunda 2002). For example, Tigranes led the Median contingent to Doriscus (Her VII. 62,1), but these were left with Mardonius in Greece and Tigranes was commanding, in 479 BC, an army corps at Mycale (Her IX.96,2), in Asia Minor; even more important is the commission of Mardontes as Admiral (Her VIII.130,2), perhaps commanding 100 out of the 300 vessels of the Persian fleet in Samos in 479 BC; this man had been leading, two years previously, a land army contingent, from the Persian Gulf and the 'islands nearby' (Her VII.80). The same happened with Artayntes, Commander of the Pactyes (Her VII.67,3) in 481 BC and Admiral in Samos in 479 BC (Her VII.130,2).

Xerxes was billeted at Sardis with his full force for the winter of 481–480 BC. Only the contributions from the European vassals had not been present there. As envoys were sent from Sardis to Europe to demand submission, an act tantamount to a declaration of war, the prospective and actual subjects in Europe would mobilize *in situ* to alleviate logistics issues. But the massive contingents recruited from Asia and Africa were camped there, in Sardis, for some months. Why not count and assign them in units there and then, allowing some more time for officers to familiarize with each other and their men and to develop some measure of cohesion? Why was this task left for after the invasion march started, in Doriscus? The only possible answer is that in Doriscus the Imperial fleet detachments, squadrons and naval districts would also converge, and this was necessary so as to see the true tallies (stragglers and late arrivals of the army included) and then at once delegate the boarders' forces to the navy and, at the same time, properly structure the land force for the initial and the next phases of the invasion. It must be noted that the initial part of the invasion, from the Hellespont to the river Strymon, was officially within the borders of the empire. Strymon was the ultimate border of the realm, as evident from the sacrifices for crossing it (Her VII.113–4; Boteva 2011), despite being a minor river with friendly territory next to it.

Thus, Herodotus narrates a major land force raised by local conscription. He gives the national/provincial qualitative makeup of this massive force, its grand total and the officials who levied it, led it and brought it together (Her VII. 81 & VII.60,1). After moving to advance base, this force, probably drilled during winter, was organized into standard units further grouped into armies. The 29 highest-ranking Imperial officials responsible for levying the host were named corps commanders and picked the commanding officers of lower echelons. All echelons up to baivaraba must have been fully manned, as argued previously. Unit commands were quite different from the natural/social chains of command used for marshalling, supplying and marching the provincial levies (Her VII.96,2 & VII.81). These original chains of command were proven effective and were retained to simplify indoctrination, training, logistics and movement through friendly territory.

Each corps probably had six baivaraba, a standardized synthesis (Green 1970), possibly of the same or kindred or neighbouring stock. The number 6, as already mentioned, complies with the 2/3 expeditionary recruitment rule. Corps were teamed to form armies either by fives, to form six such armies as is the conventional understanding corroborating the strength of Mardonius' army in 479 BC, or by tens, to form three armies. The latter is a novel proposition, more compatible with the Persian military decimal system), the cavalry high command (three cavalry commanders) and the early operational realities and choices (Boteva 2011). Still, 80 years later Xenophon assigns to King Artaxerxes II a host composed of four major armies of 300,000 each (Xen Anab I.7,12); Xenophon was actually *facing*

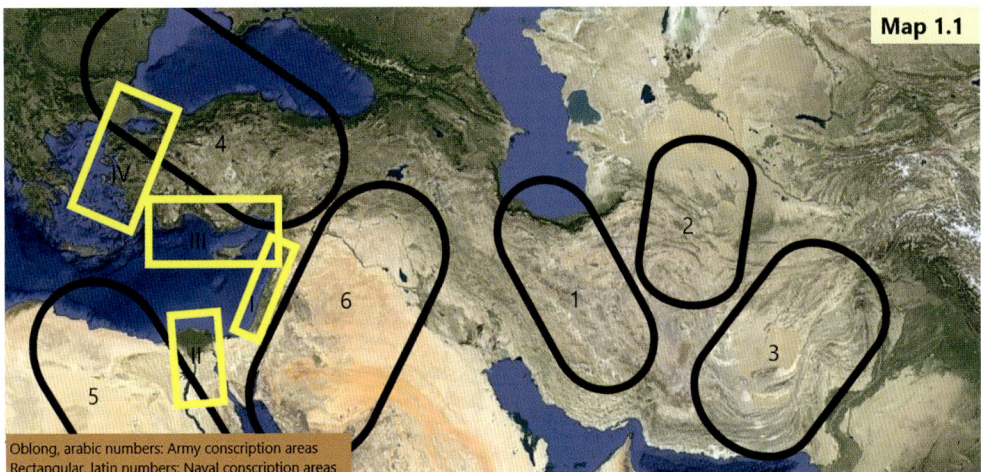

Map 1.1

Oblong, arabic numbers: Army conscription areas
Rectangular, latin numbers: Naval conscription areas

that host and conversing with men speaking with Cyrus the Younger, the impostor prince. Thus, there cannot have been any numerical misunderstanding between a liege and his generals, and as a result, the numbers of Xenophon corroborate those of Herodotus, if one takes into consideration that Artaxerxes II did not have time to muster his forces from the Far East, which may account for one more such army, while the sixth must have been the army of the Far West, going rogue after Cyrus the Younger. Thus, the building block for the Imperial host by Xenophon was the 300,000-strong army and under Xerxes there were six of them, an estimation which corroborates the 1.8 million troops reported by Herodotus.

One may attempt a rough assumption on the geographical distribution of these six commands, each producing an army, by following scraps of data in Herodotus and Xenophon. One such army must have been raised in the wider area of Iran all the way south to the Persian Gulf, including Media, Persia, Cissia/Sushan, Parthia etc. A second one from the upper satrapies – Bactria, Sogdiana, Margianna etc. and Scythia; a third from India and the SE parts of the empire. The fourth must have been Asia Minor and European lands/*Skudra*. The fifth must have been the African possessions, from Ethiopia to Cyrene and a sixth must have included Phoenicia, Arabia and Mesopotamia (**Map 1.1**). The latter three coincided more or less with the three overthrown empires, Lydian, Babylonian and Egyptian. In this light, Herodotus is perhaps justified to expect that one more such army is to be raised from the European lands of the empire and thus estimates the allies and subjects from Europe to the strength of another army, 300,000 (Her VII.185,2); which, incidentally, is the reported strength of the Carthaginian invasion army dispatched to Sicily against Syracuse (Her VII.165).

The regimentation of the Imperial army under the *Karana* is a thorny issue. In Xerxes' army (and probably in the army of the Scythian campaign) the building block was the national contingent. Some smaller ones may have been brigaded under one commander, like the Bactrians and the Scythians (Her VII.64), but basically, such contingents remained separate and did not correspond to satrapies (Barkworth 1993; Burn 1962). The number of brigades recorded by Herodotus is, as already mentioned, 29, which rises to 33 if one takes the fleet into consideration; that of the satrapies amounts to just 21, although it is hard to understand which exact instance of the Achaemenid Empire this number represents. (**Table 1.4**).

All local recruits were probably mobilized under the satrap, along with the output of the military colonies and the garrisons within the satrapy, forming the sum of the territorial forces (*spada*) available to a satrap for local defence, whence he could assume the supreme command, being named *Spadapatis*. Of these, the Persian units would be delegated to the commander(s) of the Persian home troops upon arriving at the mustering areas, whenever a royal army was raised. The Iranians of the satrapies

Table 1.4. Satrapies of Xerxes' Empire

No	Satrapy	Yearly tribute in silver talents
1	Ionia-Aeolis-Caria-Lycia-Pamphylia	400
2	Lydia-Mysia	500
3	Hellespont, Bithynia, Phrygia, Paphlagonia, Cappadocia	360
4	Cilicia	500
5	Phoenicia, Cyprus, Palestine	350
6	Egypt-Libya-Cyrene	700
7	Gandaris	170
8	Sushan (Cissia)	300
9	Babylon	1000
10	Media	450
11	Caspians	200
12	Bactria	360
13	Pactyes-Armenians	400
14	Utians, Mycians	600
15	Saka	250
16	Parthians, Sogdians, Arians, Chorasmians	300
17	Paricanians, Eastern Ethiopians	400
18	Matieni, Saspiri, Alarodii	200
19	Moschi, Tibareni, Macrones, Mossynoeci, and Mares	300
20	India	360 (Gold)

should thus be expected to band together within a royal army to form exclusively Persian baivaraba (and Median and Cissian) under the orders of the respective national commander, who recruited and led the home troops (Her VII.61,1–2). Massive Persian contingents were drawn from the military colonies/communities planted in the satrapies, and of these came the bodyguards/arstibara of the satraps. The bodyguards were probably 1,000-strong (Her IX.63,1), imitating the royal arstibara and would follow their master; they would not aggregate with home troops units. Additionally, a household yeoman cavalry force of 1,000 per satrapy should be expected, accounting for 20,000 horse out of the 80,000 total.. The latter draft had fallen to 600 by the fourth century (Xen Anab I.8,21).

Sources under scrutiny: mining and filtering surviving data

Some of the numbers of Herodotus sound, read or seem exaggerated. But this is clearly subjective; what one is prepared to believe has nothing to do with historic accuracy. The numbers should first be considered into context, which is still subjective, but allows some comparisons and assessments. And then, they can be challenged by arguments, not impressions. Characterizations like 'absurd', 'obviously grossly exaggerated' etc. are neither science nor arguments. They have to be bolstered by arguments, or else they are prejudice. The division by arbitrary denominators of the strengths reported by Herodotus or by any other source, as in trimming by three-quarters the Imperial infantry and by half the Imperial cavalry taken in Europe (Hanson 1999) is NOT a valid research, scientific or historic approach.

There are some things to remember. First, Xerxes embarked on a multi-year campaign to conquer the whole of Europe (Her VII.54,2), whatever this meant in his mind; not simply Greece, nor Athens and Sparta. This is why he sent for tokens of surrender, Earth and Water, to all the mainland Greek states (Her VII.131) and perhaps to some colonies in Italy (Her VII.163,2). Once fed by the initial success, his diplomacy would extend such demands to a new round of prospective subjects, stunned to impotence after the fall of Greece. And the juggernaut would go on, very much like Cambyses had done.

The first expeditionary period was supposed to result in the occupation of Athens, Sparta and the rest of mainland Greece. If the islands of the Ionian Sea were not subjugated in time, next year they would, to be followed by an all-out attack to southern Italy, possibly up the western coast of Greece to the Straits of Otranto, as the Carthaginians would have occupied Sicily and be able to provide assistance and support. Such multi-year campaigns were not unprecedented; Cambyses' reign was one great campaign in Africa, succeeding against Egypt, resulting in the surrender of Cyrene and failing against Ethiopia and Siwa (as described in Herodotus' Book II). Indeed, the resources of occupied Greece would be incorporated into the invading host. But, with such plans in mind, are the numbers suggested by modern scholars (Hignett 1963; Green 1970) even remotely sufficient?

Not really. The Greek resistance finally included 31 states (Plut Vit Them 20,4), of which some five were free minor nationalist islands or Imperial defectors, furnishing between one and four pentekonters or up to two triremes (Her VIII.8,1 & 82,1 & 46,4 & 48). That means 25 city-states were responsible for a massive 100,000 warriors (half of them from Lacedaimon) *plus* 40,000 sailors who could fight on land. If more states had decided to resist – an invaluable piece of knowledge which would become available reliably only in the middle of the campaign, when the Imperials would be at the kerb of the Hellenic peninsula – how many Greeks would be taking the field or to the seas? Additionally, a look at the map allows comparison of the states of the League to the Medizing states, allied or vassal ones. In this respect, the latter being able to raise (with the addition of massive Thracian contributions) twice the number of the Patriots, or six times the number from Lacedaimon, is by no means an exaggeration as is sometimes suggested (Green 1970; Burn 1962).

The second thing to consider is that in terms of ships, expeditionary fleets of 600 and the Grand Fleet of 1,200 ships-of-the-Ine are by no means incredible, nor exaggerated. Even (some) critics for the Herodotean numbers admit that vessels are much easier to count than troops (Lazenby 1993; de Souza 2003), although the Allied spy mission had no opportunity to see the Imperial fleet, contrary to some suggestions (Bradford 1980), as they went to Sardis, were apprehended and then given a tour there in land-locked areas, without any notion of checking the fleet which might have not been assembled yet. Believing that the tour was elaborately manipulated to increase their awe (Lazenby 1993) is a valid argument, although being granted permission to go anywhere, ask anything and count or see anything (Her VII.146,3) made such manipulations tricky at the very least. To question their ability to accurately observe and report and presuppose they exaggerated what they saw and counted (Lazenby 1993), on the other hand, is prejudiced and rejective and without any good reason. There is no need to believe that in the whole of patriotic Greece three men of suitable qualities could not be found. Similarly, no one doubts the number of Imperial vessels that were used to create the bridges, which is half that of the fleet. There is no rationale in doubting the ability of the whole western coast of the empire to build and man three times the vessels of the Greek alliance – and less if Corcyra and Crete had joined in.

Similarly, the idea that 1,200 was the sum of the Levantine shipping resources (Bradford 1980) is untenable. There are no indications, numbers or anything else to estimate shipping resources at large. The only available figures are these reporting actual naval resources, regarding triremes. But while the numbers of mobilized fleets can be found, by counting, spying or estimating, the numbers of potential full resources are a rather contradictory if not outright theoretical issue and possibly never recorded by any bureaucracy; much less has it been available by any conceivable channel for Herodotus. Paper strengths always refer to deployable fleets, not to end-of-times ones, where improvisation and industry might work miracles.

Every two years Darius had been mobilizing (not building) 600 vessels (**Table 1.5**); Athens built 200 in three to four years. In ten years, which would proportionately allow an Athenian fleet of 500 vessels minimum, Xerxes and Darius prepared 1,200, a mere 140 per cent more, and most likely not all of them built *de novo*. Between them, Tyre and Sidon, with the wealth from the whole commerce of the empire with the western and southern Mediterranean, if equalling

Table 1.5. Achaemenid fleets

Fleets	Strength	Campaign	Chronology (BC)	Commander (Spadapatis)
Royal	600	Scythia	515	Darius I
Royal	600	Ionia	494	Datis?
Royal	600	Marathon	490	Datis
Royal	>1200	Greece	480	Xerxes I
Royal	300	Ionia	479	Artayntes
Local/ Satrapal	?	Cyprus	498	Artybius?
Royal		Egypt	527	Cambyses
Satrapal	200	Naxos	500	Megabates
Royal	600	Thrace	492	Mardonius
Local	?	Lemnos-Imbros	512	Otanes

the Athenian effort, would account for the sum of the Phoenician fleet of Xerxes plus two 50-strong home squadrons (one for each, should such a need be required); that is two cities' worth in four years. In four years of Xerxes' preparations, plus the ones of Darius before 486 BC, why not 1,200 ships by the whole empire? In five times the time taken by Athens to build her fleet, the whole empire was able to build a fleet six-fold that of the Athenians, and three times that of the whole of the Greek Alliance at Salamis. Additional Greek vessels did not make it or did not partake in the alliance.

It is really not that much, 1,200 triremes for the Empire. This makes more believable the possibility that the line fleet of 480 BC was 1,200 new-built vessels, the vessels of the old fleet of Datis being assigned to the original bridges of the Hellespont. Once these two bridges were destroyed (the bridges; by no means all the vessels used), the surviving vessels, increased to the required number by pentekonters (Her VII.36,1), were incorporated into the final bridges built under the supervision of Harpalus from Tenedos (Rollinger & Ulf 2004). Subsequently, the bridges, having accomplished their role in allowing a relatively fast and smooth, continuous pace of crossing, must have been dismantled to better exploit the vessels, given that the campaign required massive logistics. The *old* triremes of the bridges, with skeleton crews, would have been pressed to the frontline to make up for the casualties in hulls, after the gales in central Greece, by taking in the survivors of the shipwrecked crews so as to produce more or less full crews for themselves. It is in this way that the Persian fleet made up – at least partially – its casualties before Salamis (Her VIII.66,1; Aesch Persai 341–4), obviously after the concern voiced by the High Admiral Achaemenes (Her VII.236, 2–3). It is conceivable that these second-grade vessels proved a liability in Salamis and had they taken disproportional losses, they became death traps for the Iranian boarding parties.

One must dwell on the fact that three sources, Herodotus, Diodorus and Aeschylus, report the same strength for the Imperial Grand Armada, 1,200 warships (**Table 1.6**). Instead of searching for a common tradition to be able to disprove all three, one should rather consider them cross-referenced; the more so once Herodotus and Diodorus do not match in contingent numbers and thus must have been using different primary sources. Additionally, two of the three imply (that is Herodotus VIII.66,1; Aeschylus writes it clearly in Persai 341–44) that the Imperial fleet was 1,200-strong on the eve of Salamis. In the battle of Salamis, the Imperial fleet may have already taken horrific casualties by storm and battle and still appear almost intact numerically in terms of warships. It *could have been* so, for the reasons mentioned. Whether it *had* been so, is another question altogether.

The third issue one has to contemplate is that although Herodotus' numbers may indeed be erroneous, this is on a case-by-case basis. For example, the support troops of an army may not be included in Greek tallies of land forces, with the possible exception of Plataea, and there only due to the prodigious Lacedaimonian arrangement. This is natural, as the line troops matter. But it may well be that

Table 1.6. The Imperial fleet under Xerxes

Admirals	District naval commands	Squadrons	Vessels (Herodotus)	Vessels (Diodorus)
Ariabignes	Ionians and Carians	Phoenicia and Syria	300	300
Achaemenes	Egyptians	Egypt	200	200
Megabazus	Phoenicia?	Cilicia*	100	80
Prexaspes	S Asia Minor?	Cyprus*	150	150
		Lycia*	50	40
		Pamphylia*	30	40
		Ionia	100	100
		Caria	70	80
		Dorians	30	40
		Aeolians	60	40
		Hellespontines	100	80
		Islanders (Aegean)	17	50
		Total	**1207**	**1200**
		Thrace, Macedon	120	
		Bridges	674	

Question marks denote speculation over the command assigned to the admiral.
* denotes the squadrons believed to form the Third Naval District.

in Persian practice, with the focus on logistics, especially since provisions had to be collected and transported from quite a distance, the numbers provided or used for army tallies were total human resources, including support troops and even non-combatants, from cooks, harlots, entertainers and merchants to engineers, carpenters and medics – and very possibly the naval personnel as well, as it was the treasury that was paying for all of them; the same goes for the watering resources.

Additionally, there is no reason to suppose that the contingents raised from Europe, at least all the way to the borders of Greece proper (that is, Thessaly), had not been taken into account in advance, for logistical if for no other reason. Fleet tallies were easy to produce; thus the approximate enumeration by the enclosure in a circular fence that provided a rough estimate of *land* troops at Doriscus may have been applied to land troops only and may have not yielded 1.7 million, but a number *factored* in the 1.7 million. It is important that the report concerns Doriscus but fails to mention even one of the vassals on European soil. This is a clear indication that the numbers and descriptions of Herodotus concerning the Imperial land contingents come from the official records of the Allies *before* the Persians crossed to Europe, and most probably from the reports of the spies at Sardis (Green 1970). A report including all the Asian and African troops, already assembled and with eye-witness-grade details, but not the European ones as they were not assembled, nor quantified. And with the most abstract description of the fleet, which they had never laid eyes on, but must have been informed on by the Imperial staff. Such briefing must have included a rough estimate, meaning the initial chain-of-command and *projected* numbers (ibid). Thus, Diodorus, sourcing his information from Ephorus, a native of Cyme, might have had a more accurate, *actual* tally of the Imperial fleet (Diod XI.3,7–9), which is detailed to a degree not even near his abstract description of the land host (Diod XI.9,6–7).

Herodotus is our only source that not only provides numbers, but in many cases breaks them to components and contingents (for the Army and Fleet of Xerxes and the respective ones of the Allies in 480 and 479 BC), although not always in a continuous and consistent way. He also reports intriguing details which imply an inside knowledge in some cases, but not so in other similar ones. He has no idea of the size of the armies of the Ionian Revolt or of the Cypriot uprising or of the 492 BC campaign of Mardonius, though he has an accurate number for the army of Megabazus, active ten years earlier (Her IV.143,3). He never mentions the strength of the army of Datis and Artaphrenes, but he notes that the reported strength of the army of Mardonius in Plataea includes the cavalry (Her VIII.113,3); as did the army of the Scythian expedition (Her IV.87,1). And, on top of that, in many cases, he flatly refuses to provide numbers, while other historians, with less analytical overall accounts, do so. This directly implies that he did not have, or at least he *thought* he did not have, an accurate figure or even a reliable estimate, as in the cases of the Persian casualties in the battles of Artemisium and Salamis and the Athenian army strength at Marathon, or the Allied army at Mycale.

One must thus classify the figures of Herodotus to (a) reports and (b) estimates; for the benefit of all researchers and scholars that followed, he states himself that he is extrapolating, estimating or guessing wherever such is the case (Burn 1962). He displays exceptional candour by declaring which cases belong to the latter category. The reporting is as good as the sources; the estimation is another issue altogether. For example, Herodotus flatly states that at the time the *Spartan* army was 8,000 Peers; he never states the strength of the Athenian army, nor mentions the rest of the Hoplite element of *Lacedaimon*.

In this way, there are some very interesting conclusions and observations in his narration of the army of Xerxes (and subsequently of the one of Mardonius). One should note that Herodotus NEVER states that the whole Persian host came down to Thessaly, much less to central Greece. Xerxes' massive army is credibly detailed only as far as Strymon. Additionally, and most importantly, there are very few solid figures for Xerxes' host. Some others are Herodotus' own estimations and many other scholars' extrapolations. What he does say, his *report,* is that:

- Xerxes' army had six Marshals of the infantry and three cavalry commanders; (Her VII.82 & VII.88,1 respectively).
- At one time one of these Marshals, Mardonius, commanded a 300,000-strong army, cavalry included (Her VIII.113,3).
- The infantry was divided into, or, rather, formed by a muster of 29 territorial contingents with nationalities being the organizational nucleus; a thirtieth contingent was the Corps of Immortals, 10,000 strong (Her VII.61–83).
- There were two cavalry and two infantry guard units, each 1,000-strong (Her VII.40,1 & 41).
- There were at least 10,000 Persian cavalry troops (Her VII.41,3), guard cavalry excluded, and a kindred unit of 8,000 Sagartian cavalry (Her VII.85,1).
- One year later, after Xerxes had retreated, two generals (Artabazus and Tigranes) of the 29 original commanders were found commanding one 60,000-strong corps each (Her VIII.126,1 & IX.96,2 respectively). In both cases, the new commands were of unknown synthesis and origin but irrelevant to the ones they had led the previous year (Her VII.62,1 & 66,2). Artabazus, after a somewhat complicated set of winter operations, is found with only 40,000 at his disposal (Her IX.66,2). The latter figure must account for a 2/3 expeditionary strength over a nominal 60,000 and thus sounds more plausible; still, the corps led by Tigranes in Mycale is 60,000 strong when operating (Her IX.96,2). It becomes much more plausible

that the 40,000 was what was left from the corps of Artabazus after casualties and dispatches, and the nominal strengths were 60,000 for such commands.

- Line galleys were 1,207 (Her VII.184,1), commanded by four admirals, and were then increased by 120 (Her VII.185,1); all the *original ones* were augmented with 30 Iranian marines each for the campaign of 480 BC (Her VII 184,2). Additional reinforcements, although minuscule ones, did not make it.
- The total *infantry* strength was 1.7 million men, estimated by the enclosure method (Her VII.60,1–2).
- The cavalry was 80,000 horse riders, without mentioning the method of estimation or reporting (Her VII.87); this total is contributed by seven drafting areas/nations (Persians, Medes, Cissians, Bactrians & Saka, Indians, Caspians, Paricanians) plus two 1,000-strong (each) cavalry guard units and 8,000 Sagartians (Her VII.85,1); this implies that the seven drafting areas contributed a cavalry baivarabam each, as is specifically mentioned only for the Persians (Her VII.41,3).

The estimations, on the other hand, blow such numbers out of all proportions:

- Herodotus believes that all Imperial triremes are identical and each crewed by 200 sailors, oarsmen and native marines (Her VII.184,1).
- He also understands all the 3,000 auxiliary vessels to be 50-oared galleys, although there are heavy transports, 30-oared galleys and horse transports by his own account (Her VII.97); the latter had much smaller crews.
- Moreover, he assigns 30 Iranian marines to each of these vessels, as well (Her VII.184,3). Only the latter assumption accounts for 90,000 first-class troops who must have never been there; it almost equals the Greek army at Plataea.
- He estimates the European vassals, allies and Medizers flocking under the Imperial standard to amount to 300,000 (Her VII.185,2) and these being on top of the 1,8 million. His estimation possibly stems from an effort to introduce one more army to the existing six, with its strength estimated by dividing the total levy (1.8 million) by the number of Marshals (six). In this case, one could attempt a correction: one more *corps*, for a round total of 30, is much more plausible, leaving the Immortals out of the structure of the draft.
- The estimated 1,7 million (by the enclosure method) refers to line infantry troops, as are the naval crews and the European vassals and allies. They have as many auxiliaries (Her VII.186,1), including non-combatants: wagoners, mule drivers, cattle herders, cooks, jugglers, entertainers, merchants buying slaves and loot, households with chamberlains and servants (Burn 1962). This estimate, which doubles the original, is a double extrapolation based on the Greek system

of counting Hoplites only (the Imperials might have counted every living soul) and assigning one retainer per Hoplite (Her IX.29,2). The Imperial practice might have been different, and inconsistent, depending on troop type and status. Cavalry and elites would have a higher proportion of orderlies than plain infantry.

- Charioteers and camel riders are estimated at 20,000 (Her VII.184,4). Although the Persian armed forces included camel cavalry-*usabari* (Fields 2007), at least since Cyrus II (Her I.80,2), in Xerxes' army camel-borne troops seem to be limited to the Arabian contingent exclusively (Her VII.86,2); the camels used by the Persians were beasts of burden (Her VII.83,3), not cavalry mounts.

- Herodotus never assigns a standard numerical strength to the 29 Imperial contingents; he even *says* he has no clue whether they were of equal strength (Her VII.60) and it may be a valid assumption that such data was considered secret by the Imperial officials, as was the Spartan Standard Operating Proceedure. (Burn 1962). It was no accident that the Imperial SOP was to execute the arrested spies at Sardis (Her VII.146,1), who would have been doing nothing but observing, categorizing, recording and counting. Still, supposing uniform strength for the 29 contingents is an educated guess; brigading different troops (even if their difference is ethnicity) is mostly attested in order to create units of standard size, a must for any army or for its logistics. It is a similar concept with Allied units in the twentieth century, which were brigaded together or with units of the senior ally, to create standard regiments or divisions, a fact simplifying operational planning, drilling, training, command and control but, most importantly, implementation of support, with the UN expedition in Korea being a prime example. But it is a guess, perhaps initially attempted from the audiences during the first recitation of the work; or else Herodotus would not have embarked on apologizing for not stating so.

There is one more, very similar, issue with the strength of these land army contingents of 480 BC. As mentioned before, Herodotus gives neither strength nor any basis for standardization in terms of strength. Still, it is assumed (Green 1970) that their strength, and subsequent estimations by Herodotus, are deduced from the 60,000 figure given twice, for the commands of Artabazus and Tigranes (Her VIII.126,1 & IX.96,2 respectively), no matter whether one accepts, rejects, truncates or divides by ten the said figure. Herodotus makes no hint that these commands had anything to do with the campaign of 480 BC. They are mentioned for the campaign of 479 BC and apply to another army structure. It is modern scholars who make the interpolation (Green 1970, Hignett 1963). Herodotus rather hints, indirectly, the opposite: neither Tigranes nor Artabazus command their original contingents; the former's is in Greece with Mardonius, with himself not being there, while the opposite is true for Artabazus: he stayed with Mardonius, but his original contingent is not within the ones selected. And this silence of Herodotus on the subject is very peculiar: assuming 60,000 per contingent, the 29 contingents are very close to the 1.8 million. The thirtieth contingent is the Immortals' baivarabam, of 10,000 strength and thus not of 'standard' 60,000, an issue perhaps explaining Herodotus' denial of any notion of standard strength.

Exactly at this point lies an unresolved issue: as already mentioned, the thirtieth contingent might have been the European allies and subjects, still unaccounted for in Sardis; but Herodotus suggests a whole army's worth of such troops, that is 300,000 (Her VII.185,2). If he had it right and the Immortals were the thirtieth contingent, one faces a practical dilemma: there are two ways to treat an elite guard unit. The first is similar to the WWII Waffen SS: although their units were numerically smaller, they enjoyed the status of larger conventional formations. It was not a matter of undermanning, it was matter of honour. A lower number of elite troopers could do the job of many more conventional soldiers. This is no isolated event: Special Forces units are to this day of much lower strength, even when fully manned, than conventional units of the same echelon. This implies that the one out of 30 Imperial infantry contingents (the Immortals) may well have been a baivarabam, while the other 29 may have included more than one baivaraba, and perhaps as many as six.

And there is a second possibility: the elite unit should be heavier than the draftees' to field higher strength for the same echelon. The issue is fully attested for the Roman first cohort of each Legion, being double-strength (Hygin Munit Cast 3) and is implied for the Macedonian army, with the Hypaspists being 3,000, double the strength of a typical Taxis of the phalanx (Kambouris & Bakas 2017). Had this been the case, the infantry of Xerxes would amount to 155,000, Immortals included, guards (Arstibara) excluded and with no hint whether non-combatants should be included as well. Although this might be very appealing to the 'Trimming School', the fact that Herodotus specifically states that next year Mardonius had 300,000, troops, even if taken with much salt to the tune of including the Medizers and European allies, creates the need for more trimmings; and even more if one recounts an Allied Greek army of more than 100,000, without exhausting their reserves and raised from less than half the states of mainland Greece.

In all, there is nothing unbelievable in assigning a host of 1.8 million to the empire, non-combatants included (they *should* have been enclosed and counted as they were absorbing supplies, which was the focal issue of the Imperial logistics) since the Greeks could muster 110,000 fighters without exhausting the manpower of the 31 participating city-states. A quick look at the map shows Lacedaimon, with 50,000 troops of all kinds, heavy, light and non-combatants, excluding the –

negligible – fleet; and all that at a mobilization rate of 2/3s. And then a look at the empire sets things in perspective. To raise 20 times the muster of Greece (or, rather, of the one-half of Greece) and 40 times that of Lacedaimon, seems superfluous, as Xerxes remarks to Artabanus (Her VII.48). The alternative tradition of 700–800,000 in Diodorus (XI.3,7–8) and Ktesias (Munro 1902; Burn 1962) might fit well if the 200 crew of 1200 warships, that is 240,000 or so for the war galleys plus the crews of the merchantmen and auxiliaries are taken into account, along with the non-uniformed non-combatants (artisans, jugglers, whores, other entertainers, merchants buying slaves and loot, full households with chamberlains and servants).

Providing for such numbers is another issue, and it rests at the heart of doubting the scale (not the precision) of the numbers of Herodotus. It might have been a valid argument if Herodotus was, like other ancient sources, just producing a figure. He is not, he is himself very conscientous; moreover, he states that the protagonists, both of them, were too. The Imperial staff acknowledged the issue and took measures to alleviate the issue (Her VII.50,4) while the Greek leadership tried to exploit it (Polyaen I.32,3). Apart from that, estimates based on water availability, contour and human diet patterns of 2,500 years later, physiology and bioergonomics (e.g. Maurice 1930; Delbruck 1920) are good to read, better to show research innovation, but precarious to follow.

Last but not least is the issue of cavalry. Here the numbers, for horse cavalry, are solid (Her VII.184,4) and do not include retainers, who should be counted with the auxiliaries, but do include any mounted retainers, as was the case with the Gauls (Paus X.19,9). There are three cavalry generals (Her VII.88,1), which would imply that the roster should be divided 3-ways, but this is still a guess. A further guess is that each cavalry general is assigned to one of the three invasion itineraries (Her VII.121,22–3) that might be followed by an army under dual command (Boteva 2011) or by an army group of two individual armies. There is no figure whatsoever on the cavalry number hauled by the horse transports of the fleet and no indication of who was in command of such troops and from which reservoir they originated: from the whole cavalry host, or from the cavalry contingent of one division, that may have been an army or an army group? And, which is most important, what has been the proportion of cavalry in different echelons? In two cases Herodotus provides a solid number for the strength of a Persian army (Darius in Scythia, Mardonius in Greece) and specifically states that cavalry is included. The former (Her IV.87,1) is incomprehensible: Herodotus has no numbers for the Imperial armies conducting operations before and during the rebellion in Ionia, nor for Marathon. But he has accurate numbers for the operations of Megabazus, as mentioned earlier, and for the army at Scythia, with the aforementioned intriguing detail regarding the cavalry. This information must have come either from an inscription/monument or from a Persian live source; and Herodotus has some of the latter (Her I.1,1), which explains his deep knowledge of events unfolding within the Persian Empire during at least four generations, even at times and locations without any Greek connection or association.

The issue with Mardonius' army is much more serious. As it is extensively reviewed in the respective chapter of the last book in this trilogy, suffice it to say that this inclusion of cavalry is problematic. Mardonius has four major Asian infantry contingents (Her IX.31,1–4) which must be understood to include everyone off horseback (mule leaders, pack animal escorts, waggoneers and cooks); these account for 240,000 troops if 60,000 are accepted as the standard for the national or multi-national contingents he selects. There are 60,000 missing – a contingent's worth. Where are they? One possibility is that they are the cavalry. They cannot have been cavalry, as it would mean that, if allowance is made for casualties of seaborne cavalry at sea, Xerxes took back in Asia only shreds. A second option is that the Medizers and European allies (Her IX.31,5) are actually *included* in the 300,000, which is most probable for the army of the future satrap of Greece and Skudra. Alternatively, a third option, is that one more Asiatic contingent might have escaped Herodotus' attention. It could have consisted of the smaller units of troops selected by Mardonius on merit, like the Egyptian marines (Her IX.32), who may well have been meant to serve as hostages, too. But it is hardly believable to have been so numerous as to create a whole mixed corps, accounting for the missing 60,000. Probably this secondary muster roll was primarily intended to make up for casualties in the other contingents.

The issue of the (pro-) Greek historians trimming the Allied numbers and exaggerating the Imperial ones has another aspect. It does produce an imbalance that magnifies *some* aspects of the Greek achievement, but this is only part of the truth. There is no case where the Allies or the pro-Greek historians are suspected of purposely trimming the Greek numbers, with the possible exception of Herodotus' failure to mention the Lacedaimonians who fought in Thermopylae. Even in this case, the respective figure is factored in the total Greek tally, causing no difference in terms of impression and final strength comparison!

It is quite possible that the Imperials *and* the Medizers, not the Allies, were inflating the Imperial numbers, the latter to acquire a plausible justification for their conduct, the former for much more complicated reasons. Psychological warfare was one of them, intending to unnerve the opposition (Burn 1962). But it was also a proof of the sway exercised by the liege and the efficiency of the empire. Empires need more than muscle, gold, diplomacy; they need awe and admiration. A magnificent effort to produce a vast army shows the prowess of the empire in fields not entirely military; administrative and economic efficiencies are awe-inspiring, while such a show has a detrimental effect on the morale of the enemy, especially when the latter's resolution is less than concrete (Grundy 1901). The mere notion of such numbers to be mobilized and at least obey to, if not being inspired by, the liege creates an attraction for or acceptance by large social groups within the states to be invaded or absorbed. The well-known attitude of Chinese royalties and military establishments in the early half of the first millennium BC, which revelled in numbers, is a prime historical example. Just as good as the one of the '8 squadrons, each of 8 battleships' of the Royal Navy in the First World War, and the 600-ship US Navy of the Cold War; without ever forgetting the 100,000 warriors and 1,100 vessels of Agamemnon's magnificent host (Hom Iliad II).

For the purposes of this work, the Imperial fleet is supposed to be 1,207 vessels at the beginning of the invasion, augmented by 120 from the north Aegean coast and islands and due to receive more, though few, reinforcements by the islanders of the central Aegean. The original vessels are considered to have been outfitted with 30-strong central Asian boarding parties from central Asia on top of their native marines who were at least ten. The additional boarders were counted in the army totals and were mostly cavalrymen, as there were mounts aplenty with the horse transports; the balance must have been line infantry. The Imperial land host was divided into six armies, each of 300,000 total manpower. The armies were made of 5 corps of 60,000 each; in this figure, the line baivaraba are included but also the sum of the non-combatants and auxiliaries of each corps, which include similar human resources delegated to the cavalry, *and* the cavalry. If two hazaraba of cavalry were delegated to each corps, the total of cavalry delegated to the six Marshals is 60,000 (30 corps by 2,000 cavalry each) and the infantry strength of each corps is at most five baivaraba, but not six (it is possible that they are far fewer, as few as two, and the rest are support personnel and non-combatants). The sixth 10,000 detachment might have been a 'command baivarabam' formed by the cavalry, the retinue of the commander, his bodyguard, if applicable, and every element of his staff and secretariat and possibly of the relatives, retainers and households of the senior officers. The royal train with the general secretariat, the staff of the headquarters, the royal family and household were perhaps forming a support-heavy 30th corps, the fighting element of which being the baivarabam of the Immortals and the four hazaraba of guards, both infantry (arstibara) and cavalry.

Chapter 2

The Oriental Caterpillar: Xerxes Invades

The strategic stage

Once it was decided that the campaign was to develop by land, followed by the fleet for mutual support (both in terms of logistics and operational combinations), a set of constants seemed undeniable. The concept had been tested time and again: it was successfully employed by Cambyses against Egypt (Her III.19,3; Holland 2005) and by Artaphrenes against the rebels in Ionia in 493 BC (Her VI.31 & 33). Its faulty application resulted in the disaster of Darius I in Scythia, while Mardonius was forced to abort once his fleet had been destroyed (Her VI.45,2). The only exception to the rule was the Persian Reconquista of Cyprus (Her V.116) by the army of Artybius (Her V.108), who fell early in the first battle (Her V.113), but the campaign had been victorious despite the defeat of the supporting fleet (Her V.112,1).

Common sense dictated that at least an army (group) or, at any rate, a powerful land force, was to shadow from the coast the moves of the fleet. The fleet had to make daily calls to the land if not for watering, definitely for rest. The massive crews of rowers could not be accommodated onboard, unlike other more spacious vessels of other ages. Thus, these predictable calls were windows of vulnerability, with the land army providing protection in enemy shoreline and securing watering. This was more or less how the Greeks perceived the vulnerability of the Persian fleet. At the same time, the fleet kept the army supplied and would assist by amphibious flanking or enveloping the enemy positions, should the land force be intercepted and pinned or repulsed.

In fact, it was not so, but the Allies *thought* it was and thus were selecting advantageous positions for defence. These were by necessity the shores and coves of headlands where the Imperial fleet and army/ies would NOT be in tactical proximity; the latter meaning the physical ability of each to engage in a battle fought by the other. Such positions were few.

First, the Chalcidice peninsula in Macedon, with its three promontories was such a case, the most prominent one. There was no way the Persian army would go in and out in the three promontories; they were left for the fleet to subjugate (Her VII.122–3); and even the fleet would not venture in either of the gulfs in between (Her VII.122–3). The coastal army/ies went to the cut canal of Athos

(Her VII.115–6) and from there straight to Therma (Her VII.124), to the rendezvous point with the fleet – and of course with the other armies. The fleet went through the canal, skirted the Athos promontory from the west and the next one (Sithonia, the central leg) from the east as the onboard marine forces were numerous enough (Her VII.184,2) to conduct operations to the dispersed communities but crossed to the third and westernmost peninsula, Pallene (**Map 2.1**), without entering the gulf of Cassandra (Her VII.122–3). But there was no position for the Allied forces, no secure sanctuary to fall back, no line of retreat, and thus no effort was done to intercept the invaders in the north.

The second headland was the Magnesian peninsula, defining the eastern part of the Gulf of Pagassai as it projects like a hugging arm, and runs at its full length by the Pelion mountain range. It would keep the Persian fleet at a distance from its army, as there was no way the army would enter and then backstep out of Magnesia. The army was skirting the western shore of the gulf of Pagassai and would expect the fleet to negotiate Cape Sepias and rendezvous within the gulf, at Alus (Her VII.197,1), or a little to the west, in the nice flat shore of Malis. From Alus to Malis fleet and army would actually proceed side by side – or, at least, they *could* do so.

The separation due to Magnesia was insignificant compared to the one in Chalcidice, but still, it was exploitable by the Allied forces. And there was a bonus: just south of the peninsula the great island of Euboea was situated, rather oblong in shape, lying NW-SE. If the Persian fleet went southwards, through the open sea, skirting its eastern shore, it would face an unfavourable coastline and be separated from the army by sea and land. If the fleet was going to call at Malis and skirt Euboea

Map 2.1

The Imperial advance from Doriscus to Therma. The Imperial fleet (red) sails along the coast, shadowed by at least one division (yellow), which follows the coastal road as mentioned by Herodotus for Xerxes in person. Alternative routes to accommodate parallel axes of advance (white) as reported by Herodotus may include a hard and difficult road at the north of the Rhodope range, as suggested by Boteva 2011.

from the west, it was exposed to continuous harassment from the shores and then to the straits of Euripus. The latter allowed only two vessels abreast; with at least five minutes needed for each pair to negotiate the straits, 50 hours were needed for the battleships of the Imperial navy, numbering 1,200. If the massive merchantmen and support vessels were to play any role in the logistics of the campaign, a faster, more capacious route should have been used. Probably the open sea route, east of the island would have been selected for merchantmen. Less crowded, more seaworthy and able to sail at night if need be, the merchantmen would be able to sail the eastern course in relative safety, once the Allied fleet had been destroyed. The Imperial admiralty had probably been briefed on the precipitous eastern shoreline of Euboea, if not by the Greek deserters, definitely from the abducted Eretrians (Her VI.119,2) and from the reconnaissance of Democides during the reign of Darius (Her III.135,2–3). This is manifest when they decide to sail the course in an effort to encircle the Allied fleet at Artemisium (Her VIII.7,1). The factor the Imperial admiralty had failed to correctly appreciate was the combination of the temperamental weather in the late Greek summer with the traitorous shoreline.

But the western course allowed the Imperial fleet to support the Imperial army as it ventured south. The island of Euboea created a bizarre situation. It formed straits, allowing land forces in either shore to harass a fleet, especially a massive fleet. At the straits of Euripus, a land force in one shore, let alone in both, could shoot to pieces a navy venturing to cross, possibly even with javelins and slings. Massive archery would damage hulls and rigging, pierce and neutralize or at least degrade sails and decimate rowers if not marines as well – and all these without the use of incendiaries in the form of special arrows or any kind of improvised fiery sling bolts.

On the other hand, Euboea was a land corridor. A mobile army with the most basic sea transports could land at its northern shores, overrun it and emerge to Euripus, to choke an enemy fleet advancing or retreating (Green 1970). Even if the Imperial fleet had not been assigned a massive marine force of almost 50,000 warriors (Her VII.184,2), units of the Imperial army could cross thanks to their fleet and gallop to Euripus, where they could choke the straits for the Greek navy, or swim across on horseback, or cross by a most basic bridge to flank any Greek land position north of Boeotia, or any Greek anchorage north of Euripus (Green 1970).

The third position where the Imperial army and navy would be separated was Attica. The army would enter from the NW or the N and proceed SE or S, respectively, to Athens and the SW shore and from there towards Peloponnese. Sending expeditionary forces south to Cape Sounion, and then having them retrace their steps to venture to Peloponnese was a waste of stamina, time and resources. The fleet had to round Cape Sounion and then go NW to rendezvous with the army at the SW coast of Attica to attack Peloponnese; thus it could ravage the whole coastline while doing so, without veering one inch from its destination and route.

The promontory of Argolis was a final location forcing a separation of an invading army and its supporting fleet, but the enmity of the Argives towards the leader of the alliance, Sparta (Her VII.148,4) and their affection for the Persians (Her IX.12,1) nullified any possible operational value. The ultimate position where the Imperial fleet and navy could be isolated from each other was Cape Sounion.

But the Greek calculations were inherently wrong: the fleet had a massive marine corps (Her VII.184,2), making coastal support from the army/ies redundant. The daily calling of the fleet to the coast was not a vulnerability, but rather an opportunity for ruthless aggression against coastal communities and active subjugation, as happened with all four of the already mentioned headlands which separated fleet and army – with the possible exception of the Magnesian peninsula due to destructive gales. And, even more to the point, the almost 250,000 crew and marines of the galleys alone (Her VII.184,1–2) needed water, the resources of which would be exhausted instantly in the arid central and southern Greek shoreline should a massive land force venture along the coast (de Souza 2003). Thus a land army shadowed the sailing fleet only where water was plentiful, in Thrace and Macedon; and kept their distance even on enemy shores, if the communities, as in Chalcidice, were posing no great danger, so as to manage watering resources advantageously.

On the other hand, the experience of Marathon dictated massive land forces providing full cover in calling areas where Greek armies might assemble to challenge the invader on the beach. Thus, having heard of a Greek expeditionary force attempting to dispute the entrance of the land army at Tempe with the respective fleet calling at Alus (Her VII.173,1) the Imperial Joint Headquarters must have taken care to adjust times so that the army would cover the fleet calls in Alus, Malis and, the most pernicious area, Attica. The latter was the nest of the redoubtable Athenian Hoplites who marred the prospect of elite, amphibian forces being used for the conquest of Greece and made the Imperials revert to massive land armies; the Athenian Hoplites were possibly reinforced by next-door Peloponnesian neighbours retreating from Thermopylae or emerging from the peninsula.

The starting point

For many reasons, Xerxes did not start his campaign against Greece from Babylon, at least not according to Diodorus (XI.2,3). The most plausible reason is the theory of a Babylonian rebellion in his days there as regent under Darius I. Herodotus is suspiciously silent on the matter. There are indeed no Babylonian troops in the host (Her VII.61–81), a fact in accordance with the disarmament of the Babylonians after the suppression of their revolt. The only troops from the area are the Chaldeans (Her VII.63), pure Mesopotamian stock but usually considered the *priesthood* of Babylon (Her I.181; Arr Anab III.16,5), who were brigaded with the Assyrians

(Her VII.63) – a truly minuscule draft from the second richest satrapy (Her III.92). The striking of the Babylonian titles off his official introduction shows Xerxes' disgust, a disgust resulting in horrific atrocities and looting (Her I.183) leading to the damage witnessed by Alexander III some 150 years later (Arr III.16,4), though it is not clear if the oppression was the result of a rebellion, or the oppression, especially in religious matters, fuelled the rebellion. In Darius' time, the latter was not the case, but in Xerxes' reign, it might have been, as he was a religious zealot, despite really desperate attempts with dubious arguments to exonerate him (Wijnsma 2019).

Still, there is a very real problem with the revolt(s) of Babylon. It becomes established that their dating is a matter of interpretation, not of solid substantiation (Wijnsma 2019) and the current opinion has them occurring between the rise of Xerxes on the throne and his campaign in Greece (ibid). This interpretation defies logic. The silence of Herodotus on the matter, who seems (or rather reads) extremely well-informed, is troubling. It may be explained away: the Babylonian risings might have been the reason for such long years of preparation for the operation against Greece, when Darius I had made considerable preparations himself, and there was an army victorious from the campaign to recapture Egypt after its rebellion (Klotz 2015). Still, the dating is irrational. Successive revolts, two in a matter of months at more-or-less the same area, especially in rich, flat, accessible areas, is a suicidal practice. One must admit that the two revolts would be far more in context if the earlier had erupted during Xerxes' regency, somewhere between 497 and 496 bc, possibly due to his ardent Zoroastrianism (Abdi 2007) and had been promptly dealt with, a fact that built a most favourable reputation for him for his future tasks as King of Kings. Being mutinous, the troops from Babylonia were disarmed and not included in the Greek campaign. Thus, they were conveniently poised for another attempt after the disaster in Salamis – a reason for Xerxes' fast withdrawal and his lingering in Sardis for some time, until the issue was resolved and he could proceed without any danger back to Susa (Her IX.108,2) or Ecbatana (Diod XI.36,7).

The omission of Babylonian troops, traditionally enemies of Assyria and of many other areas within the empire (i.e. Elam), shows that the multi-national conscripts of the royal army were not considered hostages in any case; or else troops from mutinous areas would have been conscripted preferably. They were drafted with a minimum of dependability as a prerequisite, which was hammered further by a variety of means into true discipline (Her VII.52,2). But they were always supposed to possess a core of loyalty to start with (Her VII.52,1). This precaution did not apply to 'contributions' demanded from new subjects who surrendered just before or during the Persian advance.

Darius had set out from Susa against Scythia (Her IV.83,2). Xerxes did so against Greece from Susa as well (Diod XI.2,3), his royal capital, although the ignorance of the Greeks on the existence of Persepolis, the secret city (Mousavi 2005) allows room for some doubt. But Babylon was not the starting point of the campaign, contrary to the repeated choice of Darius III (Diod XVII. 31,1 & 53,3). From Susa, Xerxes stayed clear of Babylon and must have moved to the whereabouts of Opis following the King's Road north-west – the Upper Road to Mesopotamia (Monerie 2019) as may have done the army dispatched against Egypt (Her VII.7) some years ago. But it is most probable that soon he veered away, for another, more traditional route. Xerxes took a right at a fork, left the King's Road and moved well to the north and entered Asia Minor by the road of Media, which is roughly Ecbatana-Pteria-Sardis (Malye 2007). This road must have been the one taken by Cyrus II against Croesus and was thus of high symbolic value. By this choice, Xerxes possibly opted for cooler climate and a better supply of fodder, water and foodstuff. Additionally, this itinerary allowed more subject peoples and contributions in materiel and personnel to be inspected, collected/selected and added to the army on the spot or follow in regular instalments.

The spatio-temporal distribution of forces and planning of itineraries

The focal point is that the Achaemenid road system, if meant to be efficient for massive troop movements, had to be used optimally. Two approaches were conceivable: the one was the use of alternate, parallel or otherwise, itineraries to

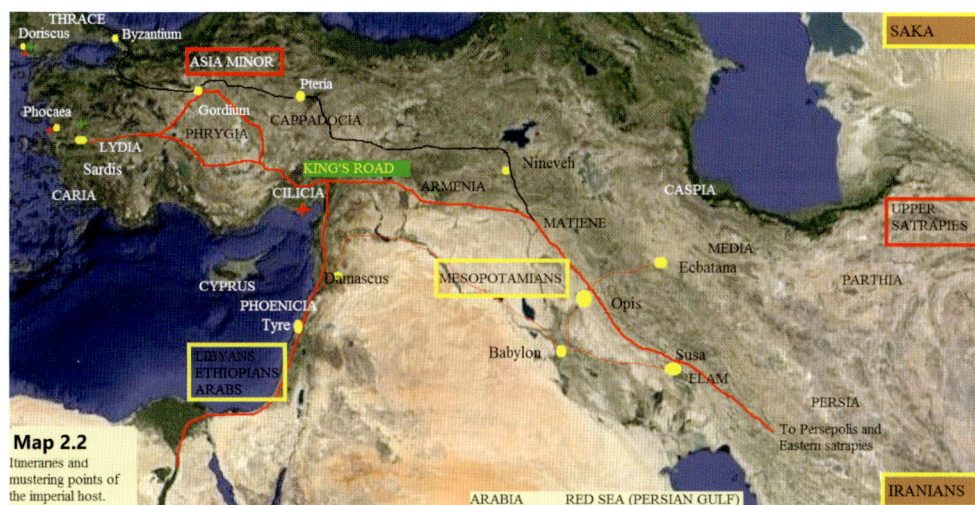

Itineraries and mustering points of the Imperial host. Stars (red for the fleet, green for the land army) denote mustering locations within the borders of the Empire. The red line shows the King's Road as per Herodotus plus the northern detour in Asia Minor and secondary branches. The black line is the northern route used before the conquest of Cilicia. Red boxes denote large geographical and administrative areas, yellow boxes troop origins or moves along the network. The mustering point of Critalla defies identification even today.

distribute the transportation load more evenly, both in terms of road capacity and of supplies along the road. The other was the sequential use of every axis, which means that troops were advancing in instalments for a depth of time, to allow logistics to play along and once more not to exceed the capacity of the roads. Both these approaches require rendezvous points along the road (**Map 2.2**), and explain many things during the invasion; for example, the assignment of two Marshals in each invasion axis (Her VII.121,3) might be an indication for the staged deployment of troops along an itinerary.

In this context, the King's Road proper, from Cilicia to central Asia Minor, was left for the troops coming from Africa who were moving along the road of Memphis to the Levantine coast, past the intersection of Gaza, where the Arabians would have poured in, coming from east to south-east. Then the movement of these units would have been northwards, taking the opposite direction to that of Alexander the Great after the battle of Issus (Arr An II.13,7), through the Syrian Gates in Cilicia, where the Assyrian and Chaldean contingents would have also converged, along with every contingent from the southern half of the Persian Empire, which would have been following the King's Road and entered Cilicia through the Gates of Amanus. Once into Cilicia, all would proceed by the King's Road to the Cilician Gates and from there into central Asia Minor. These units probably never met with Xerxes at Critalla, but converged to the second muster area, Sardis.

Critalla must have been the first rallying point of the Imperial grand army according to Herodotus (VII.26,1), found in Cappadocia but never solidly identified, as some quite strong arguments favour the location of the spot along both itineraries that cross Asia Minor from east to west (Malye 2007); still, the northern alternative is more tempting (Wilson 2005), for reasons of management of the resources if for no other. Other rendezvous points must have been established westwards. Such were definitely, but not exclusively, Sardis in the summer of 481 BC as already mentioned, Doriscus at Thrace, where army and fleet would converge in Spring 480 BC, and Therma, where the new subjects from northern Greece and the Balkan Peninsula (actually the Persian province of Skudra) would converge after pledging their allegiance to the heralds dispatched from Sardis (Her VII.32). Allied and subject contingents were also coming along to be included in the Imperial host, as it was passing by or through (Her VII.115,2).

It would be accurate, more or less, to define functionally the four known muster points as follows: Xerxes started from Susa and was leading the Guard Units (Immortals, Arstibara, and Cavalry), perhaps the Persian Home Army (Spada) and possibly other local troops, as were the Cissians. In Critalla he was joined by detachments following in his wake from as far away as India and Bactra, lagging behind as ordered, to avoid jamming the network. Units from other areas perpendicular to this axis were also likely to use the same course, as were the Medes, who probably moved from Ecbatana through Behistun to the southern part of the King's Road, and the Armenians, who would enter the axis near Nineveh, and might have been followed by the Caspians, Parthians and Hyrcanians, amongst others.

On the contrary, contingents from Asia Minor and from the south-east and south-west of the empire, that is the islands and coast of the Persian Gulf and Carmania on one hand (Her VII.80), and from Ethiopia, Libya, Arabia (Her VII.70,1 & 71) on the other, must have hit the main course of the King's Road after exiting Cilicia through the Cilician Gates into Cappadocia, to arrive at Sardis. There they had probably been preceded by Xerxes, who left Critalla and entered the King's Road at some point in central Asia Minor, in Cappadocia most likely, to follow it to Sardis. The itinerary described by Herodotus for Xerxes (Her VII.26–31) started from Critalla in Cappadocia, then across Phrygia (Celaenae, Anaua, Colossae, Cydrara) to Lydia (Callatebus, Sardis). The course of Xerxes must have been passed by some primary source, a participant or his descendant, to Herodotus because it is difficult to align, even partly, with Herodotus' own account of the King's Road (Her V.52–4). The latter is a detailed account (rivers are given in **bold**): Sardis – Phrygia – **Halys** – Cappadocia – Cilicia – **Euphrates** – Armenia – **Tigris** – **Gyndes** – Matiene-Cissia/Susa, suggesting that the historian had travelled the King's Road himself, evidently after the Peace of Kallias.

In Doriscus, the third rallying point, European units, especially from Thrace and the Euxine coast (Her VII.185,2) and the European *Skudra*-district of the Persian Empire, as well as the fleet (Her VII.59,2) would have joined in. The invasion army was morphed there. This holds true for the fleet as well: it is there that Xerxes inspects it extensively, after his first introduction at Abydos (Her VII.44) and where army units must have been delegated for fleet duty as marines to enhance native detachments.

The transformation of the army took into account the local character of the conscription; the contingents which formed the Grand Army were raised locally by the local satraps and the rest of the Imperial officials and officers, and may have been natives or appointed Iranians. Such drafted hosts mustered in several major centres throughout the realm, when mobilized centrally by royal decrees, as reported by Xenophon (Xen Hell I.4,3). Herodotus is very specific in that local dignitaries raised and led the contingents and were responsible for their training and outfit (Her VII.19,3 & 26,1–2). Given that in Thermopylae, but also in Plataea, the units were led into battle and committed by ethnicity, it is obvious that the basic, feudal nature of the army was not aborted in Doriscus for a more standardized one.

But there was something that DID change: all these units, conscripted on a local basis and led and commanded as such, were assigned to and divided by the standard Achaemenid organization and chain of command, which had been applied as a top-down institution, engulfing and reflecting the feudal muster. The brigading of different peoples under one commander, which was the practice for raising and moving the troops to the staging point, implies original, set targets for the draft of each separate contingent. Standardized command structures were introduced in Doriscus to these, possibly similar but not identical, feudal hosts. The standardization was based on set numbers of men in sub-units and units. It was the last muster before the invasion; the Strymon river must have been the official limit of the Empire (Boteva 2011), as indicated by the ceremony before crossing (Her VII.113–4).

Thus, having incorporated all his subjects' units, Doriscus was the right place for Xerxes to review and count them and to divide the musters to units, appoint commanders and, much more importantly, assign these contingents to the armies and itineraries of the invasion. This was a delicate and important task, as affiliations with the locals and special dexterities and knowledge should have been taken into serious consideration when earmarking each unit for one of the divisions.

As the Imperial army moved from Doriscus west, new subjects (including allies) along its path were sending their contributions to join or follow (Her VII.110 & 115,2) the three divisions into which the Imperial army had been divided (Her VII.121,2), each of them possibly advancing in two echelons deployed in tandem (Her VII.121,3). The final muster would have been at Therma (Her VII.121,1), the furthest possible spot for the reunion of the three divisions (Her VII.121,2–3). There, the Imperial army must have incorporated the last tributaries and allies, as were the Macedonians, and the first batch of new subjects (Her VII.122) lying off its axis of advance. Therma must be considered something between a mustering point and a rendezvous point. It was a secure vassal area, with a very large supply and logistics centre (Her VII.25 & 121 & 124 & 127), which would have never been established had it been volatile, insecure or of questionable loyalty. Xerxes never thought of creating such infrastructure in Thessaly, which medized so early as to be considered the actual instigator of the invasion (Her VII.6,2). But, on the other hand, it was a rendezvous point as the Imperial forces had crossed the borders and actively subjugated communities previously autonomous. Similar rendezvous points beyond the borders were Thessaly, Malis and south-west Attica, where army – or armies – and navy would converge.

Detailing the successive legs: The way to Sardis

Xerxes marched from Critalla due west to reach Sardis, where he established his base camp (Her VII.32 & 37,1). It was the second rallying point for the vassal units, and the winter quarters of 481 BC. A whole year had been spent from when he left his palace just to his emerging in-theatre, in Sardis, where all the Asian and African army units were to be assembled. This lumbering giant, moving at snail's pace, makes very clear the tempo of Persian campaigns westwards, every two years or so, since the Ionian revolt. Armies had moved west and arrived in-theatre possibly, but not probably, in 498 BC, and definitely in 494, 492, and 490; the last was transported from Cilicia by sea. Fully-fledged armies were taking a year to march from the heart of the empire to the western theatre; a walking distance of three months by the King's Road, according to Herodotus' calculations, but also according to Aristagoras' claims to Cleomenes (Her V.54,1).

As already mentioned, the contingents led by Xerxes did not follow the usual route through Cilicia, along the King's Road, as Mardonius and Datis had done (Her VI.43,1–2 & 95,1). The contingents from Arabia, Libya and Ethiopia must have converged to Lebanon and from there to Cilicia and then westwards to Sardis by the King's Road. Alternatively, such units might have not turned north-west to the Cilician Gates and thus to King's Road, but continued north, through the Gates of Amanus, to hit the road taken by Xerxes himself and thus meet him at Critalla. Their actual itinerary cannot be determined, but the former would put less strain on the resources along Xerxes' own course.

From Sardis to Therma

Sardis was a key point. It was there that the various detachments were integrated into an army and the Grand Army came into being. From there stemmed the subjugational diplomacy towards all the city-states of Greece and beyond, to request the tokens of submission. And it was there that the Greek spies converged

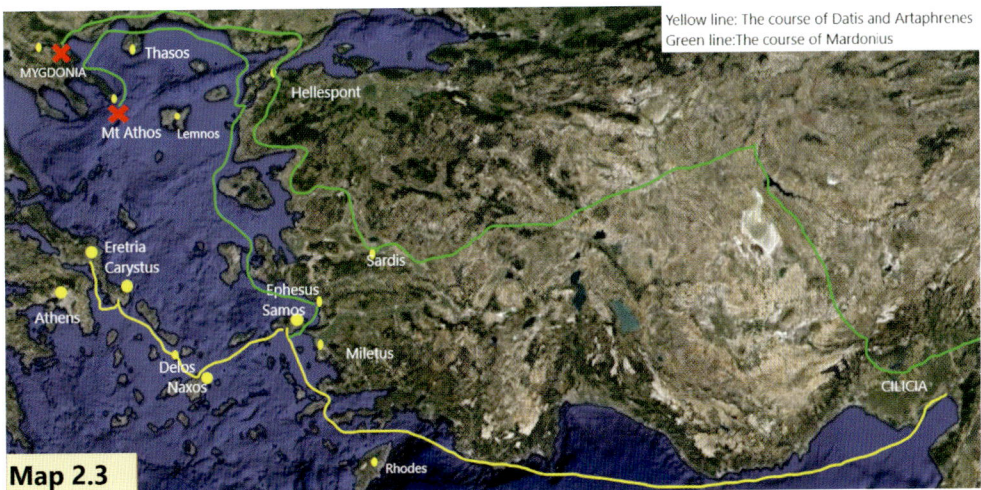

Map 2.3

to have a detailed peek at the opponent (Her VII.146,1), though the security was extremely effective for an ancient force, and one just assembled at that. The spies were captured, briskly interrogated and summarily set for execution, but Xerxes somehow was informed and intervened to pardon them (Her VII.146,3). It is important that others, *not* Xerxes, interrogated and condemned them. These functions were proceeding automatically. His intervention was needed to stop the punitive sequence and treat them as guests or envoys, so they could absorb magnificence and transmit omnipotence (Her VII.147,1) – although NOT of the fleet, which was to be forged to a fighting force later, in Thrace; possibly the next year. The whole spies' affair was the second propaganda masterstroke of his (Green 1970).

The first had been the 'Spartan Atonement'. The Persian envoys of King Darius, probably sent in 491 BC, before the campaign of 490 BC led by Datis but after the abortive one of Mardonius (Her VI.48), had been put to death (Her VII.133,1). This was predictably the doing of the infamous King Cleomenes, half-brother of the current King Leonidas (Her VII.204–5), who had a very striking disregard of religious etiquette and piousness in general (Her VI.66 & 80–1), a feature extremely un-Spartan. This was a religious crime, a trans-religious sin. A sequence of disasters drove the Spartans to atone, by sending two men to Susa to die voluntarily so as to wash off the sin (Her VII.134,2–3). Xerxes received them, but denied the offer; he said he did not care either to imitate or to exonerate the Spartans (Her VII.136,2).

Sardis had been Xerxes' winter quarters between 481 and 480 BC. Early in spring 480 BC he set forth northwards and probably followed the steps of Mardonius in 492 BC (**Map 2.3**); he crossed the river Caicus into Mysia and passed through the territory of Attarneus inland enough to keep the Cane mountain to his left (Her VII.42,1); at this point, though, there are some issues. The waypoints of Herodotus (VII.42–3) do not agree with his orientation (Her VII.42). It is impossible to skirt the Ida mountain from the east (Her VII.42,2) *and* pass by the cities of Adrammitium and Antandros (Her VII.42,1), especially the latter; nor, having skirted the Ida from the east, the Scamander river emerges at the course of the army (Her VII.43,1). The same goes for Troad (Her VII.42,2–43,1) etc. Thus, Xerxes must have skirted the Ida from the west (Grundy 1901), which is an easier task for a large army as any modern physical map can show. It may be proposed that by the same token Herodotus is somewhat upside-down in this case and the Imperial army passed west of the Cane mountain (Her VII.42,1) and thus followed more or less the shore, having moved north-west from Sardis. After skirting the Ida from the west, the army by moving north to north-east found itself squarely in the plain of Troy (Her VII.442,2) and from there, moved across the plain (Her VII.43,2) to Abydos, where the Asian entrance of the bridges across the

Hellespont was situated (Her VII.34). As the army advanced, Xerxes had time for some tourism at Troy and propaganda, pretending to be the avenger of the Trojans (Her VII.43; Green 1970). Or did he?

At Abydos Xerxes first laid eyes upon his fleet (Her VII.44) and his religious officials took pains to placate the Hellespont and secure acceptable omens (Her VII.54) for the crossing to Europe which, in terms of semantics, initiated the invasion. He crossed over the bridges, using one (the eastern) for the troops and the other (the western) for the beasts of burden and support formations (Her VII.55,1) within a week (Her VII.56,1); but this time may concern a part of the army and the actual crossing operation, especially of the supply trains, may have lasted much longer, almost a month (Her VIII.51,1). However, the month-long crossing may have been due to the destruction of the original bridges. The wording of Herodotus might well imply that the destruction occurred *after* Xerxes had started from Sardis and possibly when he was at or near Abydos. The show of lashing and fettering the sea (Her VII.35) implies the host bearing witness. The racing of the fleet (Her VII.44), a nice pastime while a new pair of bridges was launched expeditiously and the concentration of the fleet nearby (Her VII.44–5), in a most arid region, where water resources are few, can only be understood as an urgent development. A call to the fleet to come to the rescue so as to use ships and manpower for launching new bridges promptly may be assumed (Hale 2009) during which time, excursions such as the one in Troy (Her VII.43) were not only possible, but also advisable.

Thus, due to these adverse events, the crossing operation took a month (Her VIII.51,1), although the actual crossing took seven days and nights (Her VII.56,1). A 15-metre wide bridge would be easily accommodated through the decks of triremes and pentekonters, and would produce at least 10 men per 5 seconds ashore; this means something over a million men at that rate in seven days. But the delay was to prove of vital importance; when at Salamis, Xerxes had to make his moves under the impending threat of the coming winter, or, rather, of the end of the sailing season. Three more weeks and the volume of supplies spent while the host was waiting at Abydos for the new bridges might have been the difference between triumph and disaster; in retrospect, beheading the engineers of the first pair of bridges as punishment for its destruction by a tempest (Her VII.35,3) seems too lenient…

Having crossed to Europe, the Army was advancing still in friendly, Imperial territory following the contour of the peninsula, and kept east of the city of Cardia (Her VII.58,2), at the narrowest point. Cardia was a town on the western coast of the peninsula and thus the army could have bypassed it by the east only, which means the bearings of Herodotus are now correct. The Imperial army was probably following the steps of Mardonius (492 BC), who participated in this campaign and the actual road network which can be seen even today, which runs along the south-east coast for a length to cross to the north-west just after Cardia.

Exiting the peninsula, the host arrived at the first supply dam, probably at the White Shore, or at Tyrodiza, which should be located at the entrance of Propontis, on the European coast (Her VII.25). This is somewhat tricky, though. Herodotus never mentions that; his actual narrative implies that Xerxes probably took the coastal road to the west the moment he left the peninsula, although there were other options: one was to cross the mountains to his north-west to access a better route, but this was leading to a detour. In any case, according to Herodotus, Xerxes never moved east towards his massive supply dam, which means that supplies must have been ferried from there, at the curve of his path, a distance of some 60 km. The same depot must have been sustaining the Imperial host for the duration of the crossing and the trek along the Hellespont.

Once clear of the peninsula, Xerxes' army turned due west as mentioned, most likely by the coastal road, and reached the vital Imperial outpost of Doriscus at the mouth of the river Hebrus (Her VII.59). These two legs of their march were something less than 100 km each and roughly equal in length, showing the actual sustaining capacity of a depot over rather inhospitable terrain, with few local resources in terms of food and fodder. There, at the large and well-watered plain of Doriscus with the wide beaches, Xerxes organized his army for the invasion and was introduced to the whole of his fleet (Her VII.59) except for some islanders' contributions, who must have been under orders to converge to other rendezvous points, such as Therma, Pagassai or Attica (see Box 'Mustering the fleet', p.44). The inspection and parading of the navy was performed in order to instil discipline, a sense of purpose, pride and cohesion, after a necessary maintenance effort, intended to make the hulls better and watertight. This was achieved by draining, drying them, scraping seaweed, mussels and scallops off the keels to have them streamlined (Her VII.59,3), while the Greek ones kept amassing shells as they patrolled different sea routes. Furthermore, it is probable that Iranians were assigned as Marines then and there to strengthen the native boarding parties of the Imperial triremes (Her VII.96,1). This last measure included the selection and delegation of the cavalry which was to continue seaborne so as to project power ashore and to ravage deep into the enemy shoreline.

Herodotus directly narrates that the army was hammered into being there and then. The procedure is detailed, but there is one very important problem. His description of the fleet and army, both branches being there at the same time, is very different in terms of details. The description of the army, moreover, lacks any European contingent, and Doriscus was one of the finest mustering places along the road for any Thracian contributions to converge to. This implies that

Herodotus' description comes rather from the status of the Imperial army at Sardis, probably through the reports of the Allied spies. It is just as likely that the processes he reports for the Achaemenid stay in Doriscus had taken place in Sardis, except for things concerning the fleet.

In any case, keeping his original storyline, which must be accurate in context if not in timeline and locality, army tactical units were formed from the diverse contingents and squadrons, according to the standard Achaemenid decimal system (Barkworth 1993; Fields 2007) and respective commanders were appointed (Her VII.81), drill introduced and training for homogenization was undertaken. The 29 contingents of the various areas of the empire are never explicitly mentioned by Herodotus to be of the same strength; but this is to be expected a standardized military. Additionally, this would be the only valid reason for brigading together troop contributions of different nations. The alternative, i.e. assigning to all national contributions a uniform status, regardless of their numerical strength (Green 1970; Burn 1962) would have worked miracles for their morale and would allow the continued use of the chain of command which implemented the conscription and the indigenous officers. It was not so; brigading together different national contributions makes that clear. Thus, as mentioned in the previous chapter, the 29 commanders were leading single or mixed contingents of national levies and of rather standard strength – or at least similar strength – and status. A possibility would be to require simply a turnout of more than one full baivaraba for each of the 29 commanders, a fact granting equal status (Corps) but not the same numerical strength in all of them. This would be very similar to much more modern organization schemes, where divisions in different militaries have not the same number of regiments or battalions. For the Achaemenids, each corps would be anything from 2 to 6 baivaraba strong.

Drilling and exercising must have been, along with planning, the course of the day in the mega-camp at Sardis. But most importantly it must have been in Doriscus as well, where different corps were marshalled into armies (Her VII.82), the latter being assigned different invasion routes. And from Doriscus the actual campaign started.

Herodotus is explicit that during the campaign, which implies contested, if not enemy territory, the Grand Army was divided into three task forces (divisions *sensu lato*) advancing in parallel routes (Her VII.121,2–3), to cover more ground, have mutual support should one be intercepted and alleviate the fodder and water shortages. A similar approach had been enacted during the second phase of the suppression of the Ionian revolt, with three armies operating independently (Her V.116,1), although hardly for the same reasons.

The three-pronged advance occurred at least from Doriscus to the canal at Acanthus (Her VII.121,2). This strip of land consisted of friendly and occasionally independent territories. The latter were brought under the sceptre and the Imperial authority was better embedded and reaffirmed in the former. Herodotus' narration mentions Xerxes in the task force centre (Her VII.121,3) but implies a coastal location of his whereabouts (Her VII.120,1). Moreover, he implies that the three divisions converged at Acanthus although he mentions the ritual at the bridges of the Strymon (Her VII.113,2–114,1). The ceremony of the crossing implies the river was the border of the empire. It is not probable that there were bridges over the Strymon for all three routes; the most suitable part had been selected and the great flow of the river made the watering problem of the army less acute than in other parts.

Xerxes went to the peninsula of Athos, at Acanthus near to the canal (Her VII.115,2), and saw his fleet safely through (Her VII.121.1 & 122); it was a most dangerous choking point. Then, the army went almost diagonally to Therma (Her VII.124), by the fastest land route, or, at least, that was the itinerary Xerxes himself followed; other divisions could have moved differently. Near present-day Thessalonica, a mega-camp was established for fleet and army (Her VII.127,1). The fleet arrived after bringing the coast of Chalcidice and the states situated at the three peninsulas, Athos, Sithonia, Pallene (reported E-W), to their knees (Her VII.122–3).

The problem here is that although Xerxes left the Chariot of the Sun before crossing the Strymon (Her VIII.115,4), his advance from there to Therma, which was officially in foreign ground, is suggested to have been by a single route. Even if the Strymon bridges could have been established only in one location, in order to be near the depot of Eion (**Map 2.1**), the three divisions could have fanned out after crossing, to cover ground and better use water and fodder in the region. Alternatively, the northernmost task force might have converged to Therma from the north, following the valley of the Axius river to the south, after having infiltrated there at a northern latitude, possibly following the valley of Strumnitsa, as did the Germans in 1941, which implies one task force moving through, or north of the range of Rhodope (Boteva 2011).

If one wishes to be accurate, this part of Herodotus' narrative is very problematic. There is no way to reconcile his various reports on Xerxes, which is probably compiled from different sources. There are some places where there is no way to imagine three parallel courses and in some cases to identify even two is a challenge (Lazaridis 1978). Near Doriscus, for example, the terrain supports only one. Some two-thirds of the length comfortably supports two routes, with some connecting roads and paths which hardly account, in any place, for a third route (**Map 2.1**). And, finally, another part, at the area of Pangaion, supports no less than five, all converging to the lower Strymon, at Eion, the site of the bridge and the mega-depot. From there, after crossing the Strymon, two more routes continue to Therma, one straight to the west, just south of Lake Bolbi, across the width of the Chalcidice headland, another first to the south, to the root of Athos peninsula and then diagonally north-north-west to Therma. Secondary routes from this point, perhaps to the north of Lake Bolbi and within Chalcidice, allow the possibility for three routes in parallel, but Herodotus mentions this arrangement from Doriscus to Acanthus (Her VII.121,2), not from Acanthus to Therma. Even if one accepts that the northern division moved north of the Rhodope range (Boteva 2011), something quite possible if a fraction of the conquests of Darius and Megabazus had materialized as they are supposed to have been, it still leaves the issue of Xerxes' whereabouts unresolved.

The issue gets tougher: Xerxes is explicitly mentioned to have followed the middle route (Her VII.121,3), which simply means he was *not* at the coast whenever there was a northern itinerary; and at the longitude of Abdera there is. His presence at Abdera and the Delta of the river Nestos (Her VII.109) places him at the wrong position in terms of latitude. His passing *south* of Mount Pangaion (Her VII.112) in theory is reconcilable with a middle route, but one cannot reconcile his presence in Abdera (Her VII.120) with any passing near Siris to the north-west, where he left the Chariot of the Sun, before arriving at Acanthus (Her VII.116), south-east from Siris. This massive detour makes even less sense; descending from Siris south-west to the bridges near Eion may be explained: the whole army, or at least most of it, had to pass from the Eion depot at the lower Strymon to replenish their supplies, irrespective of the assigned routes, which were meant to save water resources, cover space and project the Imperial presence so as to incite spontaneous participation to the Imperial cause.

But the actual presence of the King at Abdera, and, even worse, his subsequent move north-west to Siris simply defies logic. One should conclude that Xerxes in person may have not been at all the places Herodotus mentions, especially when he mentions them as a matter of fact and not with some specific anecdote or event; but (part of) his army did and the locals preferred to extrapolate that the King himself was there. This approach may explain some inconsistencies, but still cannot resolve all of them.

The invasion plan

To culminate, the Imperial campaign had to reach Sparta, practically at the southernmost tip of Greece. From Macedon to Peloponnese there are roughly two lines of southward advance, one east and the other west of the mountain range of Pindus, which run parallel (**Map 2.4**). They run for some 350 km with only

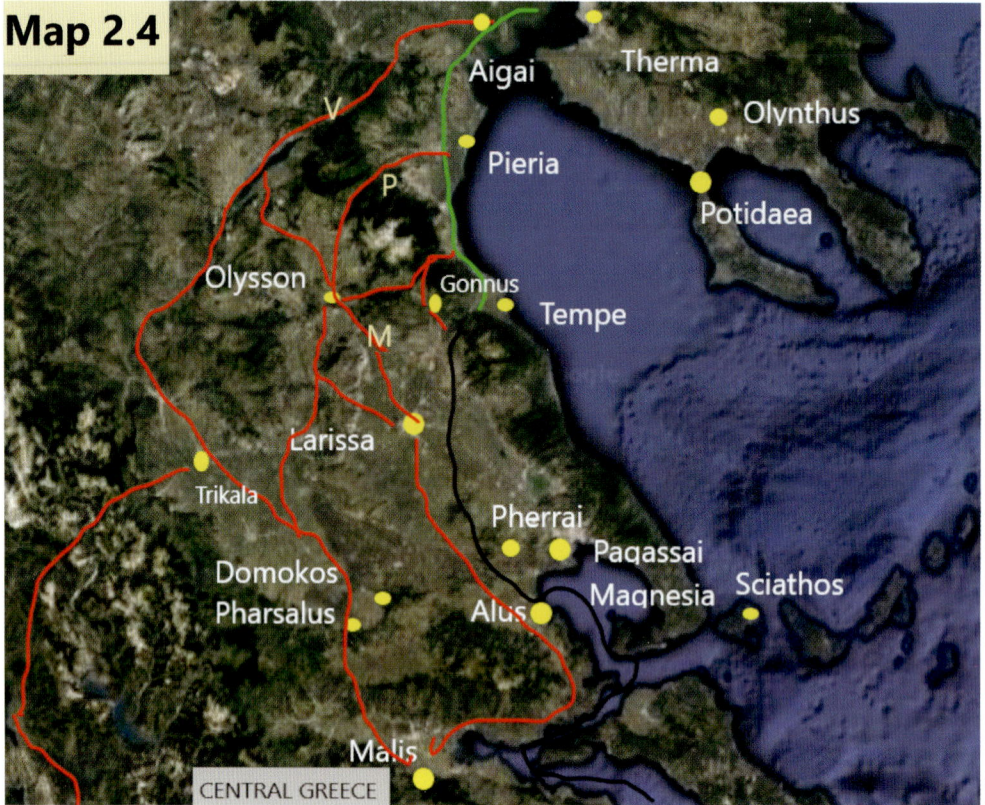

Map 2.4   CENTRAL GREECE

four connections between them: one at the beginning, roughly the course of Via Egnatia; the second at Thessaly, the third at Malis and the fourth at the latitude of the northern shore of the Gulf of Corinth. The western axis is rough for the invader but also for the defender. It has scarce resources in terms of food and difficult terrain; fodder is less of a problem and there are many streams and lakes, providing an abundant supply of water. It concludes at Antirio, just opposite of Rion in north-west Peloponnese, the proverbial back door, with something like 5 km of water between them. Still, although the defenders are bound to encounter some difficulty to deploy, the straits present numerous ambush and interceptive positions, while any invader following this route remains out of contact with friendlies descending along the eastern axis. Given the very few connections, such a western invasion force cannot be kept provisioned by supplies hauled by a supporting fleet in the Aegean, or collected along the eastern axis.

The eastern axis is somewhat complex, with a number of parallel routes and converging points. The eastern axis offers some advantages: easier terrain, proximity to a supporting fleet operating in the Aegean, but, most importantly, the territories of many Greek states that offered Earth and Water are situated along it. These had to suffer a demonstration of the Imperial power, to be discouraged from reconsidering their servile attitude. And they also had to be protected against the wrath and punitive policies of their unyielding brethren. Still another advantage was that at the end of this axis stood Athens, the primary target – the state guilty of insurrection in 507 BC, insult and invasion in 500 BC and the massive denting of the Imperial dignity in 490 BC. East, then, it was to be.

From Therma a coastal route, roughly the contemporary national highway, ran until Thebes. But there were other, parallel routes defined by the terrain. No less than four other routes connected Therma with the Thessalian plain, one of them running parallel to the beginning of the western axis. Further south, two itineraries exit Thessaly towards Malis, the gateway of southern Greece proper and converge at its plain. From Malis, there is one westward connection with the western axis and no less than three main arteries south; the coastal one which goes south-east branches further southwards in three successive places, the first two leading to Phocian territory and the third to Boeotian and eventually to Thebes. The two inland arteries also branch heavily, south towards the Gulf of Corinth (from where a westward, coastal route ends at Antirio) and east-south-east to Phocian territory and then Boeotia. Xerxes' staff had many options to keep the enemy guessing and many alternatives with which to dislodge them. Greek preference for Hoplites instead of guarding straits (Her VII.9) seems reasonable, after all.

The first objective: Thessaly

From the Strymon to Therma it was friendly, though foreign ground. Now the Imperials were entering into belligerent territory. From Therma, Xerxes launched the main part of the campaign, the invasion of Greece proper. A carpet of states terrorized to submission and alliance were waiting for his approach; the trick was exactly how to infiltrate the mountain barriers and overcome any possible Greek resistance.

The Greeks, very prudently, expected the Mega-Army to take the easy, coastal road (today's national highway) from Macedon through Tempe, the Gates of Thessaly, and ventured to shut the straits (Her VII.173,1), though, Xerxes was leaving the coastal areas for his fleet to subdue and milk for provisions and crossed the mountains with his army, after clearing/deforesting a passage (Her VII.131). Herodotus' narration is not very enlightening and seems to imply, once more, that only one route had been followed by the entire Persian army; not three, as one would expect due to the established three divisions (Her VII.121,3). In any case, Xerxes' army emerged at the rear of the Greek position at Tempe, which had been evacuated beforehand (Her VII.173–4). Herodotus states that there is a considerable time lapse between the Greek evacuation and the arrival of Xerxes (Her VII.174); it is not impossible that the Allied force withdrew, either because the position was actually

Mustering the fleet

The Imperial fleet must have been assembled initially at Cilicia – or at least so did the squadrons from Egypt, Cyprus, Phoenicia, Cilicia proper and the south shore of Asia Minor. The rest, from Caria and the whole western coast of Asia Minor, occupied Thrace and the islands of the eastern Aegean must have assembled at Phocaea and Cyme in western Asia Minor (Diod XI.2,3), or the Hellespont, partaking in the bridging operations (Plut Vit Them 16). In these waters, they had been waiting for the rest of the fleet to come from the south in the summer of 481 BC. The scarcity of water in the Hellespontine area means that the reason for the massively assembled vessels (Her VII.44–5) while the army was crossing was not a review, which was due for Doriscus, but the crossing proper, the construction of the bridges and the hauling of provisions for crews and army in view of the destruction of the original bridges.

Furthermore, if the opinion proposing that at least some of the vessels used for the final pair of bridges over the Hellespont were numbered into the 1,207 of the Grand Fleet (Bradford 1980; Green 1970; Burn 1962) it may be presumed that the royal fleet after sailing to European waters was waiting for them to catch up in Doriscus (Her VII.58), once released from the bridges which would have been dismantled upon completion of the crossing, as was the proposed course of action at the Ister (Her IV.97,1).

Additional squadrons were perhaps supposed to converge on Aphetae or Alus in Pagassai, during the last phase of the invasion and the final rendezvous might have been in Athens. Vessels that never made it to the Achaemenid navy and opted rather for the Allied fleet are mentioned to have done so either at Artemisium, individually (Her VIII.82,2) or at Salamis more organized and collectively (Her VIII.46,3), which means they were sailing to meet the Imperial fleet and were thus unencumbered in such decisions by Imperial Marines. In this, the 17 vessels reported by Herodotus (Her VII.95) to have been the contribution of islanders, obviously of the central Aegean (the ones from Eastern Aegean were counted amongst the Ionians, Dorians and Aeolians) are an oddity. Who are these 'islanders', who sent their few vessels due north to Doriscus instead of north-west as did the Naxians and Tenians?

A Lemnian vessel deserted after an engagement at Artemisium (Her VIII.82,2) and thus the Lemnians and the Samotracians may have been counted in the 17-odd islanders' vessels. But the Naxian vessels are definitely mentioned as deserting *before* contacting the Imperial navy (Her VIII.46,3), and the Tenian one in Salamis (Her VIII.82,1) is never implied to have loaded Iranian marines and have somehow neutralized them to make desertion possible

(Tarn 1908). The Parian contribution never went west of Kythnos, waiting to assess the developments (Her VIII.67,1). Thus, these never sailed to Doriscus or Phocaea; they probably had never actually joined the Imperial fleet and, on the contrary, were supposed to join the Imperial navy in spatio-temporal conditions favouring their slipping from the Allied fleet that was expected to be between the Imperial navy and these loyal subjects. Thus, after Doriscus, the muster areas for Imperial vessels must have been Therma for the ships from the northern coast of the Aegean, and then Alus, or Malis and finally, the coast of Attica, for vessels coming from the central and southern Aegean.

untenable due to a flanking path at Gonnus (as discussed later). Or, the delay of the Imperials at the Hellespont, due to the destruction of the bridges, might have made the maintenance of a massive expedition in Thessaly unsustainable for the weak, agrarian economies of the Allies though, this whole thing of early withdrawal from Tempe might be a rather clumsy effort, not necessarily of Herodotus himself, to cover up a most disgraceful fiasco.

When in Therma, Xerxes reached the decision NOT to follow the usual road through Tempe; possibly (Green 1970) after the reconnaissance conducted by himself by sea (Her VII.128), as Alexander the Great was to do before the battle of Issus (Arr An II.7,2). A quick look must have persuaded him that at Tempe it was a hard road and the best place for an ambush (Bradford 1980); or, at the very least, for a repulse by determined opponents. Thus, he went on with his original plan. Both the plan and the decision must have been brought to the knowledge of the Key-Holder of the area, Alexander I, thanks to his brother-in-law, Boubares (Her V.21,2), the Persian administrator in charge of European matters; and Alexander informed the Allied expeditionary force (Her VII.173,3).

There are two basic options if one does not feel like going coastal. One is to go westwards from Therma and follow the river Aliakmon upstream and then south-east to Volustana (modern-day Servia) pass (**V** in **Map 2.4**). The other is to go south, to Pieria, and from there to turn from modern-day Katerini west-south-west, up the Petra road (**P** in **Map 2.4**). The first option is practically the one followed in reverse by the Hellenic Army in 1912 to free Macedon from the Ottoman rule and has the considerable advantage of going through the capital of Macedon, Aigai (modern-day Vergina), where Alexander I was seated. Both options converge to Olysson, modern-day Elasson, the front yard of Thessaly, which is severed from Thessaly proper by a range where there is one pass, the pass of Meluna, leading to the great plain of Thessaly north-west of Larissa (Green 1970). Meluna must have been the pass mentioned by Herodotus as kept open for Xerxes by the tyrants of Larissa (Her IX.1).

The proceedings of the Greeks

It must have been during Xerxes' approach to, or his arrival at, Sardis that the Greeks were denied any false hopes that they would escape invasion. The preparations must have been common knowledge, as they were anything but clandestine. With Xerxes at Sardis, the obvious became undeniable; his envoys carrying requests for the tokens of submission simply made it official. Thus, what must be called the Greek Alliance was forged much earlier than the arrival of the Imperial envoys. The first proceedings must have taken place in Sparta (Hammond 1996), where the mostly Peloponnesian Allies of Sparta were briefed for the Spartan decision to resist, after some input of theirs, of course.

The Athenians may well have been represented; the whole issue must have been similar to the proceedings of the Spartan Alliance (or Peloponnesian Alliance) in Sparta, as reported later (Thuc I.67). This view agrees with the very vague description of Herodotus (Her VII.145,1) and with the assertion of Pausanias on the matter; the latter identifies the exact place of the proceedings, Hellanium, some distance outside of Sparta (Paus III.12,6). At this convention it must have been decided to form a proper Alliance under oath, the League of Corinth, and create a representative ad hoc political and military steering committee, or rather Congress, seated at the Isthmus of Corinth, with executive delegates, to determine the course of action and to conduct the war (Her VII.148,1 & 172,1). The resolution or, at least, the alleviation of enmities among all the states poised to resist the invasion, must have been a prerequisite for the formation of the Alliance. Thus, initial deliberations on the matter must have taken place during the preparatory convention at Hellanium, where Themistocles proved the key figure, along with the Arcadian Chileus (Plut Vit Them 6,2). The latter must have been the reported Tegean who, being most influential with the Spartans, advised the dispatching of the Lacedaimonian army against Mardonius in 479 BC (Her IX.9,1).

This Body of Delegates at Isthmus was the executive branch of a confederate format, allowing the term 'confederates' to be used herein, as an alternative to 'Allies'; both have been considered for this work more suitable than the 'Greeks' (or rather the 'Hellenes' as they named themselves and were called by their historians) since a minority of the Greek states and population eventually decided to resist, and a very large part sided, at one time or another and for various reasons, with the invaders. The latter are collectively from here on called the Imperials, as the Persians and the other two core nations, the Medes and the Cissians/Elamites were but a minority of the combatants in the land army and actually absent from the navy in terms of vessels.

This body of delegates sanctioned assistance missions and issued requests for help to hesitant and/or faltering Greek states, such as Thessaly on one hand (Her VII.172,1) and Crete, Corcyra and Syracuse on the other (Her VII.145,2). Additionally, it decreed that the spontaneously medizing states (but not the neutral, nor the ones subjugated by force) would be in line for harsh reprisals and 1/10th of their landed assets would go to the Oracle of Delphi (Diod XI.3,3); an excellent way to secure the assistance of the God (Apollo), or at least of the priesthood of Delphi. The other 9/10ths would probably be confiscated by the triumphant patriots, should the Gods chose to grant divine help.

The supreme command was attuned but not unified; Sparta furnished the commanders-in-chief for all campaigns, both on land and at sea, but these were working separately, supported by separate staffs/boards of Allied generals. There was no joint staff, no C-in-C in the modern sense, endowed with all assets from both military branches. The Athenians, and the Argives tried to contest the issue (Her VIII.3,1 and 148,4; Diod XI.33,4–5) but only briefly. Most of the confederates were actually Sparta's allies, in fact Peloponnesians or colonists of Peloponnesian states who flatly refused to follow the leadership of Athens, even at sea (Her VIII.2,2); the Athenians grudgingly conceded (Her VII.161,2; Plut Vit Them 7,2). The alliance would instantly double the available ships and without its land forces, Athens was doomed as it featured first in the enemy's obvious axis of advance and list of reprisals. While the Athenians made a strategically necessary concession (Her VIII.3; Diod XI.12,4; Plut Vit Them 7,3), the Argives stood by their claim so as to have an excellent pretext to remain neutral, which was pro-Persian in anything but name (Her VII.149,3). This was attributable to the crippling of their power and leadership by Sparta (Her VII.148,2) or, as some suggest (Lazenby 1993), specifically to the criminal cruelty suffered at Sepia due to Cleomenes (Her VI.75,3). The latter argument is rather far-fetched; the erosion of their power base alone explains sufficiently their mortal hatred.

The Boeotians, who had got rid of the Thessalian yoke some decades earlier (Plut De Her Mal 33) also failed to participate in the Alliance. Although uncomfortably close to Athens – and less so to Sparta – to show their true medizing colours, they only sent the minimum of reinforcements after the most extreme 'persuasion' by the Allied authorities. Plutarch's silence on any notion of participating in or being friendly towards the Alliance shows that any co-operation from their side was rather an issue of keeping a fragile balance before the arrival of the Imperials than of any sense of patriotism. The Thebans, heading the Boeotian League (Buck 1972), had a standing enmity for Athens, now being solidly sided with Sparta. On top of this, they nurtured bitterness for Sparta also, since she undermined the formation of the Boeotian League by Cleomenes' machination of the cessation of Plataea to Athens (Her VI.108,2–4). Additionally, the 'desertion' of the Spartans left the Thebans exposed to the Athenian wrath (Her V.77,1–2) by the same Spartan King (Lazenby 1993). As a result, their open siding with the Imperials, although belated and brokered by Demaratus, the exiled Spartan King (Plut De Her Mal 31), was much more resilient and ardent, as proved in 479 BC (Her IX.67), than that of the foremost Medizers, the Thessalians, whose princely house of Larissa practically invited the Imperial invasion (Her VII.6,2).

As Xerxes is mentioned to be in Pieria (Her VII.131; Diod XI.12,3), if one is not compelled to believe that his mega-camp extended from Therma to Pydna, he must have led a division by the second route, from Therma to Pieria by the seaside and then inland (Her VII.131), while another might have ventured by the first route (Green 1970), thus alleviating the watering issues and covering more ground. Both were to emerge in Olysson (Green 1970), most likely not simultaneously, so as not to congest the Meluna pass (**M** in **Map 2.4**) which lies further south.

   At this point, one has to admit that there is no comprehensible way to make Xerxes appear in Thessaly by the pass of Gonnus. This pass is accessible by the coastal road if one turns west before Tempe and is negotiable for a light force intended to turn a defensive position, but not for an army with its heavy support formations. Herodotus refers to this pass (Her VII.173,4) as the reason why the Tempe position was untenable, since an army skirting the coast southwards may use this rough pass to turn any obstacle positioned at the straits of Tempe; the Greek Alliance had not dispatched enough troops to defend both passes. Furthermore, Herodotus states that Gonnus was the last point-of-call in the itinerary followed by Xerxes, something impossible if he passed by Olysson. The correct interpretation of Herodotus (VII.173,4 & VII.128,1) must be that due to this pass, which could have been used by Xerxes to turn the Tempe position should he have moved towards Tempe, the Greek expeditionary force left the region (Green 1970). Xerxes though, who might have used the pass, most probably did not, as he had taken the upland route(s) where his engineer corps was cutting a road (Her VII.131). Even if a third division of the Imperial army did follow the coastal road to Tempe, which is highly unlikely due to the need of sparing watering resources for the fleet (if not for the triremes, then for the multitude of merchantmen), the invasion would have followed the main road through the Tempe pass and not the pass at Gonnus, given that the Greeks had abandoned their original positions blocking Tempe.

Alus and Tempe: A notion of treason and operational ineptitude

After Salamis, the Greek fleet demobilized (Her VIII.111 & 121), so the crews could attempt to save the year's produce throughout Greece, as husbandry had been neglected. In Athens, a massive effort to restore housing made them even more indispensable. Consequently, there was no wintering of the fleet; it was reassembled, at much reduced strength, next year in Aegina (Her VIII 131,1).

But even if this was not the case, or not the case immediately after Salamis, there was no possibility for calling, much less wintering at Pagassai or whereabouts. Thessaly was the winter quarters of Mardonius (Her VIII.113), while the promontory of Magnesia (with Pelion as its spine) was subjugated by the Persian fleet and the western coastline of the gulf had been the royal invasion route (Her VII.196–201). In such proximity to Mardonius' host, with Boeotia and Euboea securely under Persian control even with the main Persian army at Thessaly (evident by the complete lack of interest of any Greek army to return to Thermopylae), there could have been no Greek fleets anywhere near Pagassai after Salamis.

The only timeline allowing for a Greek fleet there is the expedition at Tempe (Her VII.173). Plutarch's incident with Themistocles proposing the burning of the Allied fleet (Plut Vit Them 20) may have taken place then and there, while waiting for the enemy. It was a monumental treason, explaining the lack of any trust of the other Greeks to his person and the privileged communication of himself while in Salamis (Her VIII.75) and of other Athenians in Plataea with the Persians (Plut Vit Aris 13). In terms of technicalities, it was made possible by the low manning of the Allied fleet remaining at Alus (Her VII.173,1) once the expeditionary force moved to Tempe, as the latter would have included many crewmembers serving as attendants of the Hoplites.

Moreover, this explains some remarks of Herodotus; the Greek fleet spending a winter in the Gulf of Pagassai, in high alert, sheltered from weather but ready to emerge to intercept convoys laden with assault troops while, in the meantime, training to a standard of tactics and to a degree of cohesion, explains why the hulls of the Allied vessels were not dried out and made watertight, which resulted in slower, heavier vessels during the operations (Her VIII.60). Furthermore, the whole defensive campaign of the Allies must be reconsidered: despite Herodotus' remarks that the Tempe expedition was launched when Xerxes was near the Hellespont (Her VII.174,1) and concluded in disgraceful retirement mere days later (Her VII.173,3), it might not have been so. A very early date would have incurred a considerable expenses to the Allied treasury but would have also stiffened the patriotic feeling before different factions might have time to present Imperial envoys with Earth and Water. Reconsidering a state's position and stance in the war would have placed it squarely into the 'rebellious subject' category, which invited harsh retaliation contrary to that of a simple foe prevailed upon in battle.

Thus an early campaign had been warranted due to strategic, not tactical, considerations, while allowing familiarization with the terrain, adaptation of tactics to available force and ground, preparations of the envisaged battlefield by sapping, trapping, morphing, denying or, simply, fortifying operations. But, most importantly, the prompt expedition allowed uncontested occupation and safeguarding of the pass against advance seizure and guarding it for the King, either by any kind of vanguard or by agents, proxies and Medizers, as were Alexander I and the House of Aleuas in Larissa, the city situated closest to the pass.

Xerxes was at Sardis, launching his psychological and diplomatic campaign and his fleet assembled nearby in Cyme and Phocaea. The Allies, possibly without the intelligence from their spies who were sent to Sardis and probably lacking any such source in Phocaea, had every reason to fear a lightning naval campaign through the Aegean, as had happened twice; once against Naxos by Megabates and Aristagoras (500 BC) and then by Datis and Artaphrenes (490 BC). Although it is never considered as a possibility, the Themistoclean naval policy and the Athenian fleet might have been designed, developed and evolved for this kind of invasion; the fast and manoeuvrable triremes intended to intercept heavily laden Imperial ones while transporting the troops of the amphibious force. A 30–50,000 army, half of them cavalry, ferried across the Aegean on 1,200 triremes and 850 horse transports (Diod XI.3,9) and landing either near Pagassai or at Tempe, meant a lightning strike depriving the Allies of Thessaly and its resources (wheat and cavalry) and knocking the door of a rather friendly Boeotia – and this very early in the campaigning season, maybe April or May, with crops unharvested and plenty of time for actual fighting. Thus, the expedition at Tempe had not been able to hold its ground, but at least denied an early appearance of a smaller Persian horde in Greece proper; and time was even more essential than troops, ships and ground.

Once the Persians reverted to a different plan, the Athenian strategy had to be reconsidered. The Imperial intention became obvious the moment Xerxes himself took the lead and confirmed the signs offered by the cutting of the Athos' canal and the creation of supply dams along the northern, land axis. In any case, trying to face the Imperial fleet isolated and deprived of any support from the land host remained an Allied priority. This principle took effect when it became obvious that Xerxes had a really massive navy that would move in parallel and possibly in co-ordination with the land army, a navy endowed with a just as massive boarding arm and fully manned. To intercept such an invasion, a true dual campaign was indispensable, as the fall of Egypt to Cambyses amply proved 40 years earlier (Holland 2005). In such a context the fleet of the defenders should be fully manned with boarders and the army would stand on its own. This was the setting for the dual Thermopylae-Artemisium campaign.

In any case, Xerxes had skirted the holy mountain of Greece, Olympus. As his host emerged to Thessaly, at its south, it became automatically Imperial territory, won by the spear. Since the holy mountain had been incorporated in his realm, the Greek Gods residing on it were automatically reduced to servitude to the Persian Gods, and their worshippers would righteously become slaves of his (Hale 2009). It was *so* simple. Xerxes was not caring a bit for the Greek Gods, as he believed in Ahura-Mazda exclusively, and perceived other gods as lying, deceitful spirits – *Daivas*. But his multi-national host must have had interpreted the uneventful passing by and occupation of the holy mountain of the enemy in the above mentioned, simple and plain terms; so would the Greek themselves, especially the Medizers. Nobody, neither Xerxes, nor his troops, imagined that the Greek Gods were lurking in the seaspray some kilometres south-east, at the cliffs of Pelion, overlooking the waves of the Aegean and aiming their vengeance at the Imperial fleet.

Once in Thessaly, the Persians took some leisure time, which meant fanning cavalry throughout the plain to deliver total submission. Eventually, they crossed to Central Greece by the easier, lower and well-supplied in water resources coastal road that followed the western shore of the Gulf of Pagassai, passing through Alus. Thus, they moved due south, and then west, to enter the Malian plain from the east, just before Thermopylae. Still, Herodotus (VII.196) mentions the river Apidanus, in south-west Thessaly (then Achaia) and by no means in Xerxes' axis of advance. Instead of supposing that a raiding party fanned out, one may well agree with enlightened scholars (Grundy 1901; Hignett 1963; Green 1970; Bradford 1980) and suppose that one division was operating in the area following a western axis southwards and probably took the Domokos pass from the city of Pharsalus straight south to emerge in the plain of Malis, near modern-day Lamia, from north-west, where it met the division(s) coming from the east.

The straits of Thermopylae were actually guarded and the Imperial intelligence had been informed on the issue (Her VII.208,1); more ominously, the plain had been ravaged efficiently (Polyaenus I.32,3). Thus, the rendezvous with the fleet – and with the supplies it carried – in the plain of Malis was indispensable since the previous rendezvous at Alus had been missed due to weather.

Part II

Thermopylae: The Most Famous Battle

Chapter 3

The Setting

A crushing show of force, intended to proactively curb the spirit of resistance of as many prospective enemies as possible, combined with the ambition to conquer Europe (Her VII.8,3), implies unmistakably a vast royal army, definitely twice or thrice the size of the Greeks united (Grundy 1901). The numbers of the latter, as already mentioned, must not be taken lightly, as is usually done by modern scholarship (exemplified by, but not limited to, Fields 2007). Only 31 city-states rallied to defend the motherland, in Plataea, in 479 BC but they fielded almost 40,000 Hoplites and a total of more than 100,000 combat-capable troops (Her IX.30). Medizing Greeks at the time of the invasion were not to be excluded as potential enemies, since Greeks had a name for untrustworthiness towards the Persian throne. This was vividly demonstrated by the Athenians a quarter-century

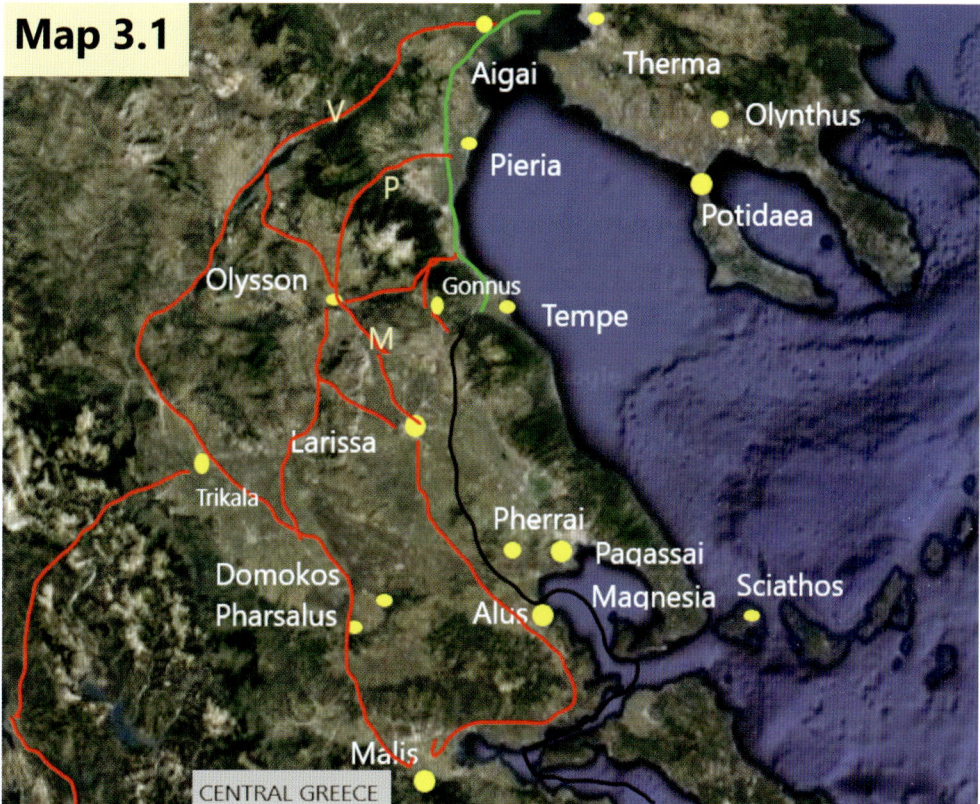

Map 3.1

earlier, when they defied their spontaneously given oaths; and by the Ionians, during their revolt (circa 500 BC), to mention just a couple. Furthermore, the definite issue of official demands for surrender was implemented long after the start of the campaign (Her VII.32) and the final answers came in while the Imperial host was halfway to its intended target (Her VII.131). Accordingly, the planning must have provided for the possibility, however remote, that a much higher number of Greek mainland states and troops would face the Imperial host in unfavourable terrain and thus were to cause significant casualties, directly or indirectly.

This royal army moves in one or more mainland routes leaving the coastal areas to the amphibious component of the royal fleet. From Therma it advances through the mountains, following one or both routes culminating in Olysson and thus circumventing the first prospective Greek defensive position at Tempe **(Map 3.1)** and emerges in Thessaly near the city of Larissa, the home of the worst Medizers, the Aleuadae (Her VII.6,2 & IX.1 &IX.58,2). Then, after receiving the surrender of the whole region, the Persian army must have continued south-south-east and followed the easy coastal road from Thessaly to Malis through Achaia Phthiotis (Her VII.196–201), that is through Alus (modern-day Almyros), the landing area of the Greeks in the abortive Tempe campaign, in the western coast of the Gulf of Pagassai.

Subsequently, marching through modern Stylis to the west, the Imperials skirted the northern coast of the Gulf of Malis. This itinerary took them over easy ground, well-provided with watercourses all the way to the Malian plain with Spercheios and other rivers flowing through it (Her VII.198). Although a secondary route, faster but harder, through Pharsalus and modern-day Domokos, might have been employed concurrently by some divisions, Xerxes himself was with the eastern group (Her VII.197,1) which included also the heaviest formations, as the royal dignity required many wagons of support and luxury materiel.

The Spartan policy, possibly doctrine, was to keep an enemy as far away as possible to spare the land and its people of devastation, a point made by Eurybiadas to Themistocles most succinctly (Her VIII.108,4). This was a very good reason for the dispatch of the Tempe expedition, a patent deviation from the standard Hoplite practice of open battle on level ground (Her VII.9B), which was probably anticipated by the Imperial staff. This expedition being prematurely aborted, a second effort was made; a small army was dispatched under one of the two Spartan kings, King Leonidas, half-brother to the maverick Cleomenes I (Her VII. 204–5) to intercept the Persian host as up to that point Xerxes had encountered only natural obstacles and the steamroller was carrying everything before it.

Leonidas may have been a man with guilt for the weird and unnatural demise of his half-brother (Holland, 2005; Burn 1962; Bradford 1980), which could have been engineered for a number of reasons. Starting with the sacrilegious manipulation of oracles (Her VI.66,2), causes go all the way to his sapping the Spartan constitution by machinating the eviction of the second lawful king (Her VI.65), to the existential nature of a power struggle between himself and his family with the Ephorate (Dickins 1912) or to conspiracy with the enemy, when he had been prosecuted. His dealings with the Arcadians during his exile caused consternation in Sparta (Her VI.74,1), which led to his restoration to kingship (Her VI.75,1) but might have caused, directly or indirectly, the passive Mantinean medizing in 479 BC and the Tegean mutiny in 470s (Lazenby 1993).

Alternatively, Leonidas may have had a death wish (Diod XI.4,4) a fact supported by the narrative of receiving funeral rites before starting his campaign (Plut De Her Mal 31). This is not as absurd as one might think; it is somewhat similar to Japanese traditions (Cartledge 2006) or very similar to the ideal of glory as projected by Homer through Achilles. Furthermore, it had a mundane political-military dimension: to win the struggle between the ideals and morale of the two antagonists (Delbruck 1920).

Leonidas had not been in line for royalty and thus he was a graduate of *Agoge*, raised as a comrade to most Spartans of his age. But still, he was much more than a brave warrior: he was an acclaimed war leader, versed in all crafts of war (Diod XI.4,2; Her VII.204), despite the somewhat malicious conviction of some scholars that there was no such training or such understanding. Limiting the Spartan training to the 'square bashing' of the British Army, whatever this might be, this position (Lazenby 1993) implies that in a lifetime of training and preparing for war the Spartans must have been very bored. Between experience and tradition some drill, which is the foundation of tactics, might have infiltrated their hunting endeavours and *Pessoi* board games, as they were able to perform army-wide manoeuvres like the Laconian countermarch (**Figure 3.1**); a safe indication of large-scale co-ordination and drill (Montagu 2006). In this capacity Leonidas' selected battlefield was the straits of Thermopylae, which control the main entrance to Greece proper (Her VII.175,1).

The two converging roads from Thessaly (**Figure 3.2** & **Map 3.2**) unite at the plain of Malis, just west of the Thermopylae straits, to continue either east or south. The former route goes through the three successive narrow corridors (Western, Middle and Eastern Gates) of Thermopylae to the main coastal road along Locris, which then turns south to the northern borderline of Phocis and subsequently, after crossing the region, enters Boeotia from the north. The other road, due south, passes off the strait of Thermopylae and is precipitous, through the Asopus gorge which is overseen and controlled by the city of Trachis, before it emerges through Doris to Phocis. Once in Phocis, it splits three ways: south to the Gulf of Corinth,

Figure 3.1 Countermarch

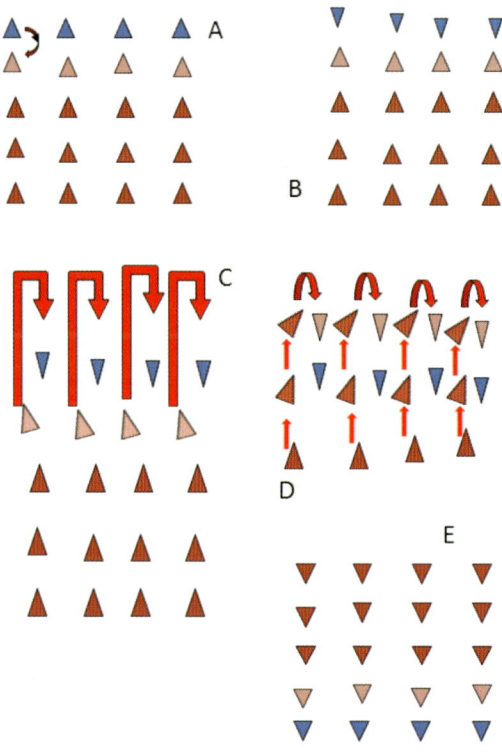

Figure 3.2

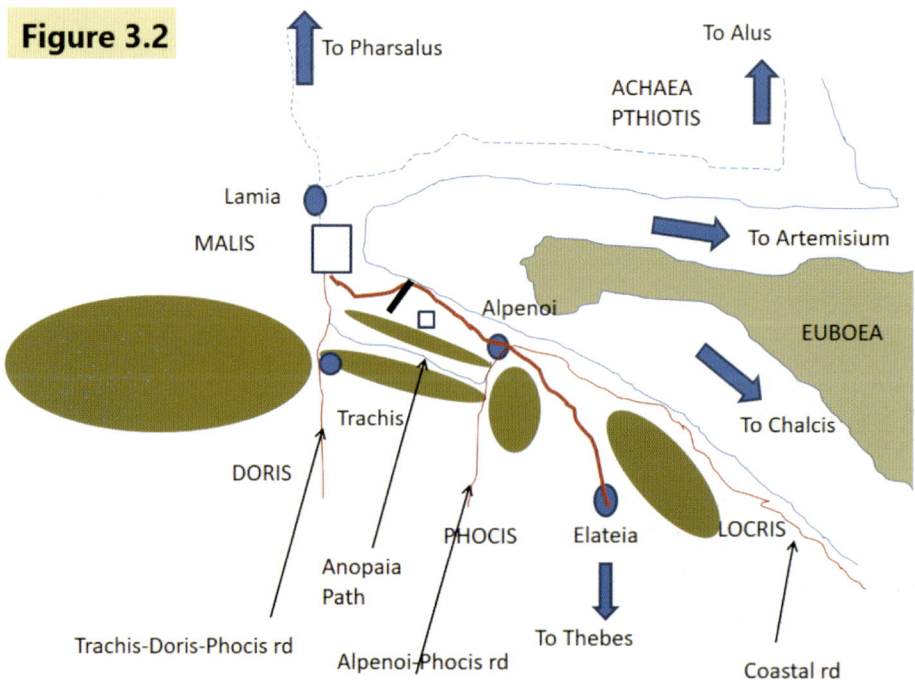

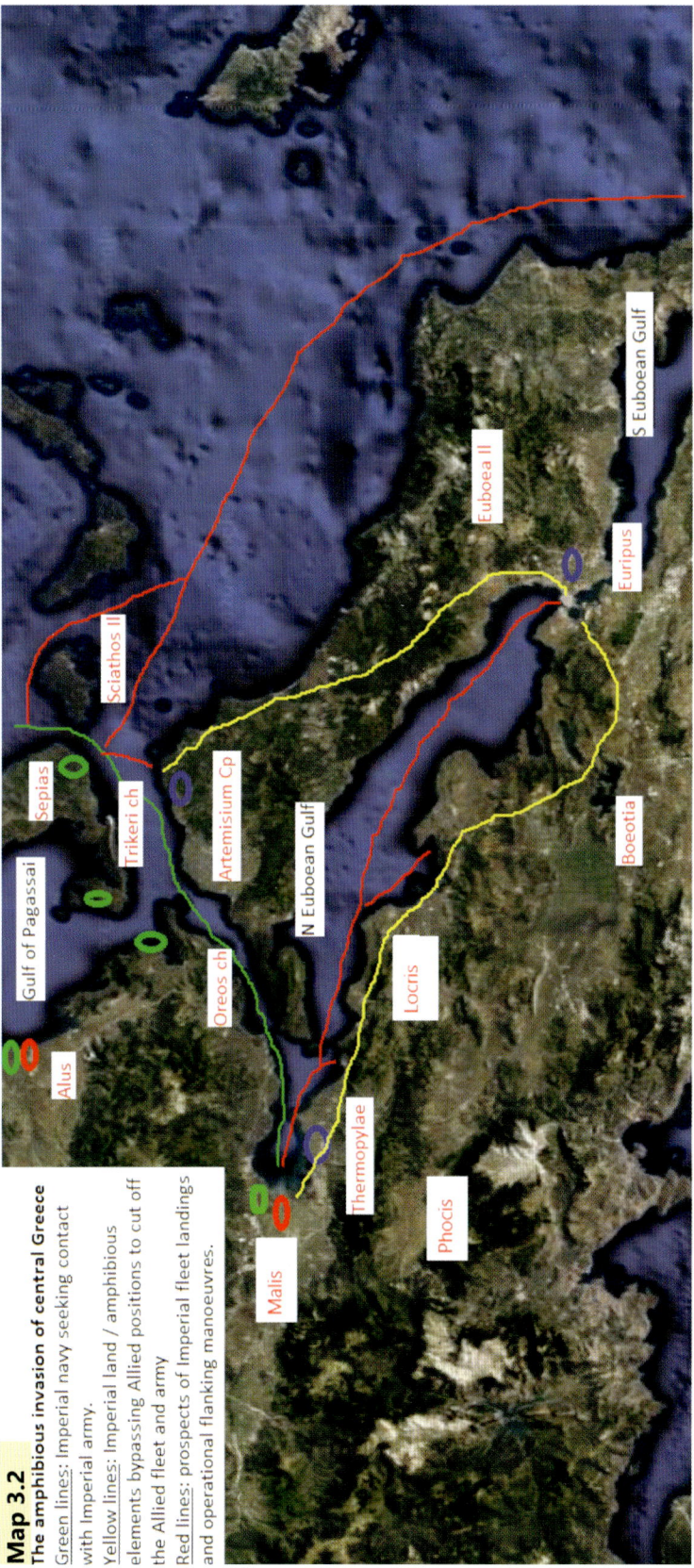

Map 3.2
The amphibious invasion of central Greece

Green lines: Imperial navy seeking contact with Imperial army.

Yellow lines: Imperial land / amphibious elements bypassing Allied positions to cut off the Allied fleet and army

Red lines: prospects of Imperial fleet landings and operational flanking manoeuvres.

The locations of Thermopylae and Artemisium were interdependent. The Imperial navy could dash east of Euboea (red line) in a wide, strategic flanking move to Attica and Peloponnese. It did actually try this route with a squadron, to encircle the Allied fleet through South Euboean Gulf. But actually it chose the western route, through Trikeri and Oreos channels to Malis (green line). From there it could outflank Leonidas in Thermopylae (blue ellipse) by landings at his rear, in Locris (red line). If the Allied fleet retreated from Cape Artemisium (blue ellipse) for an ambush at N Euboean gulf, the Imperials would land at Artemisium and dash to Euripus (yellow line) to cross to Boeotia; or to intercept the Allied fleet at Euripus by archery. The Imperial army, moving from Malis (red ellipse) through Thermopylae, could intercept the Allied fleet at Euripus by archery or cross to Euboee to attack the Allied anchorage at Artemisium by land (yellow line). Blue ellipses: Allied anchorages and camp. Vertical green ellipses: possible locations of Aphetae, the main Imperial anchorage after turning the pernicious cape Sepias. Horizontal green ellipses: contact locations of the Imperial navy with the Imperial army (red ellipses), at Alus and Malis.

east to the western border of Boeotia, or west to Delphi and Aetolia. But this road, today's Bralos pass, may have been impractical. Its mere existence at the time is debated (Grundy, 1901), and might have been available only in late summer; moreover it was more easily defensible at depth and was never used in the tens of invasions from northern to central Greece in the three centuries following this battle – an undeniable historical fact, but which may be attributable not to its non-existence or impracticality, as Grundy (1901) proposed, but to its precarious nature when defended, as amply demonstrated against Brennus and his Gauls in 279 BC (Paus X.22,1). After all, Herodotus clearly and unequivocally states that Xerxes, operating in August, finally took this itinerary (Her VIII.31).

The fact that Leonidas picked the narrows precisely to negate the enemy advantages of cavalry and numerical superiority (Her VII.177), and that this was the operational context of the previous campaign at Tempe as well (Her VII.173,1) disproves Herodotus' notorious passage (Her VII.9) that the Greeks had a stupid, unsustainable, murderous and formalized, almost ceremonial way of fighting. The Greeks knew well the advantages of fighting in straits and narrows in their country (Sears 2019), or, as seen in Plataea (Her IX.19,3) and Marathon (Her VI.103,1 & 108,1), on broken ground unsuitable for cavalry. It was for other reasons, part tactical (the excellent effectiveness of phalanx formations on the level) or of culture, finances and custom (the costs of permanent garrisons) that the Greeks were constantly choosing not to do so when fighting among themselves. And that, it should be noted, concerned unobstructed land, *not* open, not even level. Gentle slopes without pits, streams and dikes were especially favoured.

Although Herodotus implies a ready-to-go army in the whereabouts of Isthmus (Her VII.177), Leonidas must have set off from Sparta (Her VII.205,2; Diod XI.4,2–4; Plut De Her Mal 32) and collected Peloponnesian troops while advancing all the way to Corinth. Most probably he would have taken the longer road through Tegea (**Map 3.3**), not only to bypass unfriendly Argos, but to pass nearer the mustering points of the Arcadian allies (Bradford 1980), who amounted to half the Peloponnesian host.

Crossing the Isthmus and, since time was of essence (Diod XI.4,1), he must have followed the westernmost road through Megarid, without ever crossing into Attica, to emerge in Boeotia (**Map 3.4**) so as to collect further contributions from untrustworthy Thebes and from stout Thespiae (Her VII.202 &VII.205,3). This itinerary is indirectly supported by the fact that the Athenians, retreating from Artemisium, claimed that they thought the Peloponnesian army would have been in Boeotia (Her VIII.40,2); they meant the army requested by Leonidas as reinforcements, (Her VII.207) and, as a matter of fact, supposedly ready to move north right after the conclusion of the Olympic Games (Her VII.206,2). This means they had no clue whether the Peloponnesian army had moved northwards or not, a fact insinuating an itinerary not through Attica, but from the Isthmus straight to Boeotia, as does the Megarian Pass; a choice perhaps standard both at the time and later.

Then Leonidas must have continued west, to Phocis briefly, so as to take the northward road of Elateia which followed for some distance the shore of Locris, (the main highway north at the time); the coastal road mentioned previously. This itinerary was fast and took him to the heart of Locris, where he was able to turn the medizing locals to the Greek cause (Her VII.203; Diod XI.4,6), collect a promise of troops and be given access to the straits of Thermopylae, where the militia of the locals, plus the Phocian contribution, would come to meet him – as indeed they did.

The defenders: the Allied Greek contingent

The Greek expeditionary force contained two distinct elements, as already mentioned: the local and neighbouring communities that sent their entire hosts – more or less – and the contributions sent as reinforcements, or downpayments for the projection of forward defence, by distant southern Greek states. The latter were more or less token forces, according to politics. Tactical levies implied a strong commitment. A half-hearted one was obvious by sending small, standing units (brotherhoods-in-arms), similar to the 300 Spartan *Hippeis* who were actually the Spartan Royal Guard (to be discussed later). Thus, instead of some thousands, the medizing Thebans dispatched 400 (Her VII.202), possibly a special unit ancestral to the Sacred Band (Plut Pelop 18,1). This is very likely as their commanding officer Leontiades is the father of the commander of another 400-strong Theban unit which, in 431 BC, infiltrated the city of Plataea in a pure Special Operations mission (Her VII.233); it must be stated, though, that Plutarch reports another person, Anaxander, as the Theban commander in Thermopylae (Plut De Her Mal 33). Preferential drafting, as the one performed by Leonidas himself in Sparta (Her VII.205), may reconcile such an elite unit with the statement that these troops were the patriotic element of Thebes who volunteered or were dispatched (Diodorus XI.4,7). Still, it is also mentioned that during the Tempe campaign a 500-strong unit, a more standard number and under a different commander (Plut De Her Mal 31) had been contributed to the Allied cause by Thebes.

The stout Thespians, of the very few Boeotians not prone to medize, sent 700 troops (Her VII.202), which might have been their entire Hoplite army; or, alternatively, their established contribution to the confederate Boeotian army, which traditionally stood at 1,000, in here perhaps implemented at 2/3, expeditionary strength.

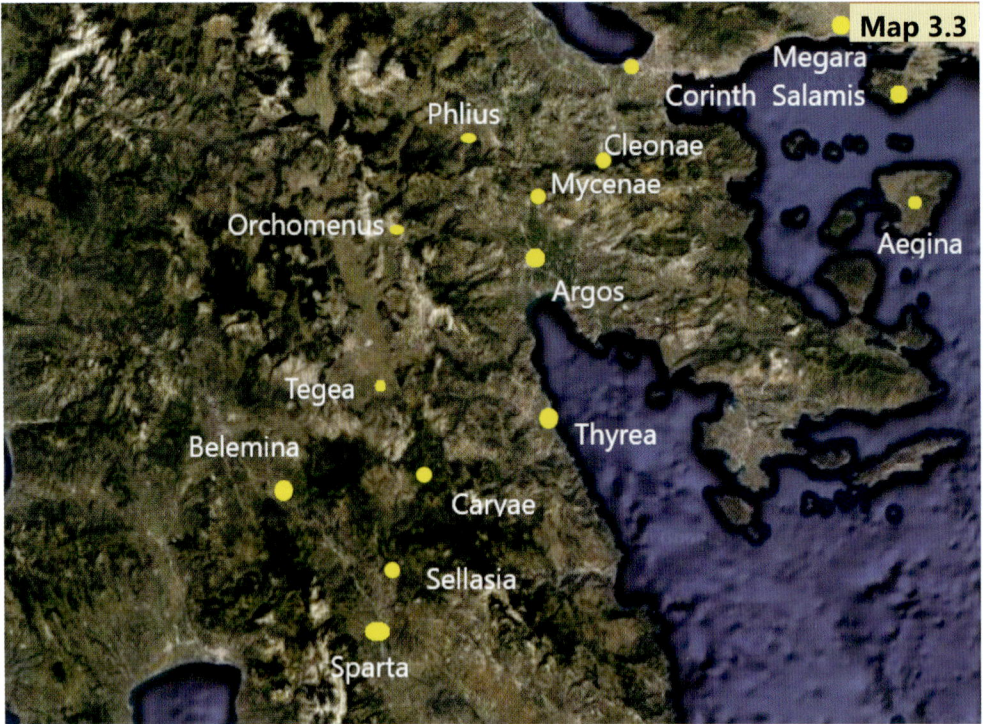

Map 3.3

Still, a year later, at Plataea in 479 BC, the city contributed no Hoplites due to their annihilation at Thermopylae (Her IX.30), so 700 must have been its entire Hoplite levy. The Thespian contribution in Plataea is considered combat troops, not logistics personnel and explicitly stated to lack *hopla* (Her IX.30). This safely

Allied reinforcements from Corinth would go, via Thebes, either up Elateia to stiffen defences at Thermopylae and Anopaia passes; or through Doris to sneak attack the spent Imperials.

Map 3.4

identifies them as light infantry and resolves incidentally the issue of the origin of the word *Hoplite*. This resolution, further supported by the combination of wording and meaning in Xenophon (Hell V.4,18) is contrary to the beliefs of many modern scholars (Lazenby and Whitehead 1996) and vividly demonstrates the nature of wrong turns in modern scholarship.

The Phocians sent an expeditionary force of 1,000 Hoplites and the Locrians their whole army (Her VII.203), which was a meagre 1,000 Hoplites (Diod XI.4,7). The latter, a small detachment undoubtedly, is rarely properly appreciated: its presence was a massive Greek strategic gain. The Locrians, current masters of the straits, had offered Earth and Water (Her VII.132,1; Diod XI.3,2) after the retirement of the Tempe task force and were ordered by their new sovereign to secure the straits for him (Diod XI.4,6). But, in view of the arrival of an army headed by the Spartans, they changed heart and sides and delivered the straits to the army of Leonidas while joining them (Her VII.203), despite the very questionable example set by Athens, which had done the same a quarter of a century ago and thus provoked the Majesty's wrath.

The Spartans were somewhere in the middle in terms of mobilization. Herodotus mentions only the 300 crack Spartan Peers (Her VII.202). These are easily identified as the *Hippeis*/Knights who fight with the king (Thuc V.72,4), drafted

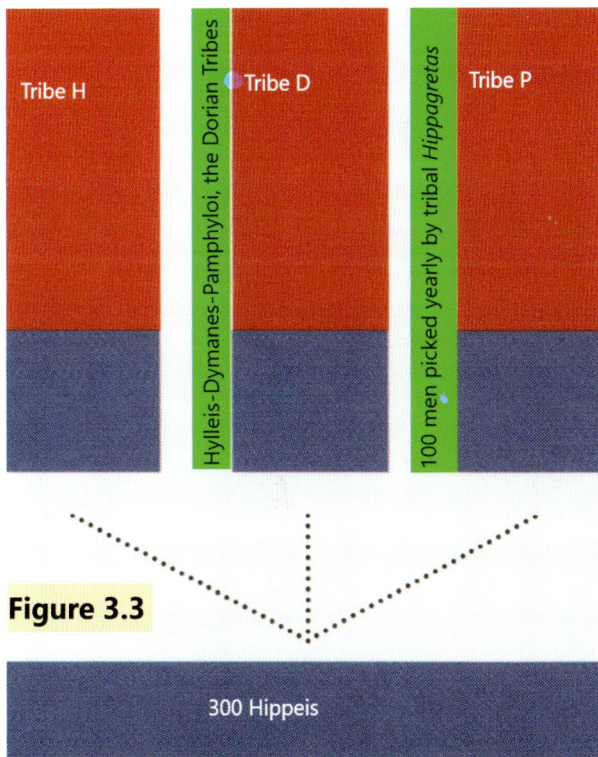

Figure 3.3

yearly by three appointed officers, the *Hippagretae*, also of yearly commission (Xen Lac Pol 4,3), obviously one from each of the three Dorian tribes (**Figure 3.3**). Each *Hippagretas* was drafting 100 adolescents, obviously from the same tribe. The name of the unit means cavalrymen and implies earlier times, when these bodyguards were aristocrats able to maintain a steed and thus rode and fought mounted (Spence 1993). Although at the time of Thermopylae the unit was strictly infantry, its *name* represented the Spartan equestrian tradition: one of the two patron demi-gods, Castor, was a famous horse-tamer; it is not without significance that the ceremonial gift presented by Sparta to Themistocles after the victory in Salamis was a fine chariot (Her VIII.12,2), a product of the luxury industry of the state.

There is no point in doubting that the 300 of Leonidas were indeed the royal bodyguard (Matthew 2013b). As a royal bodyguard is always in full alert, they could be used in distress, to buy time as happened some years later during the Helotic War, a decision which resulted in their annihilation – again (Her IX.64,2). The reconstituted corps paid homage to Themistocles (Her VIII.124,3) and it is conceivable that they accompanied Brasidas in northern Greece, in a most delicate mission far away, to stiffen the resolve of northern allies and show Spartan commitment while risking a minimum of reliable Peers. If so, the mission of Brasidas must have been similar to the one of Leonidas although in a different context and the 300 elite Hoplites at his disposal (Thuc IV.70 & IV.125,3) may have been the *Hippeis* (cavalry) of the year.

But Herodotus also mentions Lacedaimonians when narrating the battle (i.e. Her VII.208 & 211), a far wider term historically, encompassing Spartans and Periekoi. He also makes clear that the Spartans, not the Lacedaimonians, stayed to die with the king (Her VII.220); so the survivors of the rest of the Lacedaimonians were sent back, probably as the only living Laconian troopers with experience of the Persian warfighting practices. Leonidas' effort to spare some of the 300 by dispatching them home, in no small measure was intended to provide the reliable and undeniable testimony of elite members of the state to the debriefing, was nullified by the splendid pigheadedness of such troops, who flatly refused to survive by accepting menial tasks (Plut De Her Mal 32).

Diodorus directly enumerates 1,000 Lacedaimonians and 300 Spartans (Diod XI.4,5), but the Greek is unclear and may be translated as both 'and' or 'including'. The latter is preferable; previously the full strength of the force has been set to 1,000 (Diod XI.4,2 & 4,4), as correctly noticed by Flower (1998).

Should 1,000 be the total, the 700 missing in Herodotus' account might have been another Laconian unit mobilized and deployed, probably not comprised (entirely) of Peers. This leads to a division-size (*Mora*) unit of 1,000, typical in most of Greece. A *Mora* raised or stationed north of Sparta, mobilized at short notice and manned to

2/3, the standard expeditionary strength as per Thucydides for the Peloponnesian armies invading Attica (Thuc II.10,2) fits the bill. This 1,000-man total strength is perhaps higher than the Morae in the age of Xenophon (Xen Hell IV.5), but consistent with wider Greek practice and Spartan population abundance before the catastrophic earthquake of 464 BC (Diod XV.66,4). As Plutarch points out, the strength of Morae is mentioned as anything between 600 and 1,000 men (Plut Pelop 16) and such differences might stem from different manning/mobilization levels, or from different ceilings in different times/generations. A 1,000-strong territorial division is perfectly compatible with the Spartan army of the period; even in 394 BC, the Lacedaimonian contingent in the battle of Nemea was 6,000 (Xen Hell IV.2,16) in a full levy mobilization. At that time the Lacedaimonian army was six Morae, the standard provided by Xenophon (Lac Pol 11,2), thus revealing a 1,000-man Mora when top manning strength was used. Although the Mora is never mentioned by Herodotus, nor Thucydides, it is correctly suggested (Lazenby 1989) that Xenophon mentions the rank of Polemarch as the commander of Mora and Lochagos as the commander of Lochos. Thus, Thucydides is simply wrong when attesting Polemarchs as commanders of Lochoi in 418 BC in Mantinea (Thuc V.71,3) and since in Herodotus the rank of Polemarch is first mentioned (Fields 2013) for Euainetos in 480 BC for the Tempe expedition (Her VII.173,2), the Mora most probably existed since that day at the latest, although perhaps in a slightly different context.

This line of thought can be expanded to identify this Mora as the *Skiritai*, renowned to later military authors for their prowess in security, irregular warfare, and reconnaissance (Xen Lac Pol 12,3 & 13,6). If such practice can be retro-projected, the Skiritai, nimble and good in mountain warfare, were an excellent choice both for the terrain in Thermopylae and for the Special Operations undertaken (see below).

On the other hand, the identification with a Mora mobilized to 2/3 with a low fraction of Spartan Peers (if at all) is not supported by Ktesias who refers to 300 Spartans AND 1,000 Perioikoi (resolving the issue of the identity of the Lacedaimonian troops without the status of Peers) in an action where Thermopylae must be implied – but is not mentioned (Ktesias, 28). For such a forced march and given the terrain and the nature of the fighting, Leonidas might well have taken with him a unit of 1,000 young troops from the whole realm. These troops may be the ones sent as advance-guard to Megara in 479 BC while the rest of the Spartan and Allied Army were stationed in Isthmus (Her IX.14). They were the very ones executing the bait-retreat plan in the battle of Plataea (Her IX.57 & IX.85). They should have been the youngest, possibly the 20-something class, or the 18–20 and Plutarch (Moral Lac Apoph LCL 245: 350–351,15) mentions unmarried youngsters sent home by Leonidas as couriers to the Ephors. Although for this campaign Leonidas had enrolled fathers of male progeny to ensure the survival of the bloodlines (Her VII.205), on one hand this practice might refer to the knights of that year and not to other units, and on the other, although the Spartans married young and were encouraged, to put it mildly, to sire just as young (Xen Lac Pol I,6), exceptions would always present, especially in a territorial division and/or a young age-class.

Thus, with a tally of 38,000 Lacedaimonians (Plut Vit Lyc 8,3) serving from 20 to 60 years of age, that is divided into 40 year-classes, the year-class is almost 1,000 men and the 2,000 support troops sent belatedly to Marathon (Her VI.120), if drafted from the whole Lacedaimonian army and not from the Spartan Peers, amounted to two age-classes, lower than expeditionary forces abroad but nimbler, for fast access and much more than a token force.

Volunteering, Drafting and Campaigning

Practically, the usual Greek expeditionary drafting practice seems to fall under three mobilization levels. The first level is the dispatch of the standing armies, elite groups of different stock and origin in each city-state, usually called *Logades* by Herodotus (IX.21), to indicate they were under oath. Such groups were of standard strength for each city-state, but standardization did not occur among different states. This corresponds well with the renowned 'Sacred Band' of fourth century Thebes (Plut Pelopidas 18,1) through to the expanded similar corps of late fifth-early fourth centuries: '*Logades*' of Argos in Thuc V.67,2; '*Epilektoi*' (Elites) of Phlious (Xen Hell VII.2,10); '*Epilektoi*' of Arcadia (Diod XV.67,2 & XV.62,2). It also links with the past, as the suitors' oath before Helen's choice of Menelaus had been instrumental for the triggering of the Trojan War (Hes Ehoiai Fr 68.ll, 89–100).

The second level of mobilization was the whole levy ('*Pandemei*') for a short duration and, preferably, with the opponent near to home territory (Her VII.206, Diod XI.4,4). Thespiae probably implemented this level (Fields 2007), as did other states, like the Locrians who are explicitly stated to have done so (Her VII.203).

The third level, in between the two previously mentioned, is a draft of the majority of the full levy, usually by age criteria (Her IX.12) but also by any other selective way to impose quota (**Figure 3.4**). This was probably following a rule of two-thirds for the expeditionary force in large-scale endeavours (Thuc II.10,2). Multiple expeditions were not very common at the time, and thus it remains unclear whether in cases of multiple campaigns the sum of the expeditionary forces was subject to the rule of two-thirds or other arrangements were made, as in Imperial Athens (Thuc I.105,3–4) and fourth century Sparta (Xen Hell VI.4), where a number of

Figure 3.4

Full Vs quoted levy mobilization

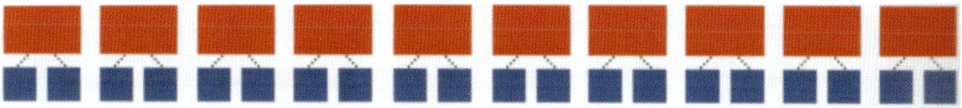

Full levy/ *Pandemei*: The Athenian army at Marathon, 490 BC, with 10 *Taxeis* (Brigades, RED), each with 2 *Lochoi* (Battalions/ Companies, BLUE). All echelons are fully manned.

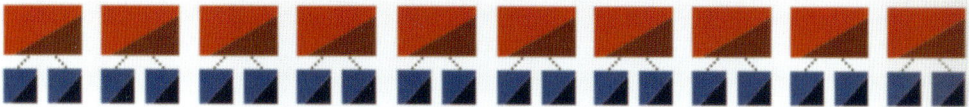

Quoted levy/*En tois Eponymois*: The Athenian army at Tempe, 480 BC, with 10 *Taxeis*, each with 2 *Lochoi*. All echelons are manned to quota, by age or by individual mobilization arrangements (darkened part not drafted).

the divisions of the army could be sent to one particular campaign (**Figure 3.5**), either fully or partly mobilized.

Herodotus never mentions the rule of two-thirds but it seems valid: the Spartan Peers are 8,000 according to Demaratus (Her VII. 234,2) and at Plataea, the expeditionary force has a core of 5,000 Peers (Her VIII.10), a 0.62 compared to the 0.66 i.e. 2/3.

It is possible that the implementation of the first level, instead of the third, by the Spartan state was causing consternation to Allies and was fully exploited by Thebes as a pretext to send a mere 400 men. Spartans served from 20 to 60 years of age, as

Figure 3.5

Full Vs partial levy mobilization

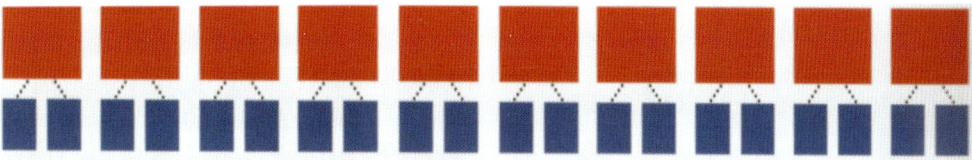

Full levy/ *Pandemei*: The Athenian army at Marathon, 490 BC, with 10 *Taxeis* (Brigades, RED), each with 2 *Lochoi* (Battalions/ Companies, BLUE). All echelons are fully manned.

Partial levy/*En tois Meresi*: The Athenian arrangement for multiple simultaneous expeditions. Only a number of *Taxeis* (Brigades, RED), each with its 2 *Lochoi* (Battalions/ Companies, BLUE) participate. All echelons are similarly manned, fully or to sanctioned quota.

mentioned earlier and the ones from 20 to 30 were permanently on alert, sleeping in barracks (Plut Vit Lyc 15,4 & 25,1) being a standing army in all but name. Their number adjusted for the total Spartan levy is 2,000. By comparison, the Athenian naval contingent in Artemisium was 127 triremes (Her VIII.1) with no less than 200 sailors, oarsmen and marines on each for a total of almost 25,000.

The 700 Thespians may have been the total levy of their city, in terms of Hoplites, which would fit well with the inability of the city to field any Hoplites in Plataea the next year, although it did furnish 1,800 fighting men (Her IX.30). Alternatively, as already mentioned, the figure 700 might be the 2/3 expeditionary quotum from a city which had 1,000 Hoplites – a full taxis/brigade. Using as a comparison a somewhat later date, the city was furnishing the larger part of a 1,000-man *taxis* for the federal army of the Boeotian League together with some minor cities (Hell Oxy 16,2–4) possibly – but not certainly – as a full-levy. Thespiae was not that close to Thermopylae to justify a full levy mobilization; thus their contribution showed a wholehearted embracing of the Allied cause.

Phocis on the other hand also sent a small expeditionary force, just 1,000 Hoplites, while the Locrians, in whose territory the battle was expected, mobilized a full levy, according to Herodotus (Her VII.203). This was amounting, according to Diodorus, to 1,000 Hoplites (XI.4,7). Had the Malians joined, as recounts Diodorus, but not Herodotus (an issue discussed elsewhere), they were 1,000 as well (ibid). Still, the occupation of their motherland by Xerxes and the full torching and devastation of their land by Leonidas before the battle (Polyen I.32,3) makes this particular contribution difficult to swallow, especially since they, as the Locrians (at least initially), figure in Herodotus' list of Medizers (VII.132).

The Battlefield

The actual battlefield was the Middle Gate of Thermopylae, the central strait of a complex of three consecutive straits of different width and characteristics, leading from Malis to southern Greece proper as mentioned earlier. Once under Phocian rule (Her VII.176), it was at the time under Locrian control (Her VII.216). The position taken by Leonidas cut the coastal road along the Euboean Gulf, a route ill-suited for a massive army as far as heavy supply trains hauling provisions and non-combatants are concerned, but rather smooth. After a distance and deep in Epiknemidian Locrian territory, which lies to east-south-east of the straits, the road branched to the coastal one proper, continuing east-south-east and another leading south-east; the latter was the easy and wide, main route into Boeotia through Elateia, and, following the flow of Kephissus river, to Thebes (**Figure 3.2**). It was a logical choice. Moreover, it was useful for combined army-navy operations if followed throughout its length along the coast, something obviously important as the Persians tried to use parallel routes of advance by land and sea. It enabled the Persian army to support the fleet from ambushes by land contingents armed with missile weapons in a steadily narrowing channel, near the straits of Euripus, as Xerxes' guides would have let him know (**Map 3.2**). It also enabled the fleet to flank with barrages of missiles any interceptive force in the way of the army, along with the standing threat of landing amphibious forces at the enemy rear (Grundy 1901).

The second approach (**Figure 3.2**), as mentioned before, was starting from the Asopus gorge. It extended south through Doris and then to Phocis, but also branched east over Mount Kallidromon, following the Anopaia path. The latter extended eastwards but at a point it was also branching south to Phocis, being a second entrance therein (after the entrance by the gorge through Doris) and north at the coastal road, behind Thermopylae and Leonidas' rear, near the town of Alpenoi; thus it was turning the position of the Allies. It was a very steep path and utterly unsuitable for a large army and its transports (Her VII.216).

This track, Anopaia, was known to the local Malians and Trachinians, to the Phocians who had suffered a Thessalian invasion from that direction and were unwilling to be in for a second treat, and to the Thessalians, allies of Xerxes and invaders of old who had discovered and used the path in times past to invade Phocis (Her VII.215; Bradford 1980). Anopaia path was an approach only suitable for seasoned task forces allowing an entry from the north to Phocis, as it was joining the route Phocis-Alpenoi, the latter being the first town or settlement in general east of the straits of Thermopylae. Anopaia continues east all the way to Elateia, where another road goes south, starting some distance east of Alpenoi, at Boagrios River and winding up to Mount Thronion. This last road was effectively shut by the defenders posted in Thermopylae, much like the coastal road skirting all of Locris to Boeotia and the main road from Alpenoi to Phocis (Grundy 1901). Actually, Anopaia should be considered a mountainous path which intersects with three north-south major arteries (except the coastal one): the road from Trachis by the gorge of Asopus to Doris, guarded by troops in Trachis proper; the Alpenoi-Phocis road, behind Leonidas' position, and, further to the east, the road of Elateia which climbs the Mount Thronion. The two latter were denied to the Imperials by Leonidas' position, as was the coastal main way south.

The road that starts from the Asopus gorge near Trachis cuts south through Doris and ultimately offers three choices and thus increases the choices of the invader and the uncertainty of the defender. The first option is through Phocis to Boeotia (Her VII.199 and VIII.31–33), the way Xerxes did select to move, as it was an easy road, well-provided with water and fodder and allowing the dispatch of flying detachments for foraging, looting and devastation. The second option was west to Delphi and the third due south to Amphissa in Ozolian Locris and through there to Crissa, on the northern coast of the Gulf of Corinth. It was an initially steep road through ravines, possibly unsuitable for a large army's transports, but leading promptly either to the friendly and well-provisioned, hospitable Boeotia, after a brief incursion to the heart of Greece; or, ultimately, to the north of the Gulf of Corinth, a very threatening proposition for the Peloponnesian states, the armies of which had campaigned north while their navies were far NE, at Artemisium, thus leaving the shoreline defenceless against possible Imperial incursions. The same road network was used later by the warring factions during the Greek civil wars (Xen Hell VI.4; Paus X.15,2) and by the Romans (Paus VII.15) during their operations between southern and central Greece.

The area Leonidas occupied was something of a tourist attraction (Her VII.176). It is difficult to envisage the terrain: the narrowest, even if as narrow as Herodotus states, only one cart wide (Her VII.200) was further east (Eastern Gate) but was not chosen as the slope to the south is gentle and might be turned by light, mountain infantry. The location of Leonidas' task force was the Middle Gate,

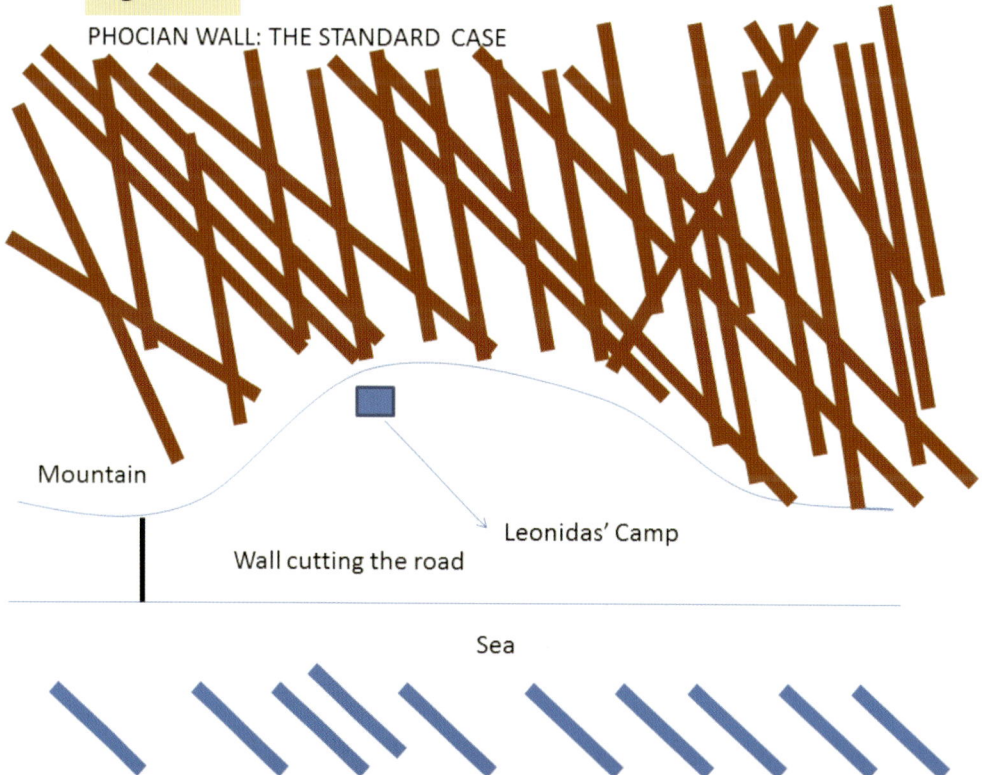

Figure 3.6

PHOCIAN WALL: THE STANDARD CASE

Mountain

Leonidas' Camp

Wall cutting the road

Sea

Figure 3.7

PHOCIAN WALL: OPEN CIRCUIT CASE

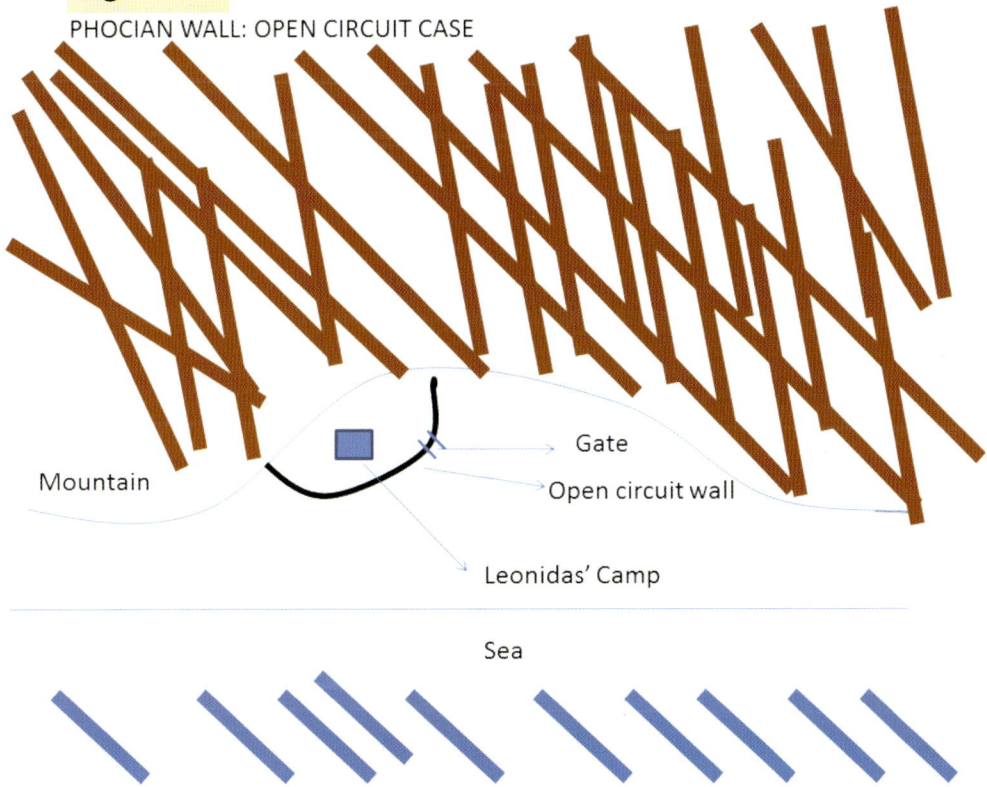

Mountain

Gate

Open circuit wall

Leonidas' Camp

Sea

somewhat wider but flanked at its south by the steep rock face of the Kallidromon mountain. What is there from the other side? Most probably the sea. This might be impassable for commercial traffic, but assault infantry would have negotiated a detour by plunging up to the chest in the sea to outflank an enemy, as happened some months later in Potidaea (Her VIII.129). No such issue was raised though; no similar action has been described. Thus one has to understand that at the time the road is considerably higher than the sea level, so as not to permit flanking, and rather precipitous: Imperial troops fallen into the sea are mentioned as fatalities (Her VII.223). Alternatively, a level but pernicious, marshy coast might be implied, making the path unsuitable for heavy formations and trains and one assumes for some supersized Imperial vehicles, especially if combined with the most narrow Eastern Gate (Rupp 2013).

A wrecked Phocian fortification (of days long past; maybe two centuries or more before) was repaired, rebuilt, revamped and used (Her VII.176). It is usually thought of as perpendicular to the axis of the road (**Figure 3.6**), something very like the Doors of Mordor in The Lord of the Rings (Kambouris et al 2015b). Indeed such works were used by the Greeks to cut off enemy forts and cities situated on promontories and were called *Diateichismoi* (wall-through). The fortifications of Isthmus, which were raised some days later (Her VIII.71 & IX.8–9; Diod XI.16,3) and once again some 115 years later, during Epaminondas' incursions (Diod XV.68,3), had been such cases. But there is absolutely no need to envision the Phocian wall thus, as there would have been very little room for pillars and a door capacious enough to allow a laden cart to pass in peaceful times, plus parapets for an adequate defence force. It may very well have been an open circuit, running *along* (not cutting *across*) the axis of the strait, as maintained by the chief excavator Professor Marinatos (Rookhuijzen 2019); both edges attached on the sheer rock of the mountain (**Figure 3.7**), allowing the stationing of a friendly garrison poised to deny the narrow passage to enemies by the most crude missile weapons, i.e. stones and javelins. This garrison may attempt pitched battle, to cut off the road in the face of the enemy, then fall back through the gates of the circuit and continue to harass the enemy by missiles from the wall, shot to their right, unshielded flank. Both Xerxes' and ancient Thessalians' cavalry and any transportation using draught animals would have been unable to pass, even if competent and determined infantry might do so, by skillfully using their shields and being fleet of foot.

The opposite argument is seemingly presented by the history and purpose of the original construction of the wall: that was to deny access for an invading force of Thessalians into Phocis; the territory of the latter at the time included the system of the straits (Her VII.176 &VII.215). Given the existential nature of the Thessalian threat, commercial/civil circulation would have not been an issue, while Herodotus' description makes clear that at this particular point the straits were not at their narrowest (Her VII.176,2). They were steep and thus not negotiable by flanking forces, but not at their narrowest (Green 1970), as mentioned earlier, meaning there might have been room for a gate, pylons, parapet walls and perhaps towers of a plain design and construction. This attests to a plausible vertical orientation of the wall, to shut off the road (Her VII. 215), furthered by fitting interpretation of the last moments of the Greek army after being encircled (Her VII.225).

The Protagonists

Herodotus explains that the name *Immortals* for the Persian elite, 10,000-strong division (baivarabam) was due to the immediate, possibly overnight making up of any casualties (Her VII83). This indicated a standard baivarabam, but of special status and privileges (Her VII.83,3); usual Imperial units were expected to operate understrength and had procedures to redistribute the available manpower for more efficiently doing so (Sekunda & Chew 1992). The name 'Immortals' was known to the Greeks far before Herodotus; at the very latest by their spies dispatched to Sardis in 481 BC. The probability that all of their sources, spies, prisoners of war, deserters, ex-medizers etc. had mistaken the Persian term *Anusiya*, meaning *Kinsman* (or other similar Greek translation, including attendant, or companion) for *Anausa*, meaning *Immortal*, is possible and even plausible (Waterfield 2006), but somehow unconvincing (Ray 2009); instead, the term Amrtaka has been proposed (Sekunda & Chew 1992). Although it has never been found or read in ancient sources, it may be a correct approach.

Still, the usual explaining away of the unit missing from the explicit narratives of the era of Alexander III the Great (Arr Anab III.11,5) is that the corps might have been disbanded after being implicated in the coup against Xerxes and the power struggle(s) since. This is even less convincing: in the battle of Issus in 333 BC Arrian directly points to Xenophon's description for the deployment around the King (Xen Anab I.8,21), a moderately informative text. But in the battle of Gaugamela (331 BC), whence the deployment plans of the Achaemenid staff fell into the hands of the Macedonians after the battle (Arr Anab III.11,3) – not to mention the archives of the Persian state some weeks or months later – Darius III had arrayed around him his Apple-bearer Guards (obviously *Arstibara*) and the 'Kinsmen' (Arr Anab III.11,5). The latter term is the most proper for translating *Anusiya*, recommends the highest honour and was eventually adopted by Alexander III (Arr Anab Alex VII.11,1 & 6) and his successors. Actually, it may have been the model for the inception of the Companion Cavalry (Arr Anab III.14,2) by the early Macedonian kings who were vassals to the Persians, as were both Alexander I and his father Amyntas (Her V.17,1 and VIII.136,1 respectively).

There are some more details to contemplate: the Immortals were a field unit of Sparabara, perhaps an elite standing army within the national Persian army, the *Kara*. The notion of *Kara* is prospective, possibly equivalent to the Homeric Greek term *Laos* which in modern Greek means 'the people'. From its full levy emerging each time, upon mobilization, the *Spada* which was the actual, drafted plus standing, army (Fields 2007), possibly enhanced by vassal units and allies. The Guards of the King, on the other hand, were the Spearbearers; the actual term is *Doryphoroi*, the direct Greek translation of the Persian word *Arstibara*, a unit in which Darius I had partaken (Her III/139,2) and most probably Xerxes too (Holland 2005). Thus, the Arstibara are the troops mentioned as Spearbearers in Greek, and amount to two *Hazaraba*, both identified by Herodotus in the Persian Parade Order with apple-like counterweights in their spears (Her VII.40,2 & 41,2–3).

It is possible that the Hazarabam closest to the King, with apple-like counterweights, are the Applebearers and are of aristocratic lineage, while the other hazaraba, with pomegranate-like counterweights, are drafted from the Immortals and made up by Persian commoners promoted on merit and valour (Charles 2011).

One cannot fail to notice the symmetry with the Hypaspist units of Alexander III (Kambouris et al 2019), which included one battalion from the entire nation (Hypaspists) and another from the aristocracy (Royal Hypaspists); still, the analogy is perhaps misleading, as the Hypaspists were a field unit and thus counterpart to the Immortals. The Immortals had pomegranate-like counterweights (Her VII.41,3) and were an elite field, not guard, unit (Charles 2011).

As mentioned above, the Argead Macedonian kingdom may have indeed copied Persian court protocol. If so, there are some deductions:

(i)   The Argead Hypaspist corps, which had been a standing army (Kambouris et al 2019) was the equivalent of the Immortals. As they accounted for the 10 per cent of the Macedonian infantry levy, if there is any institutional imitation the Persian national infantry levy must have been 100,000 at the very least, forming the backbone of the *Kara* and supported by 10,000 national levy cavalry (Her VII.41,3), leading to a total of 120,000 Persian troops, as reported by Xenophon (Cyr I.2,15), the guards not included. Perhaps this cavalry unit, diminished to 6,000, were the white-clad 'guard' cavalry of Artaxerxes II mentioned by Xenophon in Cunaxa (Xen Anab I.7,11). Most probably it was not a guard, but the national Persian cavalry draft outfitted according to the personal beliefs of the then sovereign. In any case, a decimal system emerges for the Imperials, regarding the proportion of infantry, Elites and Cavalry, as is established for the Greeks, (Plut Vit Aris 21).

ii)   The Guard of the Macedonian King, the Bodyguard (*Somatophylakhe*) was 200 men (Arr Anab IV.30,3; Kambouris & Bakas 2017; Kambouris et al 2019); most probably two units of 100 men each, which is similar to the Achaemenid structure of two guard units of 1,000 as described by Herodotus (VII.40,2 & 41.2), although the rationale of such a binary structure remains elusive. One unit for commoners and another for aristocracy as inferred by the above mentioned texts of Herodotus might be a possibility. Still, any accurate interpretation might have to consider the symbolism as a proof of the piousness of the monarch and the realm: the divine duality, the binary universe of Mithraism might be a valid origin for the need for two guard units (Soudavar 2012); or as with the Greeks and other ancient war establishments, the straightforwardness of binary command models may have been reason enough.

iii)   The Royal Bodyguards of the Argeads were seven (Arr Anab VI.28,3), ostensibly one on duty next to the king per weekday, although the number of days in an Ancient Greek week remains controversial. They might have been an echo of the seven conspirators in the Achaemenid court. There are some missing details, like the total number (the seven conspirators included Darius, while the Royal Bodyguard of Alexander were seven without counting the person of the King) but similarities are perhaps more important.

iv) A cavalry unit is expected, at least as an equivalent standing unit to the Immortals, and this should have been 1,000 strong. A second one might be expected as a mounted bodyguard, although this is perhaps notional. The description of the parade order of Xerxes' army however mentions two cavalry bodies of 1,000 each (Her VII.40,2 & 41,2), satisfying the above expectations fully. Whether one of these units accounts for the elusive 'cuirassiers' (Her VIII.113,2) is conjectural; still, one cavalry and one infantry hazaraba are drawn from the aristocracy (Her VII, 41,2); the rest (Her VII.40,2), plus the cavalry baivarabam and the Immortal baivarabam (Her VII.41,2–3) are drawn from the entire Persian nation; the Immortals actually might have included the other core ethnicities, the Medes and the Elamites, too (Deevers 2013; Charles 2011; Miller 2004). Still, this is based on the representations of the official dresses of the corps. Herodotus insists that the Immortals were Persians only (Her VII.41) and it is possible that the court attire included the national costumes of the three core ethnicities without drafting being proportional or representative of all of them; it could be a symbolism, not a factuality. Such practices can be identified even today in many guard units, which include costumes from different localities and/or from different eras; the really minuscule Presidential Guard of the Hellenic Republic has currently no less than eight official, ceremonial costumes.

Another detail of interest is that Herodotus clearly states that at one point Lacedaimonians were pitched against the Immortals. Nobody else, but also not exclusively Spartans, not just the 300. Thus, in a perfectly balanced and symmetrical action that highlights the differences of the two antagonists, a mere 1,000 Lacedaimonians of whom 300 are crack Spartan Peers were to face (not simultaneously) 10,000 Persian Immortals (Her VII.83), of whom the 1,000 are an Elite within the Elite (Her VII.41,2–3). It was the clash of the two Elites, plain, simple and without any innocent bystanders. The Persian Elite alone equals – or rather comfortably exceeds – the number of the whole Greek army; the Persian Elite within the Elite equals the total Lacedaimonian contingent.

Chapter 4

The Opening Moves

The Persian army emerged into the Greek field of view from east-north-east, having skirted the west coast of the Gulf of Pagassai southwards, after bypassing Alus (**Map 3.1**), the landing point of the abortive Greek campaign of the Ten Thousands at Tempe (Her VII.173). It was a rather easy landscape, level and well-watered and brought the Imperials opposite the great island of Euboea. They turned westwards, following the seaside to enter to the plain of Malis and the valley of Spercheios. This area is *Hellas* proper in Homeric geography, home of Achilles, the Greek arch-hero in the Iliad (II.681–5).

Since Leonidas had been on site before the Imperials, he had time to repair the ancient Phocian fortification and to establish a centre of support operations and supplies at Alpenoi (Her VII.176,5), some distance to the rear (**Figure 3.2**). The latter is a testimony to a very professional approach to operations, perfectly cognizant of logistics and its intricacies. Moreover, a concerted devastation operation to the Malian Plain had been executed. Not only did this bring plentiful supplies for the Allied army, but it deprived the invader of food, shelter and fodder (Green 1970; Bradford 1980) and was sending a message to Medizers that, even if due to compulsion, there were consequences for not joining actively in the national cause (Burn 1962); the wave of late Medizm after Tempe (Diod XI.3,2) under the pretext of powerlessness had to be contained or, preferably, stopped altogether.

It was the most logical thing to do, especially once the operative idea of the Allied plan had been to intercept the Imperial naval arm and thus derail the support and logistics agenda of the invasion force. This scorched earth policy was comfortably within the operational scope of an army only marginally short of 10,000 (Her VII.202–3). Actually, in these ravaging operations the auxiliaries of the army, including but not necessarily restricted to the followers/stewards of the Hoplites, must have been put to good effect (Hanson 1983; Delbruck 1920) and either executed the task themselves under the protection of Hoplite units keeping a watchful eye; or assisted the latter so as to double the manpower performing the task, thus ravaging double the area at a given time. The reference of Polyaenus (I.32,3) to such an incursion, carried out with extreme efficiency and skill by Leonidas, most probably refers to this operation, on the eve of the battle of Thermopylae (Bradford 1980).

The questions start from the moment Xerxes arrives at the plain of Malis and encamps. His patience, or hesitation, as he was staying immobile and waiting for some four days (Her VII.210) seems inexplicable if not ill-advised. Expecting his vast army to arrive, as it must have extended to quite a long line of march through the mountains, is the most probable reason. Additionally, the gale that wrecked the fleet (Burn 1962) would have made mud, where wagons, mounts, beasts of burden and even troops would have sunk, and possibly high seas might well have degraded the coastal road followed by the army, exacerbating the delays, the fatigue and the separation of his land units.

An approach more compatible to the bellicose nature of both Xerxes and his Persians might have been an immediate attack, to startle opponents up to this point had been elusive and otherwise unwilling to engage, as demonstrated in the Thessalian-Macedonian border at Tempe where they promptly retreated before any action (Her VII.173). Had he been mindful of his troops (Green 1970; Bradford 1980) – a view most unconvincing – why did he engage them at all, instead of bypassing the Allies through the alternative route, to Doris? After all, once the battle was done and he emerged victorious, he never led his army through the conquered pass. He went through the Asopus gorge to Doris straight south (Her VIII.31). So, given that the fleet's delay *did* cause a provisioning problem (Lazenby's 1993 efforts to deny this are unconvincing) and dumped the option of the amphibious bypassing the Allies Greek position, why had the Imperials not followed this route through Doris in the first place rather than engage in a stupidly bloody action?

One plausible explanation is that after a healthy walk of conquest, his host had *somehow* to fight, in order to taste blood and to further unnerve his opponents and discourage thoughts of further resistance. And, admittedly, it might have been his *wish* to engage, which seemed anything but stupid at the time. Xerxes and most of his generals were all convinced that their land army could beat Hoplites at any straightforward clash, as they had done in Egypt and Ionia (Lazenby 1993); especially if no tricks, as in Marathon, were to be used. Marathon was an accident; a view shared by many modern scholars (i.e. Lazenby 1993) or, else, an unmanly trick worked on vassal levies.

Under this light, it was a bonanza for him that in the straits of Thermopylae his enemies were making a stand, on level ground, ready to accept battle and with no room or ground for manoeuvring and tricks. He spotted them there and rushed to beat them there, since they were not in the mood for spontaneous flight. He mustered his army, gave it a respite, hoping, or at least expecting the resistance to melt away, and when this did not happen, he engaged confidently on level ground.

But the definitive argument is that he could not follow the alternative road. Had it been possible, after the first two days of the battle, when direct assault seemed a complete failure and a thrust in this direction would have broken the deadlock, Xerxes would have tried it. It was bad for his army's morale, not to be able to beat squarely so small a force, and that during the first actual engagement of the campaign. But there was no reason to despair – or even to become frustrated – as Herodotus says; the latter must have been made privy to the mood of the Emperor, through the Greeks of Xerxes' court, or rather their descendants, interviewed by him.

It being vital to advance, which explains the desperation and frustration, meant that if the option was available he would have taken it, even reluctantly. The evident answer is the presence of a strong and determined garrison denying free use of the alternative itinerary. A second force Herodotus knows of but says nothing about. This leads to a native population not very friendly to the Athenians in Herodotus' days. Perhaps the Malians, prominent in Diodorus' account as they furnished 1,000 troops (Diod XI.4,7) but missing in Herodotus' account (Her VII.202–3), either for the above reasons or because they were posted far from the actual Thermopylae position (Burn 1962) should be considered to fit the bill. Both Green (1970) and Bradford (1980) support such an eventuality and consider Trachis as the key of the western passes, guarded by the above mentioned contingent, if not also augmented by local Hoplite and light-armed militia. Actually, as the Malian plain had been devastated by Leonidas and occupied by Xerxes, raising troopers determined *for* the Greek cause, then and there, sounds weird. After all, one local was blamed for high treason with the Anopaia Pass, as suggested by Herodotus (Her VII.213,1). Hoplites of Trachis, on the other hand, mistakenly considered, *sensu lato*, Malians by Diodorus (XI.4,7), are a better bet, especially since the rendezvous point of Leonidas with the native and neighbouring contingents had been Trachis (Her VII.203,2) and *not* Thermopylae – a detail rarely, if ever, noticed.

Should this be the case, the operational specifics of the Greek campaign may have been very different than previously reconstructed: Leonidas might have approached the Malian plain through Phocis, intending to cast some metal into the region which had declared against the Imperials out of spite for the Thessalians early enough (Her VIII.30), and Doris, a very small patch of land and birthplace of all Dorians, to the Asopus gorge and Trachis, as the Locrians, occupying the pass of Thermopylae had medized. By emerging thus to the Malian plain, Leonidas had a privileged position and the advantage of surprise so as to ravage the flatland. Half intimidating and half impressing the Locrians he meant business, he brought about a change of heart (Diod XI.4,6) and won them over for the Alliance.

In this context, he entered the pass of Thermopylae from the west, setting the trail for Xerxes and gaining an excellent and detailed knowledge of his enemy's perspective. At the same time, the Phocian contingent would have moved from the rendezvous in Trachis up the Asopus gorge and then on the Anopaia path to position. In this way, the locals knew who climbed up the ridge, intelligence which was to prove decisive (Her VII.213,1). The above is a very convincing scenario for explaining how Ephialtes was to possess invaluable information on identity and numbers of the guardians of the Anopaia pass.

The Allied army brought by Leonidas is described in detail and with very few inconsistencies by Herodotus and Diodorus. The Lacedaimonian contingent has been discussed before. Due to the recurrence of the proposal that the balance between the 300 Peers of Herodotus (Her VII. 205) and the 1,000 Lacedaimonians of Diodorus (Diod XI.4,5) were Helots, and three Helots per Peer (Green 1970; Bradford 1980) it needs some scrutiny. It produces 1,200 men, not 1,000, as mentions Diodorus (XI.4,5). It is, much more importantly, unprecedented, even with OUR hindsight: on no occasion whatsoever are Peers known to have been followed by three Helots each. Such a theory is disproved by the account of Herodotus later on, when a semi-blinded Peer, Eurytus, was taken into the thick of battle by his Helot (Her VII.229,1), *singular*, no hint of Helots *plural* (Lazenby 1993). The notion that these 900 Helots had been emancipated (Burn 1962) is clearly retrospective due to practices of later days (Thuc IV.80); not to be rejected in principle but in this particular case simply implausible, as Sparta had no shortage of Peers as in later years whence the measure was applied. And, last but not least, Greek muster rolls mention Hoplites, not attendants. Plataea, where attendants were enumerated and seven Helots were assigned to each Spartan Peer (Her IX.10,1) was an exception due to very special circumstances.

The rest of the Peloponnesian force, which must be understood as the first ring of Spartan allies and more or less enthusiastic friends, was made up by two major 'urban' Arcadian contingents, from Tegea and Mantinea, of 500 shields each; a Corinthian of 400; a minuscule Mycenaean of 80; a Phliasian of 200; an Orchomenian of 120 and an assortment of 'the rest of Arcadia' identified (Burn 1962; Fields 1994) with the western area of the region-totalling 1,000 shields (Her VII.202). The Peloponnesian total was 3,800, very close to the 4,000 memorized in an epigram by Simonides after the battle (Her VII.228,1), and followed by an equal number of personal attendants (retainers/stewards). The entire host of the locals (Locrians) arrived, along with a 1,000-strong Phocian, a 400-strong Theban and the 700-strong Thespian contingents (Her VII.202–3).

Contrary to folklore, the nature and structure of the Spartan expeditionary force was a best guess of the available data by the Spartan government and agreed upon by the king and Ephors. It was understood that Spartan forces had to appear in the north, to stabilize the crumbling alliance and ascertain the Spartan commitment (Matthew 2013a). Leonidas though considered the mission potentially suicidal and took care to secure the best gain-to-loss ratio. The Spartans were very reverent and this reverence extended to the persons of their kings (Xen Lac Pol 13,1 & 15,9). They also had a reputation for selfishness as prominent as their expertise in war-making. For a king and some of his best troops, his guard, to be sacrificed in a magnificent way, making a declaration of grim determination, not suffering a defeat, admiration, not sympathy, would forge the Greek morale and steadfast the alliance.

The heinous omen of the Delphic oracle about the demise of a Spartan King insinuated (Her VII.220,4), without any room for alternative interpretation, the destruction, or at the very least defeat, of a Lacedaimonian army (Hammond 1996); otherwise a king could not be slain by the opponent. After all, when their king falls, the Spartan army always breaks, without an exact establishment of causality (Trundle 2013). Leonidas picked for yearly service, as king's guards, not youngsters, as had been the practice (Xen Lac Pol 4,2–3) but fathers; not necessarily middle-aged men, but fathers nonetheless (the Spartans were marrying rather young), to preserve the families and bloodlines (Her VII.205). This fact negates any second-guessing about the early realization of a potentially suicidal mission. A nation of warriors does not protect the bloodlines in conventional combat, but it does so in the face of annihilation. Thus, the Spartan understanding of the expedition was that it was absolutely necessary to carry it out; it could succeed, under a number of conditions, but it was probable that it would not and would end in defeat. The preparations were made accordingly, to cover the worst-case and most probable scenario.

Leonidas also took along as few troopers as possible, paying attention not to make a mockery of his, and Sparta's, commitment, though. Diodorus makes clear that the constitutional Spartan government (more explicitly the Ephors) considered Leonidas' mission feasible, although tricky and difficult and proposed commitment of larger forces to achieve a tangible positive result on the battlefield (Diod XI.4,3). Leonidas flatly refused and personally rated the mission as precarious, especially in the long run (Diod XI.4,4) since it was dependent on the ability of the fleet to repulse the Imperial navy, both warships and merchantmen (Matthew 2013b). He would not try to wrestle a conventional victory on the field, but would attempt to steal one following the tradition of Spartan guile, or to lay the foundations for a future one (Ibid).

In this light, the argument of Karneia festivities to honour Apollo prohibiting expeditions (Her VII.206) could not have been used seriously; the Spartans were very serious with religious commitments and if there was a taboo, the Ephors would not have proposed a stronger force. The problem is that had the idea of Karneia not been believable, it would lose its value and everybody would understand the pretence. The actual dispatch must have been authorized by some kind of remedy (Matthew 2013b); the small Spartan force used by Leonidas might imply that only those of the city would be accursed, a very good reason to expect total annihilation as a means to atone to the god for breaking the taboo. Another possibility is that the funeral games held in honour of Leonidas as King *before* he had even set foot out of Sparta, as reported by Plutarch (De Her Mal 31) might have broken the curse: by considering the king dead, the Deity might have been tricked to consider the breaking of the taboo punished. This kind of trickery was inbred in all Greeks by the myths of Prometheus who tricked Zeus and is recurring: after Leuctra, the Laws were put to sleep for a day (Plut Reg Imper Apoph/Agesil).

Leonidas asked for reinforcements once he understood not that his troops were too few to contain the enemy, but that the position was, after all, both under the control of the Allies (initially the Locrians had medized) and, after inspecting, improving and manning it, tenable, on condition of deployment of an adequately powerful task force (Her VII.207). This is a very delicate point, affecting the whole campaign. Fresh units were sorely needed, obviously to replenish casualties of physical and combat fatigue and attrition. True, it is certain that in the months between the actual campaign of Thermopylae and the abortive one of Tempe, should the timing of the latter by Herodotus be correct, the Allies must have given serious thought to the prospective suitable battlefields. In the case of Thermopylae, the Greeks made a detailed survey (Her VII.177) before having the Council at Isthmus sanction the campaign there. But before surveying the area himself and vastly improving the strategic situation by winning over all the locals – and thus leaving the enemy bereft of local supplies – Leonidas had been very unwilling to commit any significant force, or anything but a token force. The experience of Tempe was very instructive and massive expedited retreats as had happened there (Her VII.173,4) were shattering the fragile morale of the Allies, especially the uncommitted, putative ones.

The wave of Medizm after this event is tell-tale (Her VII.174 & 185,2). Neither Leonidas, nor anyone else could have foreseen a fast collapse of the defence should the conditions have proven favourable (Her VII.206.2), which they did. Thus, festivities were an excellent reason to delay a massive expedition northwards and one must in this case understand the boost to the morale of the populace by paying the God its due. Festivities having been concluded, the reinforcements would be pouring in progressively, so as not to strain the frail logistics while at the same time allowing a window of opportunity for accurate assessment of the situation by experts before committing. If the defence was feasible, reinforcements were to be committed. If not, a majestic declaration of resolve, a true blood sacrifice was prepared to appease the Gods of the Land and cast iron to the respective humans, although a retreat east to Alpenoi and then up-mountain towards Phocis, out of reach of the Imperial cavalry pursuit was practical for such a small army.

By the same token, an extraction by the fleet may well have been practical as well; the 4,000 Peloponnesian Hoplites plus an equal number of attendants minus the knights and their attendants were at most 7,400; something like 25 per vessel of the 320-strong fleet. That would get the retreating army out of the way of Imperial land pursuit and keep the triremes, which were on small boarders' complements, mobile enough for an all-out retreat. A perfect reason for the Allies to have opted in Artemisium for small boarders' detachments, had there been any need to argue for such a choice. Thus, a retreat of the bulk of the committed forces was secured, the locals by land, the southerners on deck; but the Spartan King and his guard would perish in glory should defeat occurred. A perfectly and coldly calculated Win or Die; Conquer or Perish etc. situation.

This whole machination had some weak points. The implementation of the reconnoitring campaign by a vanguard, meant that the contingent led by Leonidas was taking the field during a taboo time as already mentioned. The Knights were to atone for this blasphemy by their blood. As they were intended to perish, the sin would be redeemed, paid in blood and leaving Sparta unblemished. But Leonidas had some more first-class troops from Lacedaimon, who were not meant to perish in case of defeat, but to live and fight another day. It is conceivable that he took a non-Spartan unit (Mora) because its members were not bound by the Karnean custom and thus no divine discontent was to be on their heads. What would have been the story if the Ephors had succeeded to persuade him to take more troops, especially Spartans (Plut De Her Mal 32)? A defeatist's dream argument, that they had sinned and were for divine retribution. This is a motif regularly repeated in Greek history, due to the character of the nation's psyche, the fall of Constantinople being the most notorious example. For the other patriotic Greeks, a large Lacedaimonian army would have brought relief, not malicious questions – but this did NOT apply to the Spartans themselves!

Opposing intentions and plans

The Greek plan must have been a strategy of attrition. Killing enough opponents would not have been a viable option, but straining the logistics and draining the supplies of a vast army boxed among mountains and sea was another thing altogether; it was a prospect greatly facilitated should the delay over the Hellespont have occurred during the campaign, thus frustrating the Imperial timetable. The Decree of Troezen (Jameson, 1960-EM 13330, Epigraphical Museum, Athens) reveals that the real intention of the abandonment of Athens, a meticulously pre-planned massive operation, was to entrap the huge Persian army in Attica and destroy its fleet, thus aggravating a supply problem forecast months before by Artabanus (Her VII.49) who may, or may not, function as Herodotus' hindsight. In this light, the campaign at Thermopylae aimed at boxing the Imperial army away from the supplies of the fleet to wear it down, if not to stop it altogether. This objective is the only plausible explanation for the mission of one of the 300, named Pandites, in Thessaly during the campaign – that is behind enemy lines (Her VII.232). Neither sabotage nor insurgencies could have been his mission, as the invader had just gone through in the highlight of his power and omnipotence. A strategic reconnaissance mission must be understood (Burn 1962) and this cannot concern any other issue but the flow and availability of supplies, probably as a function of the time of the year, due to the delay in the crossing of the Hellespont.

The same is true for sapping the morale of the enemy, especially the non-Persian subject troops. It was a most attainable objective. Some bloody failures and their fragile morale, rooted on idolizing the King of Kings' power, military prowess and diplomatic efficiency (Polyaen VII.15,1) would be undermined and the same goes for the authority of the King of Kings' figure, an almost divine one since Darius I (DB 62). The prospects would then include desertion, mutiny or stunned impotence.

In this light, the campaign to Thermopylae and Artemisium must be understood as totally different from the purely interceptive campaign at Tempe, an amphibious campaign with a purely land operational dimension; there (**Figure 3.2**), the Greek fleet had been ostensibly a mere means of transportation (Her VII.173), an opinion perhaps a tad inaccurate, if a remark of Plutarch (Vit Them 20) is read within context (see next chapter). Moreover, Tempe was a focused, one-dimensional campaign with traditional joint command seeking to block the Persian onslaught. The expeditionary Allied force is not described by contingent or regarding its naval arm. It was 10,000-strong, led by a hardy Spartan General, Euainetos, a *Polemarch*, the first time this rank is mentioned (Fields 2013). Themistocles was also there, perhaps leading an Athenian land force (Diod XI.2; Her VII.173) in an amphibious operation well to the north, which thus satisfied two-thirds of his strategic considerations (an Allied campaign taking the fight as far away as possible) but not fulfilling the third, the active use of his fleet, although this is debatable. The Allied roster included a Theban contingent of 500 under Mnamias (Plut De Her Mal 31) and the figures must refer to Hoplites, implying an equal number of retainers. This causes some issues as to how many triremes were needed to carry such an army, how many of the fighting and support troops were carried on each trireme and in what kind of arrangement. The very few Lacedaimonian vessels were in no way enough for a meaningful contingent, whereas the many Athenian ones must have carried other cities' contingents as well, as were the Arcadians, for example.

An interesting remark of Herodotus (VII.177) implies that the campaign of Thermopylae and Artemisium was decided, planned and executed on the spot; no mobilization, no idling. His wording suggests a force already assembled, or stationed, at Corinth and dispatched promptly. It is correctly pointed out (Grundy 1901) that according to Herodotus the Tempe expedition took place at the time of Xerxes' crossing to Europe (Her VII.174), mid to late spring, while the Thermopylae campaign was launched when Xerxes was in Therma or soon after he set forth and the Karnean festival was still on, that is early August. There are some months in between, during which the Allies seem to have done nothing, no expedition, no fortification, nothing- – not even work in the fields, as in such a case the Athenian grain should have been harvested by July and not destroyed by the invaders, thus accounting for a lost harvest (Her VIII.142,3). This indicates rather a belated Greek evacuation of the Tempe position, probably when the defenders were informed that the Persian army was carving a route through the mountains, possibly – but not necessarily – because of their holding position; water availability was a valid reason as well.

Having to cross Thessaly on foot before cavalry, they must have retired as rapidly as possible and been very grateful to Alexander I of Macedon (Her VII.173) who must have provided accurate intelligence on numbers, but, more importantly on timing, itinerary and progress of the Persians, all data he could have been privy to AFTER Xerxes had arrived at Therma and not while he was crossing the Hellespont (Her VII.174). It must be remembered that the army with which Xerxes crossed the Hellespont was the army encamped at Sardis, observed, assessed and counted by the Allies' spying mission and thus any intelligence concerning it by Alexander I was superfluous and probably less accurate than that already available; the notion of the Greek spies exaggerating what they saw and also being tricked to amazement by cunning Imperials (Lazenby 1993) is preposterous. Not being able to select spies with a keen eye who were accurate in their reports, not easily fooled or impressed, would earn the Allies the title of the most God-beloved people in history, to be able to repulse the invader with such incompetence and naivety.

Thermopylae on the other hand was a predominantly naval campaign (Holland 2005, Montagu 2000). The Spartan reservations, due to the danger of both operational (by secondary routes and alternate passes, **Figure 3.2**) and strategic flanking (by sea raids deep at their rear, **Map 3.2**) dictated the commitment of limited forces, led by a most capable commander with an excellent grasp of all the operational and strategic parameters, not only the tactical ones. This agreed with Themistocles' wish, and need, to use the navy he created (Her VII.144) as the primary arm against the Persians, committing thus most of the manpower of Athens against the enemy, instead of the 25–30 per cent represented by the Hoplites; roughly 10,000 out of a 30,000 civic body a generation earlier (Her V.97,2).

The Peloponnesian expeditionary land force was a mere 4,000 (Her VII.202; Diod XI.4,5) compared to 10,000 at Tempe (Her VII.173), possibly to be augmented by another 3,000 troops from the immediate neighbourhood and increased to double that by the followers, one per Hoplite as can be deduced by the campaign of Plataea (Her IX.29). In short, less than 20,000, non-combatants included, campaigned to Thermopylae, compared to a little less than 60,000 for the naval contingent (270 triremes times 200 crew and marines). In Thermopylae, things were quite different than in Tempe, even at the conceptual level: operations were to develop in both elements and the two branches to campaign simultaneously and be interconnected but not form a joint force. Steps were taken to ensure mutual awareness and co-ordination, but there were two separate forces with clearly different command chains, much like the Imperials. Again as was the case with the Imperials, the Greeks had unified overall command: the Spartans were in charge.

There is one more similarity: a state campaigning in one element did not campaign in the other. Contributing to one of the two expeditionary forces fully satisfied the requirement for participation. Except for Sparta and Corinth. Sparta contributed a minuscule squadron of 10 triremes, equalling 2,000 hands, mostly Helots probably and/or Periekoi; and a small but very battle-worthy land contingent of 1,000 Hoplites plus as many Helots. This was a total of 4,000 troops with perhaps 1,100 being top fighters – really unimpressive figures. This double commitment could be considered the price of leadership; considerable Persian forces were embarked to fight as marines, although there were no Persian ships. What is weird is that except Sparta, Corinth (not Athens) also participated in both elements (Her VII.202 and VIII.1,1).

On land, a minimal Hoplite force is committed, balancing the extremely low numbers with a strong position, excellence in command, training, discipline and high symbolism. A Spartan King led an Allied, mainly Peloponnesian Army, although a token force, for the secondary, holding action against the primary enemy branch, the huge land army commanded by the King of Kings. The primary Greek force, under Eurybiadas, a non-royal Spartan (Her VIII.2 & 42), is the fleet, committed in Artemisium, poised against the weaker enemy branch in an obvious indirect strategy and with the highest level of advantages: the less obvious local knowledge of weather, currents and shores, which can hardly be reconnoitred, were surveyed beforehand. The land army had to hold the enemy long enough for the main Greek weapons, weather, shoreline and triremes, to gain a decisive victory or damage the enemy's ability to secure one.

Still, given enough time the land positions were likely to be breached, either by sheer exchange of casualties or by flanking; thus three successive ones were selected:

Tempe, Thermopylae and Isthmus. After all, despite being a one-sided carnage at some points, the battle of Thermopylae, fought under the most favourable terms for the Greeks, had a final 5:1 exchange rate, with some 20,000 Persian fatalities versus 4,000-odd Greek total killed in action (Her VIII.24–5). If deserters, wounded and prisoners are taken into account, the ratio falls further.

In the 4,000 figure, the casualties of the first days are included. These seem to be substantial, at least 2,000 and probably more. The Spartan and Thespian units falling to a man on the third day were nominally 1,000 men, and had all their squires fought and died too (the Helots most probably but for exceptions, and the retainers of the Thespians would have been a surprise), the figure rises to 2,000. The balance must have been the casualties of the first two days: included in this number is the small Mycenaean force of 80 Hoplites (Her VII.202; Paus II.16,5) exterminated to a man (Paus X.20,2) but most probably not the non-Spartan Lacedaimonian force in its entirety, which, though, must have suffered casualties. The 400 Thebans were a total loss, with their dead counted among the dead Greeks, but the survivors were taken prisoners and branded (Her VII.233,2).

Such a rate was unsustainable for the long haul and far below the 30:1 in Marathon (Her VI.117). But time was of essence. Leonidas' was really a holding force, to be reinforced as required but the main forces were kept to the extreme rear, to guard against insurrections and also strategic flanking (**Map 3.2**). The bitter lesson of Tempe had been the Persian tendency to enact such moves (**Map 3.1**); a tendency not attributable to some narration pattern or reporting bias, as sometimes proposed (Rookhuijzen 2019), but to an Imperial *modus operandi* or perhaps even SOP. Significant Allied forces would be allowed to pour north only if and when the Imperial host was fully committed and pinned.

At this stage, the main Allied arm was the navy by necessity. If the Imperial navy could be kept separated from the army, resupply would be a vital issue for the latter. The navy had no unlimited supplies and its haulers were vulnerable to storms and to surprise attacks in unknown coastlines. Practically, the Greeks had to intercept one of the two branches of the Persian War machine to win. If the Greek fleet resisted successfully, the Persian fleet could not outflank Thermopylae, neither in direct action, transporting army troops just behind Leonidas to some beach along the shore of Locris (Holland 2005), nor by landing there its organic cavalry and infantry units, an impressive 50,000 troops (**Map 3.2**). This figure is the initial strength of the Imperial Marines, 40 troops per trireme (Her VII.184,2) for 1,300 triremes (Her VII.184,1 & 185,1) and at least 30 cavalry mounts for each of 850 horse transports (Diod XI.3,9). And it could land to the northern shore of Euboea to capture the Greek base at Artemisium and from there move south-south-east through the island to Chalcis and then west, crossing the narrow channel of Euripus, to Boeotia, encircling the whole Greek expeditionary force (Shepherd 2010; Green 1970; Grundy 1901).

If Thermopylae held, the royal army could not threaten Euboea through Chalcis nor the mooring base of the Greek fleet. The royal army could, in principle, outmanoeuvre the Greeks, by crossing at Chalcis and then galloping north-north-west to the Greek anchorage at Artemisium to deliver slaughter to the crews and burn or capture the vessels. Moving north and further to the west, they could descend on Aetolia, as did Brennus in 279 BC (Paus X.22,3). But this detour was leading out of the pre-planned access itinerary, where allies and supplies had been gathered, and into broken terrain, far away from the fleet and the supplies it carried, while also making a mess with the fine timing arrangements between the two Imperial branches.

Finally, and less probably, the Greek fleet of some 270 vessels (Her VIII.2) could easily embark the whole of Leonidas' army of 8,000 (Her VII.202–3) by adding 25 men in each vessel and landing them near the Imperial mooring, thus eliminating the fleet on the beach, in a surprise action before the Persians could establish communications between army and navy – or it could, if Xerxes had not endowed his triremes with 30 marines each.

All the above explains why Xerxes attacked. He simply did not want the Greeks staying there unmolested. The pass of Thermopylae was of little consequence by itself, but it was a part of the Allied defence complex and the only position exposed to a land offensive. By simply being there, Leonidas guarded the rear of the navy by not allowing the Persian land army to cross to Euboea, but also by allowing Greek reserves to surge to Euripus to interdict any naval outflanking. Additionally, the small garrison in Trachis could bury any Imperial incursion through the gorge, under tons of rocks and stones, as was to happen in 279 BC against the Gauls (Paus X.22,1). It was the combination of the Allied positions and forces which made the mix extremely flammable. If the defenders of Thermopylae were beaten or thrown back, the road from Alpenoi to Phocis would open and be used to turn the defence positions by Trachis, or bypass it entirely (**Figure 3.2**).

Xerxes' waiting for four days before attacking (Her VII.210) was not just to muster his lumbering, gigantic army, which took days to concentrate in a position (Bradford 1980). He was also waiting for his fleet (Green 1970, Bradford 1980), at the same time perhaps hoping that the size would strike home the correct message to the opposing Greeks. The fleet could flank the Greek position by landings, assault it by the use of 'naval archery' as executed by the Athenian fleet against the Gauls in 279 BC (Paus X.21,4) or make it irrelevant by using Euboea as a land corridor for parts of the army (Grundy 1901). Not seeing the fleet was ominous. Meeting a blasphemous rejection of his extremely generous proposals for an honest surrender

(Diod XI.5,4) rang a bell. The terms were generous given that Sparta had not been entitled to spontaneous surrender by offering Earth and Water (Her VII.32) and were only extended due to the critical turn of events. Ordering the assault to eliminate the land element of the Greek resistance was, under the circumstances, more than a reflex reaction from the Persian High Command, whose instincts were true. With Leonidas gone, the whole defence plan was shattered: the Greek navy withdrew, the Persian navy made contact with the army, normalizing supplies and the pass to Doris was free. After all, their previous knowledge of the Greeks did not indicate any risk of failure if a direct assault was attempted on level ground against Hoplites; Marathon had proved the risks inherent in the opposite proposal. Seen under this light, frontal assault against Leonidas was anything but poor tactics.

Chapter 5

48 Hours or Less: The Battles

Xerxes would rather have the Greeks retire by themselves so that he could hunt them down with his cavalry (Her VII.210 & Diod XI.6,1). Modern scholars think he attacked reluctantly, as light oriental infantry attacking Hoplites in a narrow front seems rather poor tactics, and this must have been obvious to their command (Bradford 1980; Green 1970). This may be a retrospective projection. Xerxes indeed would rather have his opponents removed without battle, which is indicative of a competent general; or their position turned by an amphibious operation, but there is no hint that he considered a direct assault a bad choice, much less one prone to failure. The last confrontation between land armies of the Empire and Greeks had been at Marathon; the empire was defeated, but the crack Imperial troops had summarily pushed back for quite a distance, if not broken and pursued, the opposing Athenian Hoplites (Her VI.113,1). Details might have been scarce for the Imperial staff, but in Greece, the legend of Marathon was popular and widespread and many details or conclusions might have been drawn. The Imperial headquarters had every reason to presume that the assault troops would defeat the Greek units, since this time they seemed immobile, dug-in and thus vulnerable to mass archery and unable to implement a more effective defence. And, more importantly, this time there were no vassal weaklings at the Imperial wings, as the front was very narrow.

The mission was assigned to the Median contingent (Her VII.210; Diod XI.6,3). Diodorus had a nefarious scheme (XI.6,3) to have them bear the brunt of casualties as he considered them politically unreliable; an intention which would explain the suicidal order to capture the Greek Hoplites alive (Her VII.210). This opinion of Diodorus is plausible; their former supremacy over the Persians is a legitimate factor, as he correctly points out. Their adherence to non-Zoroastrian, or rather no Mazdaic, religious practices, headed by Magi, is one more reason, both in terms of religious Zoroastrian vehemence and of the bitter past of an alleged coup by a Median Magus just before Darius' reign (Her III.61,1; DB 11), as detailed previously (Kambouris 2022). This was exacerbated by a Median sedition (DB 24). But as the Medes and Cissians are the two main components of the Achaemenid empire after the Persians, a model of precedence may have been at play: the two senior associates are called upon to brush aside the enemy at the first clash; once it proved not to be a mere skirmish, the Persians are called, against an obviously exhausted opponent, to display the superiority of the Master Race.

The problems start with Diodorus' remark, a most plausible one, that the offspring and relatives of the Marathon casualties were brigaded with the Medes, as having the most powerful motivation; that is, revenge (Diod XI.6,4). Herodotus, on the other hand, mentions the Cissians (the Elamite natives of Susiana, where the main capital, Susa, lies) as brigaded with the Medes (VII.210). When enumerating the invading host, these two nations are separately and consecutively mentioned, under different leaders (Her VII.62); thus their grouping together in Herodotus' narrative must have a meaning missed ever since, as Diodorus' account has the Cissians follow the Medes, but as a totally different entity, grouped with Saka (Diod XI.7,2). In both narrations, the first day closes with the attack of the Immortals (Diod XI.7,4; Her VII.211).

And here comes the problem with the progeny of the casualties of Marathon. Sons or brothers, do they form a part of the Median contingent, or are they another unit brigaded to the Medes for this specific field assignment? With 6,400 dead at the very least, how many are these, and are they of one kin and nationality? A significant proportion of the Imperial casualties at Marathon were from the encircled centre, with the best troops, who were Persians and Saka, but no Medes according to Herodotus (VI.113,1). Other subjects were massively killed in the two flanks and more might have drowned in the marsh, whose corpses must have not been found and counted and thus add to the 6,400 figure. There is no answer to this problem.

The Median contingent attacked time and again (Her VII.210,2) but to no avail. As the Greek phalanx was jammed in the narrows, it follows that the attackers could not launch a full scale attack. No matter whether the diverse ethnic contingents of the Imperial host were baivaraba or corps made up by more than one baivaraba, anything from two to six; no matter whether they were of uniform strength or not; a hazarabam would have been the tactical unit for any single attack. Given the width of the strait and the need of the Imperials for room to manoeuvre and launch their attack, half a hazarabam, 500 men, was the most for any attack. More such units were used successively.

The repeated attacks (Her VII.210,2 & Diod XI.7,1–2) of the first waves met with a stout defence. It is unclear what troop type attacked in Thermopylae; the surroundings did not lend to the sparabara as compact Greek phalanxes would offer small, hard and difficult targets to massed archery while enjoying dense, unarmoured and insufficiently shielded masses for collective, disciplined spearing (Ray 2009). Takabara light infantry, endowed with Close Quarters Battle kit and protected by their crescent shields up to a degree, raised from the reserves of the national levies, especially of the Persians (Xen Cyrop I.2,13) but not exclusively so, might have been a solution. Their onslaught would be meant to infiltrate into the dense Hoplite formations to erode them, and was launched possibly under cover of volleys of special archer units or standard sparabara. The small, round or irregular-shaped shields mentioned for Cissians and Saka, but not for the Medes (Diod XI.7) imply that not all the Achaemenid Iranian infantry were sparabara, contrary to some contemporary views (Ray 2009; Sekunda 2002; Sekunda and Chew 1992) and possibly targeteer-rank infantry was at some time tested as a means to unlock the access to the straits, conceivably augmented by archers; to suggest these latter were Saka armed with more powerful, composite bows (Ray 2009) is legitimate, but nothing more than that.

If, on the other hand, conventional sparabari were used, volleys would have been fired to force Hoplites into a defensive posture, if nothing else, before the Medes would have attempted close contact. At the very least this should have happened after the improbable but still quite possible first effort to tear down the Greek formation and arrest the vile *infidels* alive (Her VII.210), which would have ended in a bloodbath. The small depth of phalanx task groups and the very small front denied both high-arc and diagonal modes of shooting and thus any practical result to such suppressive fire. As a consequence, archery came to naught and the shorter Persian spears were rarely brought into action as the longer Greek ones caused carnage from standoff distance (Her VII.211,2) against unarmoured or lightly armoured opponents, especially the rank and file behind shield-bearing dathapata file leaders.

The result of the fight was largely due not only to the difference in spear length, but also to the ineffective and perhaps few shields of the Imperials (Diod XI.7,2–3). Even when a spara, which is rather large, had been available, it still was a shield designed for lightness and stopping missiles with low momentum and high kinetic energy. Spearthrusts are not very fast, but have higher momentum, exercise tremendous pressure in small surfaces and pierce wickerwork much more easily. Moreover, should the attackers have been able to reach the Greek line, the shoving of the phalanx would have brought them down, out of balance and open to spear-thrusts, while the Greek large, stout Argive shield and panoply warded off the thrusts of the short spears. There was no lack of valour nor of experience; still, the attackers were repulsed repeatedly. Each wave must have been engaging for half an hour before being recalled, without achieving any success, but having suffered incapacitating wounds aplenty and quite a number of fatalities. Successive waves were thrown in and were pushed back promptly, much faster than their stamina would dictate, due to the murderous nature of the fighting. They were finally recalled and retired under orders (Her VII.211,1), without any ill-treatment or spite for lack of valour, aggressiveness, daring or mettle.

At this point, a pause is needed. The order of Xerxes to 'bring the defenders alive' may, just may, be hiding another line of thought and tactics. The Imperials must have taken a good account of the defeat in Marathon, no matter how much they had downplayed it. They did not want to let it happen again. It must have been a staff exercise 'How would you react had you been Datis'. The advance at the run and the determined attack against the comparatively weak wings were identified as the key issues. In Thermopylae, Xerxes, once battle became inevitable followed the best possible tactics, contrary to some scholars' beliefs (Green 1970; Bradford 1980). He attacked on level ground with good assault troops; bad tactics would have been to assault the naturally protected position controlling the road to Doris, where the citadel of Trachis lurked over rocks and peaks. In Thermopylae, it was good ground, against an obvious target, enemy land troops. Shooting at them would allow them the opportunity to charge at the double and catch the archers before the latter could change weapons and perhaps formation to go for close-quarter combat. An *Imperial* running charge, *without* archery barrage was tantamount to an innovation and Xerxes wanted to test it. He could startle the enemy Hoplites and perhaps catch them in attack formation before they were able to form for defence or launch their attack. Perhaps not all Persians believed in the new assault tactics: Mardonius, either from belief or from experience did not try it in Plataea; he preferred the standard Achaemenid massive archery barrage before a charge.

Eventually, the experiment did not work, as the Hoplites were very fast to transform from attack to defence formation, or at least faster than the Imperials had estimated. In Thermopylae they may have been all the time in a defensive mood and mode, except for the last day which was once more a surprise. Thus, they could adopt tight formation, project their spears held firmly underarm (Matthew 2012) and let the charging Imperials get impaled on their spearpoints, or literally crashed onto their shield-wall, to a stop. Then the Imperials were speared at will by the much more penetrative Hoplite spears, designed to pierce at least body armour if not shields also and aimed accurately at unarmoured body parts, such as the face, neck, groin and thigh.

In general, Herodotus' detailed account is more reliable than the somewhat sensational one of Diodorus. Still, Herodotus reports only the Medes attacking (Her VII.210,2–211,1) although originally he made clear that the mission was entrusted to both Medes and Cissians (Her VII.210,1). But he never mentions a thing about the Cissians; it was as if they never engaged. On the contrary, Diodorus reports that Cissians relieved the Medes, thus in part corroborating the initial account of Herodotus and he adds the Saka as a third contingent. Since the Saka were brigaded with the Bactrians (Her VII.64,2), who were never mentioned as taking part in the clashes of the first day, perhaps Diodorus added them to the list due to their prominent role in Marathon, as second in valour only to the Persians (Her VI.113,1).

Enter the elites

The Medes having fought either alone or with some company by other contingents, were definitely and bloodily repulsed. The bloody failure at the very first instance of actual resistance was a PR disaster for the Empire. Empires are cemented by myths and beliefs and the trick is to have and sustain a myth more powerful than reality; this is the economy of aggrandizement. And this myth was now hacked to pieces by the Greek spears. Still, the continued waves and the massed archery (at some time it would have been called upon to support the assaults) would have caused wounds, exhaustion and casualties. Xerxes had no idea of how the Greeks were moving; his sight, when his infantry engaged near the Middle Gate must have been limited. Accordingly, he tried, very logically, to deny any respite, any reorganization, any breath to his enemies – and perhaps he was still under the false assumption that he was against the Lacedaimonian contingent spotted out of the wall by his mounted scout (Her VII.208). Hence the decision to commit his best troops was a correct one, to literally save the very nasty day. Had he waited for the next day, the pain of the wounds might have taken some wounded Greeks out of action, but the night respite would have allowed a reorganization of their units, a possible arrival of reinforcements and, most of all, a mental reset in both camps establishing the Greeks as the victors and the Imperials as the vanquished, at least for the day. If the sun was to set without him breaking through, he was vanquished; if he succeeded, nothing up to that point mattered: it would have been a hotly contested victory. Thus, with invincibility on the table, Xerxes committed the Immortals: 10,000 Sparabari, unmistakably so due to the description of Herodotus that 1,000 with golden pomegranates as counterweights to their spears were encircling 9,000 who had silver pomegranates as counterweights (Her VII.41). The bearers of the golden pomegranates were the dathapata file leaders.

Herodotus provides two pieces of information within the main body of the narrative. The first is that the Immortals attempted a number of different tactical dispositions in their repeated attacks, including the attacks in groups (Her VII.211). Whatever this was, the message that these troops were better-trained and much more versatile than other units is unmistakably driven home. The second is that the Immortals had some grounds to believe that they were bringing the Lacedaimonians to a breaking point and thus, once the latter were turning to flight, they were giving chase only to be counter-attacked by the supposed fugitives with disastrous results and massive casualties (Her VII.211,3).

The Immortals were in for a nasty surprise. Till this point, the Greeks were rock-solid, in the defensive, a metal wall on which wave after wave of Imperials had been broken. Contrary to some views (i.e. Ray 2009) there is no indication that they advanced, attacked or did anything else than enduring and then rotating to catch their breath and sponge their sweat. But the Lacedaimonians changed the game with the Immortals, emerging forward, to a wider spot with space behind them, so as to be able to use mobile tactics, as described later in this chapter in detail. By any account (Her VII.211; Diod XI.7,4) the Immortals were badly mauled. The counter-attacks meant that running Immortals in hot pursuit crashed onto a fully deployed and solidly set Lacedaimonian phalanx, which advanced briskly and was thrashing the disorganized Persians. The latter turned to flight and were fleeter than the advancing phalanx, but the very narrow exit, the Western Gate, meant that some were trapped in for just enough time for the Spartans to slay them. The Immortals, once disorganized and possibly having their dathapata, with the spara shields, obliterated at the first phase of the Spartan counter-attacks, as they were closer in their pursuit to the fleeing Hoplites, were unable even to pretend to form a solid front and contest the issue. They were unshielded troops with short spears, although possibly armoured by scaled cuirasses (Seevers 2013), fighting against a fully organized phalanx with Argive shields and Hoplite long spears – the perfect setting for a true carnage.

And this was happening to the best unit, THE elite baivarabam of the empire. Xerxes' strategy was backfiring. The Imperial army had other Persian guard units, such as the Applebearers and Arstibara, but the Immortals were the elite field unit, at least of the infantry. Their slaughter was sapping the Imperial authority. From the viewpoint of the Imperial host, the Western Gate would have been the Gates of Hell: units were going in and human wrecks, bits and pieces with horrific wounds were coming out. The carnage was unnerving; each fresh Imperial unit taking over the attack had to go through the bodies of their comrades heaped and still hot and bleeding. But the sorry condition of the units retiring under orders was unnerving to all. Xerxes was right to be uncomfortable: a spark of defeatism could induce a massive panic to his host, which would fast lose any faith in his Divinity and invincibility and thus might consider mutiny.

Moreover, although the Immortals were replenished instantly (probably overnight) from other Persian units, the disruption of the cohesion and of the aura of invincibility of the unit meant a window of opportunity for massive uprisings and mutiny, as the Corps was functioning as the ultimate Military Police in a multi-national, heterogeneous and not very enthusiastic, nor deeply motivated, army, which was cemented thanks to imposed discipline by rewards and especially punishment (Her VII.103). Jumping on his command throne (Her VII.212), Xerxes could not have been more justified to worry for the future of the campaign; and all that was happening in the first encounter with the enemy!

The disciplining of the Imperial army would have taken a good part of the comparatively short late summer night, while the Allies would have been thrilled by their success. Even against the Immortals, there were rather few fatalities. The Greek weapons were reusable, but their continued use would have resulted in high attrition, as the usual clashes involving Hoplites were violent but brief, with few exchanges of blows. The rotation rate of the Greeks taxed the individual task groups lightly, a good prognosis for an attrition fight. With the encircling squadron of the Persian fleet not surviving a second gale (Her VIII.13) and thus not being able to resolve the deadlock in Thermopylae, the Imperial staff had to do it the hard way.

Herodotus' account for the second day is abstract but compatible with the one of Diodorus (XI.8,1–3), which describes a continuation of the previous practice, with picked troops attacking by waves in the expectation of a sudden collapse of the Greek defence due to attrition (Her VII.212). This approach would lead to the depletion of the more battle-worthy Imperial units, a very poor choice for a protracted campaign with a multi-national army, but it was perhaps inevitable in a crisis. Herodotus gives no clue on the units engaged the next day (Her VII.212); Diodorus (XI.8,1) mentions that they were chosen on merit – most probably reputed – but still coerced, motivated and pressed by military police to keep up the fight (Diod XI.8,3). A better interpretation would be that contingents with equipment suitable to face off the Hoplites, such as the Lydians and Assyrians (Her VII.74 & 63) would have been chosen.

But another line of events is conceivable; an approach followed, according to Herodotus' detailed account (VII.223,3) during the fighting of the third day. This time a more concise attrition strategy might have been formed. Having re-established the discipline, successive waves of disposable and possibly unreliable troops were thrown onto the Greek defenders. A very stringent system of enforced field discipline, with impromptu flogging, pushed unenthusiastic troops to continuous assault, thus tiring, if nor wounding the defenders and blunting and damaging their weapons. The deadly spears of the Hoplites, longer than the Imperial ones and perfectly suited to the confined struggle within the straits between close but separated bodies of troops clashing frontally, had a tolerance in thrusting and penetrating human bodies, especially through reed-and-leather shields, and then being retrieved. Their points could break, detach or dull and the shafts could be hacked by sidearms, especially axes and hatchets, broken by bare hands or shattered by sliding forces. Once spears were broken, the stout Hoplite shields, with practically unlimited resistance to arrows, would give way after high numbers of blows by hacking heavy weapons, clubs, spherical spear-butts and even spearpoints thrusting with enough determination or despair. And it was not an issue of destroying the weapons of all the Greeks: if one contingent was disarmed to a degree that the fight would come to individual, hand-to-hand combat, with swords, the Imperial mass would achieve a breakthrough and perhaps face with higher spirits the remaining Hoplite units, held in reserve, in more favourable terrain, perhaps out of formation.

This last possibility, along with the indignation caused by the shortage of supplies, the delay of the fleet and the massive loss of Imperial face might explain the remark of Diodorus that in the second day Xerxes, unwisely, engaged his best units (Diod XI.8,1), encouraging them with promises of bonuses and threats of capital punishment. A line of disciplinary troops, possibly a Hazarabam of Arstibara, as the Immortals were licking their wounds, was posted behind the deployed units, conceivably at the Western Gate, to deny retreat (Diod XI.8,3) and, most importantly, flight – except under orders. Using numerous picked units in such confined space meant by definition that assault groups were supposed to be relieved at given intervals.

The massive bleeding of the Imperial army on the second day must have had a naturalizing effect rather than a sapping one, as described by Diodorus (XI.8,4). It might have led to questioning and doubts regarding the divine image of Xerxes, a huge drop of morale at the prospect of entering in the slaughterhouse to be butchered (Diod XI.8,4) but in the mid-term, this was hammering his huge host into a single army. Different nations were bleeding together under His Majesty's gaze, all contingents participating in the blood sacrifice.

The casualty rate may have been much slower and lower than implied in texts and movies. It must have been considerable, but the ratio of thrusts to actual kills must have been rather low. The lower it was, the more exhausted the Greeks would have been and the more damaged their weapons (Holland 2005). Additionally, as discussed previously, the casualty exchange was probably less lopsided. Xerxes now had nothing to worry about in tactical terms; his army and campaign were safe from any unfortunate events on the field.

The evolving greater picture

The operational situation for the Imperials was murky, as the Malian field provided no supplies due to the foraging and scorching performed by Leonidas' army. With the stocks collected from Thessaly growing thin and the region stripped of any remaining quantities, while the fleet was both blocked away and suffering massive losses in merchant vessels laden with provisions, things were going sour. Each day of delay the provisions available to the Persians, on their axis of advance in Boeotia, would diminish due to consumption or picking clear by the enemy foragers, if not altogether destroyed by an Allied campaign of active scorched earth as in Malis. Additionally, the water, the most important variable in the Imperial plan, would be exhausted, and under the hot Greek sun disease would inevitably break out: this multitude of men and beasts, malnourished and dehydrated, producing massive amounts of bio-waste in a limited area meant that not only smell, but actual infections would start plaguing, incapacitating and demoralizing the Imperials. Once intelligence on the conditions in Thessaly arrived, Leonidas would have been able to estimate, crudely, no doubt, the tolerance of the Imperial supply system. And in such a case, the entire Greek army might be able to deliver a crushing blow (Matthew 2013b).

With the Greeks it was different. Herodotus (VII.206,2) is very clear that at least officially the defence of Thermopylae was expected to last for quite some time, giving ample margin for sending reinforcements. And the Greek army had not encountered any surprises. The small size of their force, which, if the terrain is taken into consideration, compares *favourably* with the one dispatched at the Tempe expedition, allowed relatively easy acquisition, securing the flow of supplies (Matthew 2013b); the ravaging of the plain of Malis might well have amassed supplies for men, as there were very few beasts, for the duration of the campaign and also some for the anticipated reinforcements. The stout defence they were able to present was exactly what they must have been expected to do. Doubts and fear, at least initially, were expected, but the verdict of battle and the results in a wider context were nothing more – or less – than a correct forecast becoming true.

Additionally, the size of the army of Xerxes had nothing to do with the Greek ability to hold the pass. It would have been crucial in a field action, but the main impact would have been in terms of attrition. Thus, the remark of Herodotus (VII.207) that Leonidas, seeing the enormous size of the enemy, asked for reinforcements might be out of time or context or *both*. If nothing else, the size of the Persian army was rather accurately recorded by the spying mission to Sardis (Her VII.146,3) or known to exaggeration as an unnerving policy of the Imperial intelligence staff (Holland 2005). It could not have been *greater* than expected, although the spectacle could indeed cause some awe. As a result, Leonidas could not have been impressed by an enormous size, let alone staggered and requesting immediate reinforcements. The sheer size of the enemy would offer him a most important strategic advantage: the fast consumption of supplies and the starvation of the whole host (Matthew 2013b).

This problem of the Imperial staff must have been grimly, and only partly, alleviated by the loss of the more disposable troops, an event which was also keeping the mind of the soldiery away from their stomachs and towards the immediate danger of the Greek spears. As their demise was also degrading the arms and armour of the Greeks, the human waves, a practice recurring in Iranian history (i.e. during the Iran-Iraq war of the 1980s), was indeed a logical approach. The continuous use of the Greeks' edged weapons was blunting them. Thousands of not particularly strong, nor well-weighted hatchet blows would splinter a Hoplite shield, crush a helmet, break a sword or spear shaft. Thus the demise of such troops was by itself productive. If they scored a hit, even *more* so.

The proper instigation for Leonidas to ask for reinforcements would have been the successful implementation of the probing action of the expeditionary force: multiple contingents from different states, proven to fight and co-operate most effectively and holding the Imperials in an advantageous position, in combination with the success of the naval strategy of denial off Artemisium. Any attrition of his force might have made his request a tad more urgent, but it was definitely *after* the successful test of arms – an event counted upon by the Allied high command – that the request must have been made. A need to initially stiffen and subsequently replace the units most savagely tried against the Imperial waves (**Map 3.4**) is the first and most obvious reason for asking the expedient dispatch of reinforcements.

Another, even more plausible, reason is that such reinforcements could be used to secure the Anopaia path, which was not known to the Allied headquarters and decision-makers until the task force of Leonidas was on the spot. Just a fraction of the expected troops would be more than enough to turn the higher ground defence into a rock-solid one, with many troops to spare for other, more direct needs and assignments.

And the third reason might have been that there was a window of opportunity for the Allies to deliver a crippling blow to the Imperials. Once Leonidas saw them coming in masses to a thoroughly ravaged area and possibly knowing of the tempests to the east, he saw an opportunity for the main force to arrive from Doris to the Asopus valley and conceivably deliver a blow from the rear to the pinned, thirsty and hungry men of Xerxes, low on morale, calories and stamina, before any intervention by their navy in terms of supplies (Matthew 2013b).

One may doubt the optimism in the Greek camp, or the ability of Leonidas' force after the first two bloody days to still hold the Imperials at bay. But that their stellar tactical performance would have been the only trigger for a more substantial force to risk north of the ready-to-medize Boeotia and without any possibility of evacuation by the sea, cannot be doubted.

The latter has not been fully developed by modern scholars as a dimension of the Thermopylae campaign. The southern expeditionary force was 3–4,000 Hoplites (Her VII.202) with as many auxiliaries at the very least. These 8,000 men did move to Thermopylae on foot, to collect Boeotian contributions (Her VII.202 &205), but could have been evacuated by sea as already mentioned. The 270-ship Allied fleet originally dispatched (Her VIII.2,1) should thus embark only 30 men apiece to make an evacuation. In this case, they would be loading the triremes with just over 40 men, the number used by the Chians 14 years earlier for the sea-fight at Lade (Hcr VI.15,1). Numbers become even more sustainable if the full fleet strength of 320 triremes is taken into account, as previously done, and the pentekonters which were vessels for long hauls. A massive army, on the other hand, would not be transportable by sea if things were going sour.

The Climax

Still, at dusk Leonidas had one solid reason to worry. He had done his duty, he bled the Imperial army and could hope to stop the Imperials then and there, as he was unimpressed by the enemy and had taken all due precautions. He suffered casualties, that is a fact, at least 2,000 men if one takes into consideration the final body count and the proceedings of the last day. The human waves and, more to the point, the vassal units carefully selected (equipment, valour) and competently handled (enforcement, motivation) thrown at his army during the long and bloody second day were taking their toll and in retrospect this was important: more than a quarter of his army in two days were killed in action, which could upset the timetable of the Allied campaign.

On the other hand, the Imperials were pinned and making no progress. This would invite the spectre of hunger and, to a lesser degree, thirst, but also bad temper, low morale and poor hygiene; and the campaign might be aborted then and there (Shimpson 1972). The Phocians were holding a most advantageous position squarely on the Anopaia Pass and there was no reason to doubt their ability to hold it. If an Imperial force was to appear there, it would most probably be assault troops, sparabari, and not lighter kinds as some scholars tend to presume (Shimpson 1972). The beauty of the Sparabara was that it was line infantry, but just as good due to nimbleness and weaponry in broken, hilly, urban or mountainous ground (Diod XI.6,3). Modern scholars (Green 1970; Burn 1962), suggesting that Spartan officers or counsellors should have been dispatched to enforce discipline and proper guard and picket function, fail to appreciate all aspects of the concept of delegating, especially in truly allied or confederate, not vassal/subject, armies, and the concept of attrition. Leonidas could spare no troops for a plausible threat, while the multitudes in his front were factual, actual and lethal.

But Leonidas had every reason to doubt the ability of the fleet to keep the Persians off (Holland 2005). Up to that point, he would have a crude estimation on casualties due to the gale and the limited engagements, and also of the abortive mission around Euboea, which at the time had been neutralized. But the fleet had not taken on the still sizeable Imperial navy head-on, and thus he had every reason to doubt Athenian boasts and feel that his success might be nullified by a naval reverse.

In the light of this, within the glory of victory but seeing the seeds of failure, Leonidas would have jumped at the opportunity to end the war that very night by assassinating Xerxes (Diod XI.10,3), a notion perhaps suggested by the net result of the semi-successful operation of Brygi tribesmen against Mardonius (Her VI.45). Herodotus is not very clear on the circumstances of Mardonius' injury back in 492 BC; surprised in his tent or while trying to rally his troops to counter-attack? Although the raid ultimately failed in its immediate objective, as Mardonius and his army, despite the casualties, both survived and continued to operate briefly, the result was the abortion of the campaign; a huge strategic success. That was what Leonidas wanted and Hellas needed. But on the other side, the Imperials might have incorporated some lessons learnt in their standard operating procedures (SOPs) and doctrine due to this incident.

It is not that the Persians were particularly susceptible to chaos and utter defeat when losing their *Karana,* the head of armed forces. All armies using non-equalitarian principles (which means almost every single army in history, with few exceptions) are vulnerable to decapitation strikes and the Greeks of the classical age were by no means an exception (Montagu J.D. 2006). Even the versatile Spartan armies were feeling uncomfortable whenever decapitated, as recorded by Xenophon (Hell I.1 and VI.4). Equalitarian Athenian forces were supposedly more resilient and it is not a coincidence that an Athenian, Xenophon, reset the mercenary army of the 10,000 after the treasonous apprehension and execution of their generals (Xen Anab III.1). At Marathon, the death of the Head of the Army, (Her VI.114) had little effect on the already gained victory and the handling of the troops to secure, conclude it and return to Athens to avert a landing. The factual high command, the panel of ten generals commanding the tribal divisions suffered only one killed in action. These facts notwithstanding, it was a safe bet that slaying the divine monarch would cause insurmountable chaos, especially if some of his staff, preferably all of them, were gone with him. Thus, both antagonists had good reason to try unconventional methods to break the deadlock: Xerxes because it was threatening and Leonidas because it might prove unsustainable. He doubted he could keep it up for any meaningful amount of time and definitely not until reinforcements started pouring in.

Xerxes was able to detect the path to the rear of Leonidas, thanks to the spontaneous offer of a native of Trachis, Ephialtes, who obviously eyed a lavish reward (Diod XI.8,4; Her VII.213,1). This of course brought a price on his head later (Her VII.213,2) but there are some issues of great importance and rather obscure details in this. First, Herodotus mentions other possible perpetrators (Her VII.214,1) and given that such an infamous act after the defeat of the invader would not secure fame or wealth, one should contemplate the motivation of wildly different storylines. Clearly, either Ephialtes or the group of the other two traitors mentioned by Herodotus presented the solution and guided the Persian troops, but not both. As Green (1970) correctly observes, there are a number of possible names that might have informed the Persians on the track, but only Ephialtes seems to have been able, or willing, to act as a guide and thus provide both a sense of security and immediate and direct guidance, advice and troubleshooting, should the need be.

On the issue of informing the Persians, it is a miracle that so *few* people tipped them off and that only *one* had been willing to guide them. What about the willing Medizers, the Thessalians, who had used this same path beforehand to conquer the stout Phocians (Her VII.215) who were defending Thermopylae with staggering success, in a context parallel to the current? Yes, it was in generation(s) past, but not one of them had kept the event in memory, nor actual relevant details? Herodotus is unfriendly to them throughout his work, he could hardly have been expected to exonerate them.

The inability of the Persians to find the track for a week or so shows that they may have come from a mountainous country but were not mountaineers, at least not in any tactical context. Throughout the campaign, mountains were on the Greek side, from the refuge and guerilla warfare of the Phocians on Parnassus (Her VIII.32,1 and IX.31,5 respectively) to the campaign of Plataea (Her IX.19,3).

Still, the contact with Ephialtes might have been the work of the other two. One was a native of the area just subjugated by Xerxes (Antikyra, opposite to the northern shore of Euboea) and the other a national of Carystus, a state subjugated by Datis ten years previously (Her VI.99,2). Both were lacking local knowledge *sensu stricto* but might possibly have been effective agents of the King's benevolence and his current wishes and needs to the local populace, in the hope of some intimate knowledge of the terrain.

The other issue is the selected unit. Diodorus (XI.8,4) mentions 20,000 troops but both himself and Herodotus (VII.215) name Hydarnes as the commander, and the latter explicitly states that he led his own unit, which is none other than the Corps of Immortals (Her VII.83). However, the Corps was only 10,000-strong even if its paper strength is assumed; it should have been reinstated to nominal strength after the bruising of the previous day almost overnight. Badly mauled, disheartened and rushed after that brief respite into a special mission without any time to re-acquire cohesion as a unit, its men were once more the obvious choice due to a simmering longing for revenge, their assured reliability, efficiency and discipline. The fact of reverting to this battered unit, after it suffered such an ordeal and with little respite, points to a more or less shaken morale, if not also discipline, among the Imperial host and the need to cover this very Corps with the glory and credit of the final victory, so as to restore its shaken image (Bradford 1980). The military police heavily armed with whips were called upon to enforce the suicidal attack orders of the next day (Her VII. 223,3). This implies exactly such issues, which would adequately explain high-profile moves later on, after the battle, to assert the invincibility of the King of Kings and hammer discipline anew, such as the sponsored battlefield tourism (Her VIII.24).

Herodotus is very clear that the whole unit had been dispatched and Green (1970) sees no reason to disbelieve that it was indeed committed *in toto*. Actually, if one takes into consideration that the Greek army was in total some 15,000 men, with an advantage of position, anything *less* would risk being outnumbered in a very precarious location. There is no reason whatsoever to think of *fewer* troops being dispatched, but to entertain the ages-long sport of 'trimming the Persian numbers' for no good reason. The opposite, to accept Diodorus' figure of 20,000, with a second, probably Persian, baivarabam is not bereft of merit and reason, according to the above; but it is unsubstantiated and unwarranted.

The raid

Leonidas at that point would have collected accurate intelligence on the mountain treks and on the disposition of the Persian royal camp, with the palace-HQ-tent of Xerxes occupying a huge area, being highly visible, prominent and guarded by at least one guard unit (Hazarabam) of Arstibara (Holland 2005). The son of a despot who gained the throne by murdering in a coup his predecessor should have been extra cautious, especially in hostile territory and have taken all possible measures to guard against enemy assassination attempts. The mere size and complexity of the interior of the command tent, along with the numerous Arstibara guards, equaling a small army, made any small-unit operation impossible.

The Spartans had thus deliberated upon a decapitation effort, as a matter of tactics or as a desperate solution, as recounted by some ancient sources (Diod XI.9,4; Plut De Her Mal 32) and accepted by very few modern scholars (Green 1970; Bradford 1980). If indeed so, the task would have required a trained unit of top physique and cohesion, to negotiate difficult terrain stealthily and quickly, infiltrate or invade the tent and kill everybody in it to effectively decapitate the Persian army, if not the whole state. The murder of the *Karana* might not be enough, as happened in the battle of Kosovo in 1389 AD where the Sultan Murad I was assassinated but his staff kept it secret and the army won against the Serbs. Thus, the killing of 'almost everybody' found in the royal tent headquarters (Diod XI.10,3) was not impromptu; it must have served the double purpose of making sure Xerxes would not escape disguised as someone else and of killing as many members of the

Persian chain of command and administration, to break down the functioning of the administration machine, collapse the command and control of the army and instil terror into the troopers.

Either bad luck or some precautions taken by the Royal Security Detail, possibly advised on the practices of *Krypteia*, the Spartan equivalent of Intelligence Service (Plut Vit Lyc 28,1–3) by Demaratus, the exiled Spartan king, resulted in the total failure of the attempt. The King was not in his tent (Plut De Her Mal 32), perhaps by luck but possibly as a standard precaution (especially when in enemy territory) and the executioners must have fallen on the Arstibara. The element of surprise being with them, they must have killed quite a number plus any number of officials found in the tent. Maybe some of them were impersonating Xerxes for such an eventuality; this practice may have been familiar if not usual in some eventualities concerning the Royal Person (Her VII.15,3), despite issues of decorum (Her VII.16). The commotion must have been considerable and the chaos within the Persian camp hazardous in its own right. To exterminate or eject the intruders, the Persians had to wait for first light so as to detect them amongst the shadows and the chaos (Diod XI.10,4), encircle and shoot them down.

Such events may explain why the final wave of attacks, against the defenders of the pass, took place at noon (Her VII.223,1) and the same happened with the attack of the Persian fleet against the Greek anchorage in Artemisium (Her VIII.15–6). The order must have been issued simultaneously after mopping up.

Chapter 6

The Final Day

The Persian climb started after dark (Her VII.215), to keep hidden from prying eyes and the task force must have left the camp from near the King's emplacement, which was upstream and practically sealed off from the rank and file of the vassals. When at the plateau, by daybreak, they must indeed have surprised the Phocians and suffered so themselves (Her VII.218,2). But the Imperials found their footing promptly, seized the initiative and reacted faster (ibid) as they were elite troops and on alert. Ephialtes knew who the Phocians were and soothed Hydarnes (Her VII 218,2) by revealing their identity. He may have spotted them during their movement into position, had Leonidas approached the theatre from the Trachis-Doris-Phocis route, through the gorge of Asopus; in such a case the Phocians, to get into position from Trachis, followed the very route Hydarnes was following. Alternatively, Ephialtes may have surveyed the area himself before going to the Persians. In any case, he had neglected to mention to the Imperial staff that some troops were stationed there (Bradford 1980). Understandably so, to avoid causing any alarm and reluctance to engage in such a risky endeavour, as would be natural due to the enemy being positioned favourably. Such reluctance was a luxury Xerxes did not have at the moment, but Ephialtes did not know it and had no intention of risking the rejection of his offer and the loss of the expected lush dividends for his assistance.

A limited barrage of arrows, maybe one or two per archer from the leading hazaraba was enough to displace the Phocians to a position where they would pose no threat to the Imperials (Her VII.218,3) given the disparity of numbers. It was a storm of some 4,000 missiles, but the Immortals did save most of their arrows – almost all of them – for the struggle ahead. Still, the rather anxious question of Hydarnes upon sight, whether the emerging opponents were Lacedaimonians (Her VII.218,2), shows vividly the awe already stricken into the hearts and minds of this unit after the initial exchange of pleasantries two days earlier.

At about that time, deserter(s) from the camp of Xerxes brought word to Leonidas (Her VII.219,1). As the vassal Greeks of Xerxes were manning fleets, how these compelled patriot(s) were following Xerxes and the army is a mystery, since they were coming from Cumae in Western Asia Minor (Diod XI.8,5) which furnished a naval contingent (Her VII.95,1& 194,1; Diod XI.3,8). There were vassals and advisors, like the Peisistratids and Demaratus, but the obviously lowly deserter(s) are a mystery. The Persian secret service might well have kept a stock of 'deserters' to plant impressions and false information (Holland 2005) to manipulate the enemy.

Later, Allied outposts came down the mountain and brought the same news (Her VII.219,1). Had they been from among the Phocians, Herodotus would have mentioned it to exonerate the latter as much as possible for their dishonourable behaviour. So, where and why had they been posted? In this combined campaign the Greeks are establishing an elaborate system of surveillance/early warning, logistics and communications showing a deep understanding and a scientific and professional, not amateurish, conduct of war. But Leonidas had shut the backdoor (at least he thought so) and was facing the Persians head-on. Was this piquet force dispatched to observe the Persian camp and report the possible success of the assassination squad? Or to inform should the Imperials opt for an assault to Trachis?

In any case, Leonidas was informed of the Persian manoeuvre and, as described elsewhere, decided to order the majority of his army to retreat, knowing that half of them would probably take up arms with the invader in the very next days (Locrians, Malians and Phocians). But he preferred to have them doing so half-heartedly and with a feeling of shame instead of providing motivation to their relatives to seek vengeance by forcing them to stay and perish. As the Imperials were on the Anopaia path, they would descend to Alpenoi, following the last part of the Phocis-Alpenoi itinerary and thus denying it to the retreating Greeks. The latter had to move for some distance on the level and very suitable for cavalry pursuit coastal road east of Alpenoi into Locris, until the ascending path near Boagrios river, the road to Elateia, up Mount Thronion, where they would be relatively safe from cavalry pursuit (Grundy 1901).

Leonidas himself, along with his bodyguard would hold the position to the death, investing in the shame of the survivors to trigger a more determined response at a more opportune time and place. The Thespians volunteered for a share in immortality in a Pan-Hellenic scale, as only the heroes of Homer had ever done up to that point. The Thebans most probably did too, as keeping a force amounting to 40 per cent of his loyal troops in a hostage capacity would have been a very unwise policy for Leonidas; a fact not lost on Plutarch (Plut De Her Mal 31). And this is particularly so if one considers that Leonidas did not even keep anyone unenthusiastic about the prospect of a glorious death (Her VII.220,2). In this light, any suspected treasonous snakes would have been expelled from the Phalanx of Glory and sent, under guard, to Isthmus (Plut De Her Mal 31).

Additionally, these Thebans were an embarrassment for their medizing city (Diod XI.4,7). Unwanted back as survivors (Burn 1962), they were possibly selected amongst the patriots of the city to man the elite unit of Thebes in an impromptu fashion as happened with Leonidas, in order to appease the Allies. This would furnish the added advantage of having such reactionaries conveniently out of the way should the Imperials win (Green 1970). So, these Hoplites were fighting without a tomorrow. They were probably volunteers, set to spare their city from the stain of Medizm it was going to acquire. After the Persian victory, the medizing governing faction of Thebes would really love to have them disappear, to be spared the uncomfortable dilemma over an infamous deed of surrendering them for punishment to the Asian ally and master or an in-house liquidation of any such men, so as to leave no loose ends (Lazenby 1993). And among all such considerations, Leonidas dispatches couriers to Sparta. What was he communicating to the government of Sparta and/or to the Greek Council at Isthmus? Could it be to stop the relief army cold at Isthmus and NOT advance further northwards?

The late time of the assault of Xerxes at the pass (Her VII.223) on the third day implies either that he intended to allow his enemies a last-minute change of heart leading to headlong flight, so as to launch against them a murderous cavalry pursuit with no danger for his troops; or that the camp was in an uproar which delayed the usual early dawn onset of hostilities by the Persians. Otherwise, he would have attacked as early as possible to pin the Greeks, make any kind of expedited retreat impossible and grind them down while also taking their attention away from the flanking force, which was elite and had to be both protected from further casualties and be the harbinger of victory which the lesser, vassal troops could not achieve. Alternatively, to spare some of his troops, Xerxes could have waited for a commotion among the Allies, or for a prearranged signal, so as to move concurrently with Hydarnes' arrival.

But this is an embellished theory. The Imperials were definitely prepared for a gruesome attrition fight, as military police units were whipping, if not executing, beaten troops to keep them attacking (Her VII.223,3). This practice is not reported by Herodotus for the first two days when the attacks were expected to result in a decision, even by attrition. Diodorus, on the other hand, reports such measures on day two. (Diod XI.8,3). The motive for this costly frontal attack was obviously to tire, exhaust, weaken in stamina and numbers while practically disarming the Hoplites with waves of expendable and ill-disciplined vassal units so as to spare the encirclement troops who were Persian elites. But it also herded unstable and demoralized Imperial subjects (Diod XI.8,4) to their duty, to erase any doubt or treasonous thoughts, while keeping the defenders pinned so as not to run or concentrate on the flanking force.

The sortie to immortality

Leonidas seized the initiative, whatever the reason the Imperials had forfeited it. His advance in the open (Her VII.223) might be explained as an effort to give a final blow to the Persians, taking them by surprise while they were still in turmoil. A small push off the cliff, in case the King had been incapacitated; the triggering of a massive response that would expose the beheading of the command structure. Once that prospect had failed, he – or his surviving troops – fell back within the straits and took a position to be evacuated by the fleet.

But this is hardly believable: in such a case Leonidas would have covered his rear with the rest of the army, posted to guarding the narrowest part, the Eastern Gate (or the wall at the Middle one), in an inversed disposition, to ward off the Persian flanking force, and he would have thrust with his meagre force in deep and compact formation to pierce as deeply as possible into the Persian camp and lines. More to the point, he would have done it at daybreak at the latest, to combine with the nocturnal terror caused by the raiders and to cover his approach for as long as possible. It was not the case; Herodotus explicitly states that he had his line extended (Her VII.223), that he moved in response to the Imperial approach and had sent the rest of the army away (Her VII.222).

This might smell desertion (Her VII.219,2), according to some scholars, at least to a degree, where the apparent lack of morale and enthusiasm and the mutinous spirit obliged Leonidas to grant or even order a retreat (Her VII.220,2), which he volunteered to cover so as to ensure the survival of some thousands of probably elite, battle-hardened Hoplites, invaluably experienced against the Imperial troops, from Persian cavalry pursuit (Holland 2005). The latter is a tricky concept: whether the ground had been suitable for cavalry and for how far such ground was extending to the south is one issue. The descent of the Persians from the mountains eliminated a possible mountain escape route, safe from cavalry interference. Xerxes (Diod XI.6,1) seems poised to such a conclusion perhaps as a focal strategy. This may explain the specifics of his descent to eastern rather than to western Thessaly (which was closer) as an effort to outmanoeuvre and encircle (any) Greek expeditionary force at Tempe. Holland (2005) goes far enough to suggest that the deserter(s) who brought word to Leonidas (Her VII.219,1) were planted and their arrival timed so as to deny any active countermeasures by Leonidas, but to allow expedited retreat. This concept, of course, would have required the Persian cavalry probing the Greek positions first thing in the morning, not after the early noon coffee break.

There is one key factor, though, that weighs against plain desertion (Grundy 1901): failed two-front defence (Bury 1900; Grundy 1901; Pritchett 1958) which may have been inapplicable due to the terrain at the egress of the path near Alpenoi

(Burn 1962) – or even rearguard action (Ray 2009; Fields 2007; Holland 2005; Lazenby 1985; Shimpson 1972; Green 1970; Burn 1962). The same factor supports a decision to cause maximum casualties, carnage and awe (Hignett 1963) while providing a gallant gesture (Green 1970; Hammond 1996). It is the offensive deployment to an extended line (Her VII.223,2). This serves one purpose only, to expose as many troops to enemy contact so as to maximize enemy engagement and casualties in shock combat. It might be pressed somewhat, to intend to blunt the enemy attack by high attrition, or to overthrow the enemy (Roisman 2017) and even reach the position of the King, posted with his guard at the rear (Ray 2009) in an attempt to decapitate the invaders.

But the latter presupposes the King being in the field, a notion ill-substantiated for the case of Xerxes by any source, and especially by the narrative of Herodotus (VII.223,2). The former is less absurd, once someone accepts the extremely low figures of Xerxes' host proposed by modern scholars (Ray 2009; Hignett 1963 *i.a.*). Any understanding of a reasonably sizable Imperial host, engaging at leisure, should find the notion of an extended front of less than 1,500 Hoplites charging so as to penetrate or overthrow and wheel an enemy without the advantage of a deep and compact formation a tactical impossibility and a blunder clearly unworthy of Leonidas' generalship and Spartan prudence. Still, this headlong assault might have given Diodorus' source the mistaken idea that THIS was the attempt against the King. In such a case the figure of 500 (Diod XI.9,2) is credible if it refers to the Spartan Hippeis and the Thespians, minus the previous days' casualties and without the Thebans.

The offensive intentions of Leonidas, to gain time or drain blood or both (Delbruck 1920) were hampered by his ridiculously low numbers. The result was that he could not attack openly, fully seizing the initiative, which would be beneficial for the pursuit of his plan. He had to wait for the Imperial attack, after the morning libations and prayers (Her VII.223,1), possibly before the Imperial troopers had been in assault position, as they were doing the previous days, so as to surprise them but definitely after they had started moving, something reminiscent of Marathon. He advanced to meet the enemy with as wide a front as possible so as to stun them, to dislodge and surprise them out of battle formation and cause maximum casualties *before* the arrival of the flanking force. The depth and width of his battle formation are impossible to estimate, since the casualties of his three divisions are unknown and – despite Ray's (2009) best but unsubstantiated efforts – impossible to determine, as is the width of the field where he engaged. Still, truly the deployed phalanx must have been articulated in three major divisions, Theban, Thespian and Spartan. The idea that the Thebans were on the left and thus were cut off from the other two divisions when Hydarnes' troops intervened

(Ray 2009) is valid and perhaps ingenious. On the other hand, there is no reason to assign the right flank to the Spartans. It was the position of honour (Rey 2011) and the usual one for the commander (Hanson 1991), but Leonidas at the time must have been beyond such niceties, and by posting his Spartans at the centre he had every reason to believe he could better control the engagement and maximize the damage. As shown clearly by Agis in Mantinea, in 418 BC, the Spartans could well post other Allies at the right and be themselves and their King, where they thought it advantageous (Thuc V.67,1 & 72,4). Xerxes, contrary to the view of Ray (2009) would have never exposed the Persian troops to any additional dose of Spartan terror; losing them was both losing kin and losing control over the vassals.

The finale

The Imperial officers – even if their timing for the arrival of Hydarnes had been a bit off – took every contingency into consideration. They were prepared for another bloodbath, by encouraging most persuasively their vassals to the attack without thought of retreat. And this well-oiled coercion machinery implies they were actually anticipating a new carnage *and* that they had the time and luxury to apply such measures. Flogging might have been the least of the disciplinary actions but the most spectacular, as stabbing a 'yellow friendly' fleeing in terror from a fight is trivial within hundreds of stampeding, terrorized troopers in full flight.

It is obvious that the Persians could keep the fight on for days and that a vassal dying by a Greek spear was not a casualty but rather one step towards blunting or, preferably, breaking a spear (Holland 2005). A vassal drowned in the marsh – the seaside of the strait was probably marshy and not a cliff, as shown by recent research (Rupp 2013) and already mentioned – was a lost opportunity for some damage to Greek weaponry; and a vassal eviscerated while hacking without result on an Argive shield was a positive factor weakening the said shield, one step towards smashing it. The remark that in the end, most Greek Hoplites had only swords and some not even these (Her VII.225,3) shows clearly the success of such a well-thought, albeit machiavellian, practice.

Leonidas fell and his body was recovered during this, the most gruesome, phase of the fight. Once the troops of Hydarnes approached, the Greeks were tipped off and retreated under pressure. Herodotus is a bit unclear; they retreated, for whatever reason, behind the rebuilt Phocian wall (Her VII.225) but it is not clear whether they did so by entering through the gate behind the wall or retired east, behind the axis defined by the wall as to the pass. Obviously, the first possibility, implying a *Diateichismos*, a vertical wall sealing the pass, is easier to accept than the latter, which presupposes a wall controlling, not fencing off the pass; but in that case, they should have manned the wall and shut the gate. No matter how few, without manning the wall and shutting the gate there was no logic in taking refuge behind it. And Herodotus is clear: they did nothing of the kind.

When the flanking troops arrived, the surviving Greeks just retired to a hillock (Her VII.225,2), without any real prospect. These survivors were, at least some of them, crack Spartan Peers, trained to keep their head through waves of adrenaline, and the rest of them were Thespians. Their retreat (Her VII.225) makes no sense. It might have been a sign of despair, as it was the wrong thing to do. Presenting an almost disarmed and static target, the last survivors were executed by massive archery (Her VII.225,3) by Hydarnes' troops, who had encircled them and fired swarms of arrows over, between and around their few, smashed shields; shields too heavy to hold for hands fighting berserker-like for some time. It is questionable whether any Imperial troops, seeking revenge, tried to exact it up close and personal and thus got engaged in close quarters with whatever means the Greeks found handy.

The only possible explanation would be a retrospective projection of the fight against the Celts in 279 bc, when the Athenian navy beached and evacuated the once more encircled defenders of the straits (Paus X.22,12). Such an arrangement might have been attempted in co-ordination with the fleet back in 480 bc. There was no reason to think that the Persians, after two consecutive fighting reverses and two massive storm hits in just a week (Her VII.191 & VIII.9–14) would offer naval battle. Thus, a massive disengagement might have been attempted after having delivered a slap at the Persian land army early in the day and should the night raid have failed. The Theban troops might have been included in the evacuees, for the reasons mentioned before. If this was Leonidas' intention, it failed as well.

The whole tale of the last stand, to its gruesome details (Her VII.25), would pass to eternity, but most of all, to the faltering Allies, through the eyes of Abronichus the Athenian and his crew of the liaison vessel, who informed the Allied naval camp of the disaster that had befallen the land force (Her VIII.21). The Greeks who sided with Xerxes, such as the Peisistratids and Demaratus, are the most probable witnesses and ultimate conveyors of the events of the last day (Macan 1908) *and after it*. But the sanctioned liaison officer Abronichus is the best bet for quelling the unwarranted doubts of modern scholars (i.e. Flower 1998) over the reporting of details of the last moments of the defenders to the rest of Greece and Herodotus.

The surviving Thebans, seeing no ships, broke and surrendered upon encirclement, having faithfully fought up to that point and exonerating themselves from any suspicion of treason. They were captured, but only after some of them had been murdered unarmed and yielding by hot-blooded Imperials (Her VII.233,2). They had fought to the last minute and were talking eyewitnesses of the events. Asking for mercy by citing their city's Medizm and stating that they fought against their will (Her VII.233,1) was the most logical thing to do (Ray 2009) and possibly the *only* thing to do. They persuaded nobody, least of all Xerxes. But since he had to encourage surrender for the next stages of the campaign in order to spare his troops any further bloodbaths, he pardoned them indeed; after branding them as slaves (Her VII.233,2) so as to help them keep their allegiances steady and refrain from boasting of their feats of arms against the King's men. Still, these branded survivors supposedly bore their scars with pride after the war, as a proof of their mettle and their sacrifice for the Freedom of Hellas (Plut De Her Mal 33).

Chapter 7

Analysis of the Components of the Battle

Tactics – I: Relief by exchanging and rotating units

The main effort of the Allied commander-in-chief, that is Leonidas, was to block the way through the straits by Hoplite phalanx detachments and keep it so. The detachment that drew the first blood remains unidentified. What is of special interest, though, is that individual detachments, or task groups, were up to the task and found adequate means to plug the passage and produce an effective barrier to the enemy assault waves. Leonidas is explicitly mentioned as using and rotating homogenous detachments (Her VII.212,2) as task groups; consequently, they must have been formed by dividing the contributions of some city-states, had they been large, or by grouping other such, when too small.

The smallest were the 80 Mycenaeans, too low to be considered as a task group. The 300 Spartans were definitely able to fight by themselves and this is a comfortable minimum for a 10 to 20m-wide Middle Gate as estimated recently (Rupp 2013); 250 would also have been possible: two shields per metre of front produces a rank of 20 to 40. Thus, 250 men are enough to array at a depth of 12 to 6. Leonidas, though, would have considered psychology and prestige and would not have used detachments smaller than his own elite on their own. Consequently 300–500 shields are the detachment strengths that allow effective defence while keeping maximum homogeneity. The two 500-strong sovereign Arcadian contingents from Mantinea and Tegea would have been the strongest task groups, possibly matched by the Locrian detachment divided into two task groups and the pooled Arcadian contingent of 1,000 men divided to two 500-strong task groups as well.

A better economy could have resulted in 8 or even 10 still reliable task groups of 300-odd shields each from these 3,000 troopers, instead of only 6 groups of 500 shields each. But fighting in complete uniformity and possibly in whole units /subunits of their respective home armies must have made these men much more confident (Rey 2011; Ray 2009); it is important to remember that in phalanx warfare familiarity among closely-packed Hoplites had been a crucial factor (Xen Lac Pol 11,7).

The Thespians and the non-Spartan Lacedaimonians would have formed two 350-strong task groups each, while the Corinthians and the Thebans one task group of 400 shields each. Last, but not least, the Orchomenians, Phliasians and Mycenaeans would have been pooled together to one task group of 400 shields. Thus, if homogeneity and not numerical uniformity had governed Leonidas' disposition of troops, 14 task groups would have been formed: one mixed, three Lacedaimonian, three Boeotian, two Locrian, four Arcadian, one Corinthian), which were to rotate. The Hoplite phalanx supposedly fought effectively for a short time only, perhaps an hour or so (Hanson 1991, Sekunda 2000 & 2002). This is not attested in any source; numerous events narrated by Herodotus clearly describe prolonged and bitter fighting between Hoplites and non-Hoplite troops (Her V.119,1 & VI.29,1), while the Athenian feat to fight and win Marathon, fast-walk the Marathon race – more or less – and be able to fight again, demonstrates the excellent stamina and endurance of Hoplite militias. Still, modern scholarship considers rotating and relieving a physical necessity (Adcock 1957; Sage 1996; Hanson 1999; Holland 2005) and had it been so, Leonidas' men could carry out a 14-hour late-summer day by engaging just once each. If 1,000-odd units were used, each task group would have engaged twice, as the 7,000 Hoplites would suffice for 6 task groups of increased homogeneity: two Arcadian, one Boeotian, one Lacedaimonian, one Locrian and one mixed (Corinthian – Phliasean – Orchomenian – Mycenaean).

The rotation of these phalanx task groups had been quintessential. Leonidas knew perfectly well that once his small army pushed back a number of assaults and nullified the Persian effort of overthrowing the defenders, the Persians would automatically revert to an exhaustion and attrition approach (Her VII.212,1), which would be amplified by their lighter battle kit under the summer sun. Thus, to avoid attrition of any kind, he had to rotate his men frequently and fast (Her VII.212,2). Rotation of units plugged tightly into straits needs space and time. So, after a respite of their enemies' charge, which would have been achievable if an efficient killing rate could be sustained, the relaxing of the tight, close order of the frontline unit to a more open setup would allow pouring in a fresh task group through lanes between neighbouring files while retiring the spent one (**Figure 7.1**).

The Greek tactics mentioned by Herodotus imply a universal drill in Hoplite armies of passing units through each other's lines in order to rotate them in combat. This is easily done in exercise and is the logical solution for such problems since the invention of trained and drilled infantry. But it establishes that the Hoplite infantry of many Greek states, not only Sparta, had the ability to manoeuvre under pressure. Not only they were able to execute drill under pressure, but did it paired to other similar troops, with whom they had never trained before.

Given that the Hoplites would have formed in maximum density with shields interlocked (*synaspismos*) to withstand the shock of the attack, to shove back and to defend against archery volleys, the compact files had to gain some depth to relax

Figure 7.1

Unit relief through files

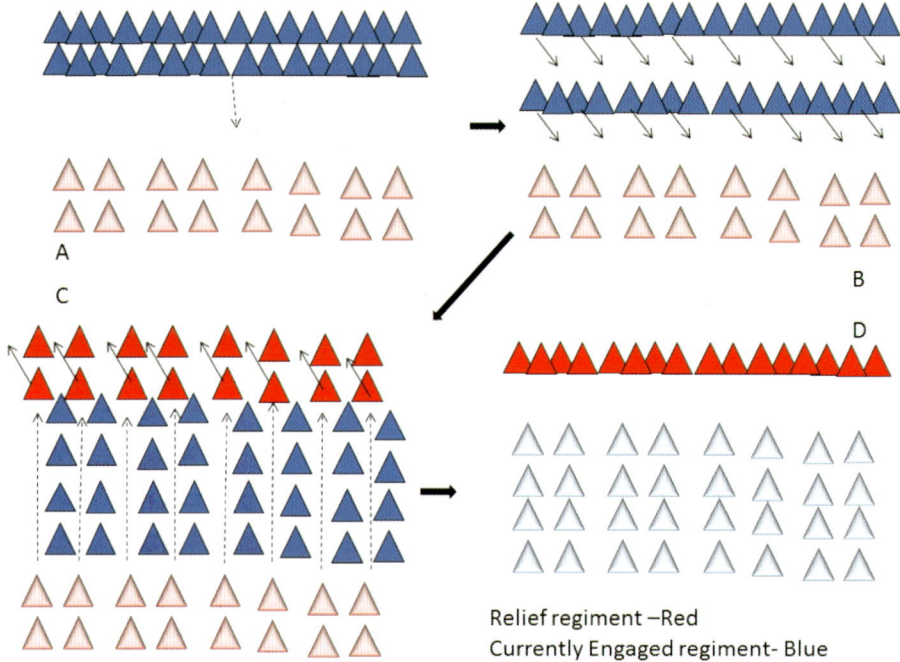

A

C

B

D

Relief regiment – Red
Currently Engaged regiment – Blue

the succession of lines (**Figure 7.1**) and then each second file would have been inserted, man by man, in its left or right-hand neighbouring one, creating one-man lanes while doubling the depth. Thus the files of the relief unit would slide in between by the lanes at the double, while the front line unit moved backwards. Once the positions had been swapped, each even number of a file of the relief unit would step left (or right) and front, to close the formation before the rear rankers advanced to lock the new formation solid. This is easier said than done, but a number of the units present were elite standing units and the four days or so, while Xerxes was waiting idle, plus the days the Greek army occupied the position before his arrival (Her VII.208) would have been put to good use to make so simple a drill common practice.

Tactics – II: Feigned flight and Ekdromi

More impressive is the 'feigned flight' of the Spartans (Her VII. 211). Contrary to the account of Herodotus (**Figure 7.2**), it should have been similar to the *Ekdromi* attested much later by Xenophon (Hell IV.5,14), although executed in inversed spatial terms. The engaged line cannot retreat in the face of the enemy – especially of a more numerous and lightly clad enemy – *en bloc* without suffering casualties.

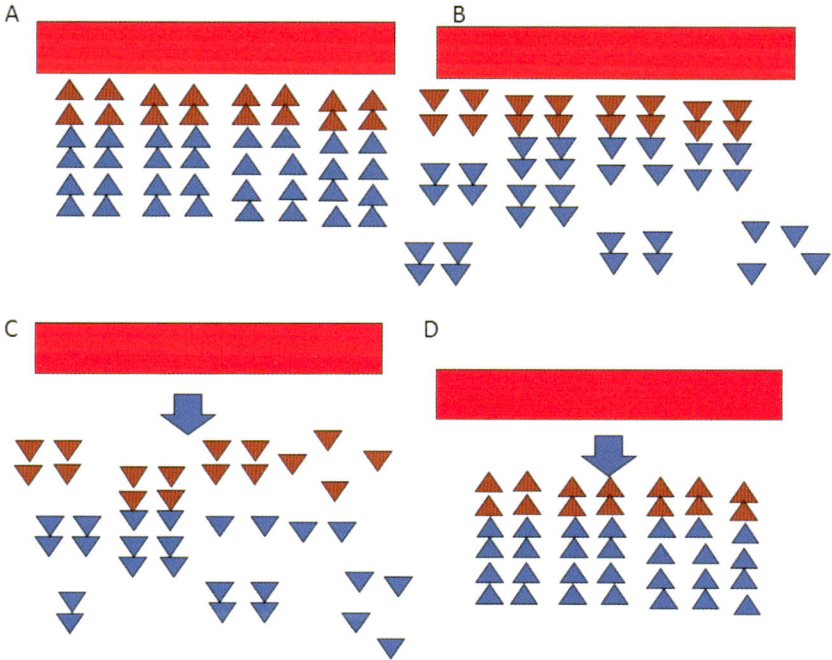

Figure 7.2

FEIGNED FLIGHT

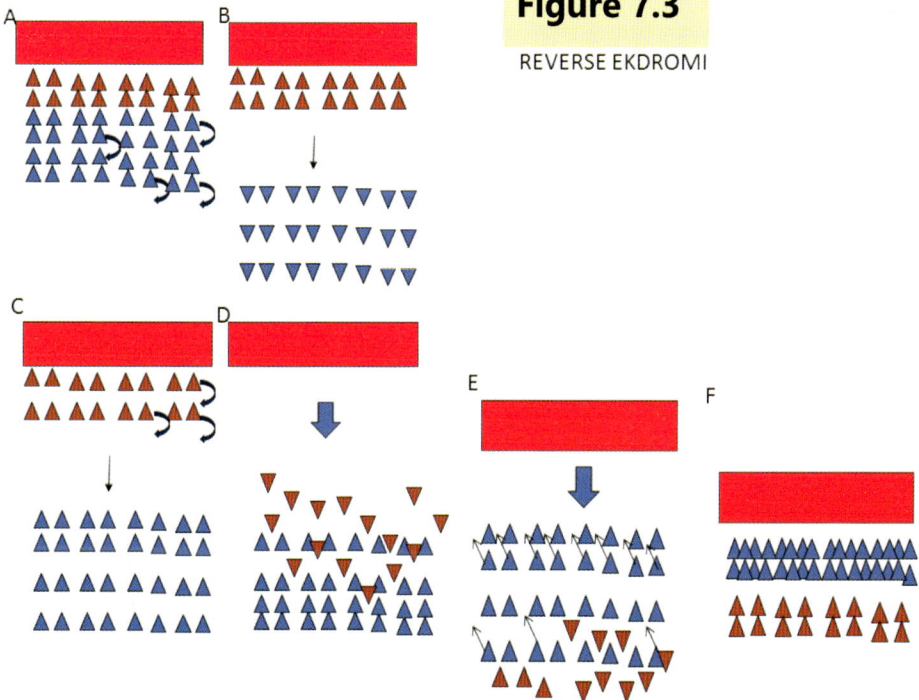

Figure 7.3

REVERSE EKDROMI

Thus the less fleet portion, the veterans posted in the rear ranks, retreat first at the double, unnoticed by the enemy, to reform promptly at a distance. In such cases, the original battle order cannot be recreated and one should fight next to any random comrade, something that 'only troops drilled under Lycurgus' laws can do' (Xen Lac Pol 9,7).

Subsequently, the fleetest troops, who have remained engaged with the enemy, must break at once and gain some strides – four to six – while their opponents are startled. After that, since they were not facing missile troops but shock infantry, they must keep and even open the distance and cover their backs with the shield for fear of the occasional javelin or stone. Having the enemy hot on their heels, they cannot instantly regroup and turn, even if perfectly trained. It is much more likely that they would retire through the files of a line formed by the ones who had retired first (veterans) and are unnoticed by the pursuers. After they pass through the spaces between files, the line will be sealed in less than three seconds, the running troops regroup and catch a breath behind the last rank of the new line and then join the files to reinforce it in shoving (**Figure 7.3**).

Tactics – III: Special Operations/ Decapitation strikes

Herodotus has no idea of Special Operations and cannot even imagine them. He is narrow-minded in military matters. Speaking of the diver Skyllias, he disapproves of the lore of him swimming a great distance without coming to the surface, considering it impossible (Her VIII.8). He never wonders if a very human device, like a combination of straw (as snorkel) and stones (as weights) might make him stay undersea without being seen, which was the factual meaning of the lore. He was simply under the surface: nobody counted his breaths. In such a mindset, the notion of Skyllias cutting the anchor ropes of the Persian fleet and thus maximizing the disastrous effect of the storm off Pelion (Paus X.19,2), is unthinkable for Herodotus and for many a modern scholar (i.e. Lazenby 1993).

It is no great wonder then that he says nothing on the assassination attempt mentioned by other historians (Diod XI.10; Plut De Her Mal 32). Many modern scholars, from Macan (1908), Burn (1962), Hignett (1963) to Hammond (1996) and Lazenby (1993) disbelieve it, while Green (1970/1996), Ray (2009) do not. It was very Spartan (Paus IV.4,3), and very logical to try an attempt; it was also Spartan not to talk about it (Thuc V.68,2), especially at a time when previous friends had become mortal enemies and any detailed account of past battles might be used to deduce their current operating procedures and *modus operandi*. Assassinations and Special Operations were an integral part of ancient Greek politics. Trained professionals were available, although not in abundance. The Spartans had a name for such attempts and skills due to Krypteia (Plut Vit Lyc 28,1), their very own Secret Service with missions centred on gathering intelligence, state security and assassinations, in some cases even involving the Kings themselves as operators (Paus IV.4,3). Flower (1998) noticed the Krypteia connection but failed to mention that the 300 Knights in this campaign are older, more experienced than the usual draft and perhaps selected with this chapter of their CV in mind, as well.

But the story of Diodorus (XI.10), recounting the event, is not satisfactory. The tent of the king would have been as far as possible from the enemy's line of access. The two armies were distant enough for the sentries to detect a massive approach, even performed as clandestinely as possible (Diod XI.10,1). The version of the crack unit sent, not led, by Leonidas, is a much better bet – and here Diodorus (XI.9,2) might have had it right, concerning the number of raiders involved: 500. The lore[*] wants them to have swum from the Greek position to their objective: enter from somewhere with a smooth shoreline so as to plunge silently, but with the necessary gear, walk-swim the distance to the river, then upriver to the tent of the King. Still, although clandestine enough, the distance and time start to become an uneasy factor, and the task force has to move upriver skirting the length of the entire Imperial encampment, as the King's tent was always upriver, to draw from clear and pure water (**Figure 7.4**).

As it is a clandestine operation and the instigators perished, we may never learn the exact facts, but it is very conceivable that the story is somewhat distorted. A just as clandestine and faster approach, straight to the tent of the King, would have been by marching the opposite way than that of the flanking force of the Persians (Her VII.215–21). In the dead of night, the two groups might have lost each other easily – or rather the Persians may have lost the sneaky Greeks. This would have been especially so if the latter were acknowledged 'Special Operators', as Skiritai might have already been (Xen Lac Pol 12,3 & 13,6; Thuc V.67,1) and members of Krypteia surely were (Plut Vit Lyc 28,1). This version, suggested by Pressfield (1998) in the best-seller 'Gates of Fire', explains very well why Leonidas did not try to intercept the flanking force, although he was informed early enough (Her VII.219). There was not enough time to reinforce the Phocians (Holland 2005), but he could try to intercept Hydarnes somewhere along the descent path or to shut the Eastern Gate off with some units (Montagu 2000). It is true, in any case, that the terrain might have not been steep enough and advantageous at the Eastern Gate. Given that the Persian force was numerically strong and their descent offered their archery considerable advantage (Ray 2009), a double interception might have been ill-advised.

---

[*] The movie 'The 300 Spartans' of 1962 shows a seaborne night raid.

Figure 7.4

THE NIGHT RAID TO PERSIAN CAMP : SEABORNE AND MOUNTAIN APPROACHES

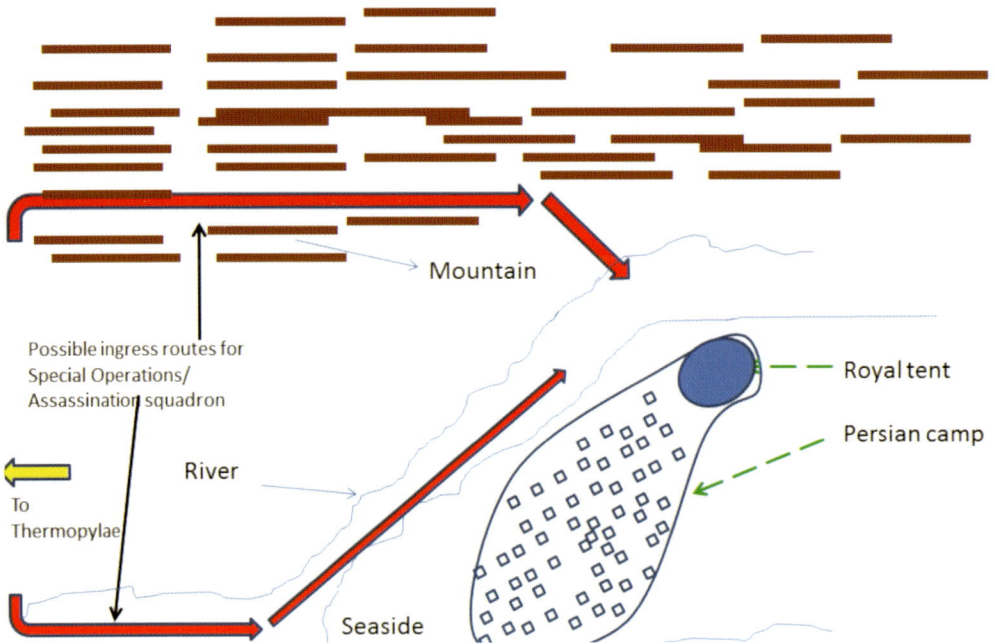

Leonidas did not want to have any noise or commotion in that area, so as to keep the guard of the Persian camp down. The attempt was made and had some Persian officials killed, such as the two brothers of Xerxes (Her VII.224), who cannot be explained as casualties in any other way. Neither the attrition approach nor the assault attempts of the Imperial army included risking higher officials, much less princes.

This assassination attempt, along with the carnage and consternation of the two previous days, the loss of his relatives and the old case of the murder of the Persian embassy (Her VII.133) allowed, or imposed on Xerxes the ill-treatment of the corps of Leonidas (Her VII.238), considered at the same time sacrilegious, criminal and blasphemous to Gods and humans. Not that other propaganda dimensions are to be dismissed: from the intimidation of other prospective blasphemers considering resistance against the divine order of Ahura Mazda, His truth and His acolytes, as prescribed in the Behistun inscription for insurgents (DB 32 & 33 & 43 & 50), to the mundane factuality that the head proved to everyone the demise of a Spartan King (Bradford 1980). Such proofs of barbarity were very effective in disciplining the oriental host and the Greeks did reciprocate with the crucifixion of Artayctes, the Persian governor of Sestos (Her IX.120,4). But the outrage caused among his Greek followers, supporters and would-be subjects could be placated best by claiming vengeance for another outrage, as happened with the torching and wholescale slaughter in Acropolis, some days later.

Command structure and formats

There is also another issue, little-noticed but of paramount importance: the method of command. It is often discussed but rarely, if ever, well understood in technicality and detail; nor is it compared to later and modern practices. The Greek way was to lead and the commander, once the battle-order was set and the missions or objectives delegated (if any), was taking his position in the line to fight. In some cases, as in Marathon and Plataea, a degree of overview and control was secured by the commander-in-chief, in order to intervene and orchestrate more elaborate actions, and in Thermopylae, the exchange of detachments (Her VII.212) shows such a command and control function properly exercised by Leonidas; but possibly it was set in motion so as to function by default should he be unavailable.

But what about the Persians? They are often ridiculed for erecting, manning and operating a lavish observation platform, at a proper, commanding feature of the landscape, for Xerxes (the Commander-in-Chief/*Karana*), with every possible comfort and luxury as mentioned for both Thermopylae and Salamis (Her VII.212 and VIII.90 respectively). There were royal scribes, taking notes (Her VIII.90). Really, one can wonder what difference there is between Xerxes' establishment and nineteen-century or even twentieth-century observation posts for commanders and staff. Is there a conceptual difference between the Persian establishment and the well-provided, guarded, conditioned and even cozy American headquarters, especially general headquarters, like that of Eisenhower's in Second World War Europe?

Moreover, no such establishments are mentioned for any subordinate commanders, who also partake in the battle, at least when things go sour or become critical; Mardonius was killed-in-action in Plataea (Her IX.64) as were other Persian commanders in Mycale (Her IX.102) and one admiral in Salamis (Her VIII.89). Thus, there simply was one more level of command in the Persian structure, reserved for the King-of-Kings or any other *Karana* assigned by his favour. This might be the true meaning of Xerxes thinking that his troops in Artemisium fared ill due to the lack of his presence (Her VIII.69). It may have been not just the watchful eye of the King, set to administer rewards and punishments (Diod XI.8,1), but also that of the Supreme Commander, properly supported, to direct the battle against a sneaky enemy, take the right decisions and delegate tasks. This of course meant that the Greeks did not need to fool the Persians; it was enough to fool Xerxes, as supposedly happened in Salamis (Her VIII.75).

In Thermopylae, this leadership concept is obvious and proven true: the Persian High Command, despite the dismal battlefield performance, never lost control of their troops and the battle. Always at the ready; reserves lined up and sent as required (Diod XI.7,2), retreat allowed (Diod XI.7,4) or denied (Diod XI.8,3), panic waves contained (Her VII.212). But, most of all, providing adaptability: from the decision to attack with the elite troops on the first day (Her VII.211), so as to take defenders unawares, to the change of method on the second. The storm tactics of the first day (more than one – Her VII.211) changed to the attrition attempt of the second day (Her VII.212) and to the pinning and flanking of the third (Her VII.213&223).

Xerxes' throne and observation post at Thermopylae should have combined the view of the prospective battlefield with security and safety. One could thus deduce that it should have been posted over the First Gate, high up for a better view but not on the main ridge; should the main ridge be attainable by that position, his troops would have flanked the position of the Greeks. This projection suits well with the throne platform mentioned in Salamis (Her VIII.90,4; Plut Vit Them 13,1) and stands against the notion of an Emperor-General ranking among his troops as proposed by Ray (2009) in a debatable interpretation of Her VII.223,2. The argument that Persian Emperors were actually taking the field is based on the examples of Artaxerxes II and Darius III who are of a later date though. Neither Xerxes in any operation after being named heir, nor his father Darius I are known to have posted their royal persons among their vassals in the line of danger – not necessarily the first line.

Additionally, and contrary to some modern criticism (Fields 2007), the Greek organization was tactically much more elaborate and useful than the Persian one. The Greeks used a binary model, and the Spartans extended it to the lowest levels, which was the critical difference; it made them an army of officers (Thuc V.66,4). The binary structure revealed by Xenophon (Lac Pol 11) or even a quaternary structure, implied by Thucydides (V.68,3) for the Spartans, requires the commanding officer to oversee two or four subordinate units, a task perfectly doable if not easy, as demonstrated by the contemporary insistence on such command systems. The very straightforward and managerially more effective Persian model, by contrast, which is celebrated by modern scholarship, (Fields 2007) requires any commanding officer to oversee ten subordinates – a task achievable only if a commander is to assign and supervise the most basic functions. Obviously, the subordinates being grouped by five within the same echelon partly addressed this issue and provided a structured binary leadership adequately flexible in both tactical and support considerations.

Operations

The clash in Thermopylae was the first land battle for the host of Xerxes. It emerged victorious, but the lessons learnt were coming at a hefty price. The exchange ratio as detailed by Herodotus was nothing impressive, a mere 5 to 1; 20,000 Imperials for 4,000 Allies, in whom helots and other attendants were included (Her VIII.25,1–2). The carnage within the confines of the battlefield was disheartening, nonetheless, and Xerxes understood well the power of impression. As his fleet made contact, at last, unloading some supplies (many more were lost to the gale off Sepias), the army was licking its wounds and most of those Killed in Action were buried clandestinely so as to create a positive exchange ratio (Her VIII.24–25). The crews of an underperforming fleet, responsible for the fuss in the first place (had it made the timetables, the Allied defence would have been turned), were invited to dispel any rumours about the land army meeting with any kind of reverse (Her VIII.24).

It is striking that the Imperial army, although victorious in a decisive and clear-cut manner having nothing to do with the events at Artemisium, and having obliterated their enemy, gave no chase nonetheless. Xerxes had with him a comfortable force of cavalry, as he engaged them in racing games in Thessaly (Her VII.196). This cavalry force was not engaged during the battle and thus had suffered no bruising; still, he did not launch them to pursuit against the retreating Greeks who may have had a 10-hour head start, which is 40 km at the very best. It may have been that dusk and possible ambuscading disheartened the Persian staff after the bitter experience of Spartan fake retreats; or that the fugitives would have reached mountainous routes (i.e. the road of Elateia) that would not be negotiable by cavalry. Whatever the case, Xerxes opted for consolidation and securing the battlefield, while engaging in shaping the surroundings for his fleet to watch and admire, as their morale was even less victor-grade than that of the land army. Possibly he proceeded also to unlock the access through the ravines under Trachis, where the Malians would have surrendered immediately once the position of Thermopylae was breached. But that was all.

As the fleet and the army were reunited, for the first time after encountering resistance, the respective staffs met as well to exchange views. The main issue here was that the evidence implied a most nefarious prospect. The army had no answer for the Greek tactics of Hoplite warfare if these were adapted to broken ground and straits, something unexpected. Each defensive zone had quite a number of them allowing the invader a number of options in operational manoeuvring. Though, if a large Greek army took the field, to guard all the passes of a line, the Persian army could do little to force them and the fleet might not be the answer. The decimated merchant fleet could deliver less and was too terrified to over-perform, which was the only way to make good the numerical deficit. With time becoming still more of essence, amendments were in order.

Xerxes was a very intelligent and meticulous man. He noticed that things went just as Demaratus had predicted (Her VII.102) and that meant excellent knowledge, power of deduction and relevance despite his years in exile. He asked, as a consequence, his opinion for the next phase of the campaign. The ex-Spartan King eloquently obliged; usually when judging his suggestions one tends to forget the precise timing and the origin of his deductive ability. Knowing the Persian preponderance for flanking, especially for deep turning moves at the rear of the enemy with independent task forces, he suggests a deep naval campaign to establish a naval base just off Sparta at Cythera (Her VII.235). The 300 vessels, one Naval District Command, he proposes (Her VII.235,1) are 12,000 boarders' worth, 50 per cent more troops than the Spartan peers (Her VII.234,2); 60,000 total troops and mariners, more than the entire force Sparta sent to Plataea. The vessels were a quarter of the original navy (Her VII.89,1), as Demaratus ignores the magnitude of the losses due to storms and battles. At the time, with the Imperial Standard being in Malis, his priority is to sap any prospect of the Greeks manning another line of defence, so as to open the road to Attica and to the first objective of the campaign, Athens. With a threat at their backyard, the Spartans would not campaign north of the Isthmus; without the Spartans, neither any other Peloponnesian nor the western Greeks were likely to do so, accounting in total to 50–60 per cent of the projected enemy field strength. Athens was assuredly doomed.

Demaratus' old friends and comrades in Sparta were of the same opinion and refused to be drawn north of Isthmus. There was no need for the campaign at Cythera, the Spartans would spontaneously revert to a policy safeguarding the(ir) rear. Even south of Isthmus was considered far too north. Dismantling the Greek Alliance and opening the gate of the peninsula was NOT the issue in Demaratus' advice; it would be the issue of Artemisia's advice, just before the battle of Salamis (Her VIII.68), with Attica already occupied, burnt, and purged. But Salamis was not in sight at the time and Demaratus considered the Greek fleet destined for Isthmus, as it was indeed. His advice was meant to bring the Imperial standards to Megarid, at the doorstep of Peloponnese, while taking out Athens, Aegina, Megara, with as little fuss and casualties as possible. That meant preferably without battle and definitely without the Lacedaimonians in any such battle.

Demaratus had no information about the even more sorry state of the Imperial fleet compared to the Army. Eventually, the army conquered; the navy had not. It was the land victory that unlocked the stalemate and high admiral Achaemenes was furious, possibly after having heard a good deal of swearing by his pious but demanding kingly brother. Thus, when he heard of another plan for dividing his fleet he threw a tantrum (Her VII.236). Rightly so; had he not succumbed to the temptation to try to encircle the Greek fleet, he might have won from day one, as he would have been spared 200 vessels, most seaworthy after the initial gale. It cannot be said whether the fatal flanking attempt was his own idea and now regretted it or somebody else's which he condoned; still, the other brother, Ariabignes, a brave and

A flair of tactics

Whether Leonidas fielded against the Immortals the whole contingent of the Lacedaimonians or some part of it remains controversial; the rotation implemented by the Greek Army deployed just a portion of the available Lacedaimonians at a time. Sound deployment practices point to whole units/subunits being used to maximize cohesion and use the standard command structure and chain. Still, the Lacedaimonians were trained to fight next to any other Lacedaimonian (Xen Lac Pol 9,7), not needing the personal bond necessary for typical Hoplites so as to project solidarity and cohesion. Additionally, the Lacedaimonian military structure was very detailed and explicit, going down to subunits of perhaps 15 men with proper commanding officers. It allowed, as a result, considerable flexibility in adding troops to adapt the width and depth of a phalanx to the field and ground.

On the other hand, it is safe to suppose that Leonidas probably refrained from applying against the Immortals the same plugging model used previously with devastating defencive efficiency. In that case, small task groups filled a narrow space with both flanks anchored on natural obstacles and remained nailed in there in compact formations, rock-solid against waves of attackers. A more offensive approach must have been selected against the Immortals, which would present a tactical surprise and, at the same time, offer the prospect of a more substantial victory against the hardest nucleus of the enemy army. The main body of the Herodotean narrative (VII.211) is the proficiency of the Lacedaimonian Hoplites in feigned retreat and timely counter-attack in perfect co-ordination, which is discussed separately.

Hence, an advanced position between the Western and the Middle Gate would have been selected, in order to extend the front of the phalanx, so as to increase the killing rate by engaging at once more men and, most importantly, invite more enemies into a wider killing ground, which would work as a trap once they were put to flight by feigned retreat and counter-attack. For a feigned retreat, Leonidas needed space behind his formation; to lure enemies, he needed space in front of it; thus he must have deployed his phalanx at the widest spot between the aforementioned gates.

It is important to remember that the Lacedaimonians had to be really fleet of foot to be able to perform mobility tricks to the lightly burdened Asiatics, although some of the latter might have been endowed with iron-scaled armour (Her VII.61). This is far from certain; the cuirassiers, spoken of as a unit (Her VIII.113) and probably identified with the troops endowed with the scaled armour, may have been cavalry rather than infantry. The latter possibility fits well with the scaled cuirass of Masistius, the cavalry commander under Mardonius in Plataea (Her IX.22), and with the existence of bizarre metal helmets in some but not all Persian cavalry (Her VII.84), a piece of armour rarely identified with Persians in Greek art and literature. It is much more believable that a unit with helmets, in an army which issues them sparingly by tradition (Xen Anab I.8,6), should have also been issued with the just as sparingly used metal body armour.

just man (Plut Vit Them 14,3), fought memorably, but rather recklessly in Salamis (Her VIII.89,1; Diod XI.18,5). It might have been his inclination, but also it might be an indication of remorse or shame and an effort to atone by personal bravery for disastrous errors of judgement. Sending away what amounted to one District Naval Command to one of the three most capricious promontories of Greece, Cape Maleus, responsible for the wanderings of Odysseus, was a bit too much. In any case, the Imperial admiralty was set to no more division of fleet assets; in Salamis, it will happen again by the personal deliberation of Xerxes (Aesch Persai 364–71).

The expeditionary Standard Operating Procedure was for the fleet to subdue the coastal areas by landing infantry and cavalry parties (Her VIII.23) and for the army to strike inland. The latter very probably enjoyed fleet transportation for replenishing its provisions. The coastal areas, including Euboea and the eastern and southern coastlines of Attica, were delegated to the fleet, which carried a landing force of more than 45,000 first-line troops, 40 marines per ship times 1,200 capital vessels (Her VII.184). This is a conservative estimate, as the native boarding parties were at least ten-men strong since the lowest unit of the Achaemenid army was the dathabam (Her VII.81) but were not necessarily restricted to this strength. Higher deck strengths were not impossible.

Chapter 8

Invading the South

After Thermopylae, the Persian army was really vast for the mission at hand. It was a waste of resources and bad practice, logistics-wise, not to put this numerical superiority and the high morale after the victory to good effect so as to expand the direct invasion footprint. Western Greece, west of Pindus, was not included in the operational plans of the Persians, although it became an important front during the Peloponnesian War (Thuc III.94–5). It is plausible that operations in that area were meant to develop after the subjugation of Peloponnese, with the fleet moving northwards into the Ionian Sea to proceed to the invasion of Italy.

The Persian High Command knew the geography of Greece due to the expatriates; thanks to the mission of Democides; due to the numerous emissaries sent to demand Earth and Water and, most of all, due to Demaratus of Sparta (Her VII.209). He must have informed Xerxes that his own ancestors, the Dorians, failed to invade Peloponnese through the heavily fortified Isthmus (Her IX.26), but succeeded by emerging at the north of the Gulf of Patras and crossing at Rion, by ships built in nearby Naupactus (Paus X.48,10). Given that NW Peloponnese (Achaea) was medizing heavily (Paus VII.6,3), it was natural to attempt a crossing there, especially after the carnage at Thermopylae, which could get worse at Isthmus. Demaratus directly suggested so (Her VII.235,4), to both spare his past and future subjects and to increase his own and their future usefulness as instruments of the Great King, under the auspices of whom he was to be restored to his throne (Radford 1980). Thus, the Persian army, once in Boeotia, should have sent a division of some strength SW to subjugate western Phocis and Aetolia and cross into Peloponnese by ship to friendly territory in Achaea, thus flanking the defences at Isthmus and dividing the defending army. The rest of the army could advance to Athens to deliver punishment.

Although we do not fully appreciate it, this is exactly what happened! This course of action may have been decided after Thermopylae, at the staff meeting (Her VII.234–235) where Demaratus proposed an amphibious landing at Cythera. His proposal was rejected, but another might have been processed, presented and perhaps sanctioned. So, a change of plans is possible after Thermopylae: The Persian army did not cross through Thermopylae, along the coastal road, possibly

Green lines: Imperial moves to Thebes and Delphi.
Red lines: prospective, supposed and suggested imperial moves after Thermopylae.

Map 8.1

because the marshland at the seaward side made it impractical, at least for the laden wagons and the pack animal trains (Rupp 2013). It poured south through the gorge of Asopus and the straits of Trachis (**Map 8.1**), which were unlocked automatically once Thermopylae had been breached. First in their path as they emerged through the Bralos pass was the region of Doris, which remained unscathed as it had medized (Her VIII.31; Diod XI.14,2) but possibly because of its insignificance, poverty (Grundy 1901) and, once it had never raised a weapon against the Persians, to not infuriate past and future Dorian slaves of the Great King who allegedly originated from there.

Then the invasion force reached Phocis following the flow of the river Kephissus and entered Boeotia from the west. Phocis was devastated ferociously and completely due to its stance before and during the battle of Thermopylae and to the enmity of the Thessalians who were important to the Persian cause (Her VIII.32–3; Diod XI.14,1). But the trek through Phocis to Boeotia does not agree with the map of destruction of Phocian cities and sanctuaries looted and razed, as recounted by Herodotus. Some of the latter were not along the axis of advance, like Hyampolis and Abae (Her VIII.33). Naturally, raiding forces were detached from the main body of the army to fan out to pillage, ravage, forage and devastate; this is perfectly in line with the report that the Thessalians were guiding the Persians so as to leave nothing unscathed in Phocis (Her VIII.32,2). Such a raiding detachment proceeded to loot the Oracle at Delphi (Grundy 1901).

An alternative view, which is not exclusive to the above, sees the destruction of the whereabouts of Hyampolis and Abae as proof that after Thermopylae a separate detachment might have eventually followed the coastal road past Thermopylae into Locris, brought it into submission and then turned inland, to Elateia. From there it entered into Boeotia from the north, to meet the main army coming from the west, after incinerating Phocis. Under this light, one may understand an omission of Diodorus who clearly says that after Artemisium the Imperial fleet raided Histiaia in northern Euboea and then the coast of Euboea and Attica as it progressed south (Diod XI.14,5), but does not mention the coast of Locris. Either Locris remained unscathed, or it was assigned to the land army, but not to the one headed by Xerxes as this was moving through Doris and Phocis (Her VII.31–5; Diod XI.14,1–2). The first option is not plausible. Locris had medized and then experienced a change of heart and followed Leonidas, delivering the strategic position of Thermopylae to him instead of safeguarding it for Xerxes as instructed. This was a very bad precedent for the Imperial dignity and foreign policy. Thus invasion, devastation and punishment were imperative and an army detachment invading through Thermopylae might have taken over, leaving to the fleet the other shore of the straits.

After thoroughly reducing Phocis, the main Imperial body under Xerxes continued SE to enter Boeotia in the area of Orchomenus, accepting the surrender of all Boeotia west and south of Lake Copais (Her VIII.34; Diod XI.14,2) while levelling Thespiae (Diod XI.14,5) due to their commitment to the cause of the Greek Freedom and their participation at Thermopylae to the bitter end. It subsequently reached Thebes. The city was sitting on a rather strategic position (Grundy 1901), near the end of the main N-S road from Larissa and Lamia to Athens, while plugging the main passage of Boeotia towards the south: the flimsy strip of land between Helicon range to the SW and the marshes of Lake Copais to the NE. Another road, from Chalcis in Euboea to Kreusis in the Corinthian Gulf (west of the Isthmus of Corinth) was passing through Thebes (Grundy 1901), a very dangerous option as, if followed, it would bring the Imperials just opposite of the Peloponnesian shore, without the obstacle of the Greek fleet, which was deployed east of Isthmus.

In this context, one may see, for the first time after Acanthus, three Persian groups operating separately: One – hypothetical – past Thermopylae to Locris and then turning to the south by Elateia to meet at Parapotami with the second, led by Xerxes through the heart of central Greece, while a third group moved from Parapotami via Panopeus and Daulis to Delphi for either a limited looting operation against the Sanctuary (Diod XI.14,2; Her VIII.35) or for expanding the ravaging operation to a mission of conquest, by bringing the W-SW part of Locris and Phocis to heel while opening the back door of Peloponnese in the triangle Naupactus – Rio – Calydon.

According to Plutarch, Thebes medized at that precise point and the city was introduced to the King's benevolence due to Demaratus, understandably enjoying high favour at the time, who was guest-friend to Attaginus, a leading Theban medizer (Plut De Her Mal 31). Obviously, there was some fuss due to the Theban implication at Thermopylae, an unfortunate event where their official state participation was undeniable due to the surrender of the survivors under the evocation of their mother city.

Contacts and a degree of understanding must have been reached previously; otherwise, there would have been no Earth and Water from Boeotia when Xerxes was at Therma. But *before* that, the position of the city was ambivalent, as it sent a token force at Tempe with the abortive expedition (Plut De Her Mal 31). *After* the ceremonial offer of Earth and Water, a Theban expeditionary force fought at Thermopylae. This is directly attributable to Leonidas; Herodotus implies a somewhat heavy-handed policy on his behalf, while Plutarch, striving to exonerate the spontaneous medizm of the city by discrediting Herodotus, provides some details: Leonidas, *en route* to Thermopylae, went through Thebes, no matter which approach he finally took to the straits (**Map 3.4**) and requested the high privilege to sleep in the sanctuary of Hercules, the local demi-god. This was granted to him as a unique exception (Plut De Her Mal 31) even though the Kings of Sparta were accepted throughout the ancient Greek world as blood descendants of Hercules (Her VII.204) and were thus entitled to it by default. This request and its satisfaction create some interesting questions but did produce a spirit, however (dis)honest, of goodwill and the Thebans sent at Thermopylae as many troops as he had requested (Plut De Her Mal 31).

The last allegation is inaccurate. Leonidas requested that they partake, as do all the like-minded Greeks and the Thebans, ingeniously, did so by sending a special unit, practically their standing army to represent them (as did Sparta and all the Peloponnesian cities and the Phocians as well). NOT their full host as would have been the case had they been truly allied-minded, as were – and had done – the Thespians (Her VII.202) or the Locrians (Her VII.203), who had initially submitted to the Empire but were turned by Leonidas (Diod XI.4,6). Thus, Herodotus' affirmation that they sent troops with little zeal because their allegiance was with the Imperials, must be quite correct. They had declared for the Empire, especially after the abortive Tempe campaign, and were not ready to about-face as fully as the Locrians did. So, the unit they dispatched must have been made up entirely of volunteers, who would be blamed individually for their conduct should Xerxes reach their walls. At the same time they were shirking devastation by the small army of Leonidas which was there and ready and by their neighbours, both within and beyond the Boeotian borders. The volunteers, of course, were the patriotic element of the city (Diod XI.4,7) and their number might be due *not* to the dispatch of an elite unit, but to the inability to find enough patriots to muster a 500-man unit as the one sent to Tempe (*before* Thebes had declared its submission) and equal to the commitment of Tegea and Mantinea.

Had it been so, some reports of Herodotus may be seen under a different light. At the final phase of the battle of Thermopylae, the Thessalians informed the Imperials that the surrendering men who claimed Theban origin, so as to be spared, were indeed Thebans and their city had already capitulated (Her VII.233). Plutarch argues that as they were enemies because the Thebans had broken the Thessalian hold on Boeotia (De Her Mal 33) this was not possible; but it *may* have been, if the Thessalians did so to instigate the Persians *against* the Thebans, implying directly that these opponents had capitulated before and they were renegades, not legitimate enemies. Thus, the good services of Demaratus had to be purchased to placate the King (Plut De Her Mal 33). Furthermore, as the Imperial juggernaut advanced southwards, there were Macedonians sent by King Alexander, an enemy of the Thessalians (Plut De Her Mal 35) but a very reliable ally of the Empire and linked to it by matrimony. These Macedonians were tasked with identifying the Boeotian cities and territory (Her VIII.34). This was vital, as there were no clear markings between Phocian and Boeotian territory for the Imperials to stop massacres and pillaging, which had been the order of the day in Phocis (Her VII.32,2; Diod XI.14,1) and the Thessalians, serving up to that point as guides promoting the devastation of Phocis (Her VIII.32,2), might have been tempted to err intentionally when in Boeotia and not inform their masters promptly…

It must have been at this point that the majority of the Thebans embraced the policy of Medizm (Her IX.87,2); Attaginus would have presented himself as the only possible intermediary to appease the King. Attaginus' very logical arguments to the King would have been that he and his friends had forestalled any *effective* Theban commitment to the Thermopylae campaign, but for a token force (comprising only self-declared reactionaries). Even this token force was only exacted when a whole confederate army appeared at their doorstep, with a very menacing resolution from the League, to take all the land from any spontaneously medizing city, split it to the member states and consecrate 10 per cent to Apollo of Delphi (Diod XI.3,3).

Even more logical sounded the explanation that had it not been for such imminent risks and dangers, the Thebans would have medized readily, out of spite for Athens and bitterness for Cleomenes (Lazenby 1993). The latter was the notorious slayer of the Imperial envoys and had machinated the joint Peloponnesian – Chalcidian – Theban campaign against Athens only to desert them to be bruised by the new, massive, Athenian Hoplite phalanx (Her V.74–7). The prospect that this treason was due to the undermining of Cleomenes by the Ephors and Demaratus and not to Cleomenes himself (Dickins 1912) would not change the Theban feelings, arguments or posture; after all Demaratus, the sworn enemy of Cleomenes was at their door and a friend of Attaginus. Consequently, it was their proximity to a very hostile Athens, to which they had suffered a recent heavy defeat, circa 507–6 BC as mentioned above, and a potentially much more hostile Sparta which, under Cleomenes, undertook an active counter-medizm series of campaigns in Greece as far as Samos (Her III.54,1) that made them keep quiet and not declare for the empire more decidedly.

Under this light, and perhaps to the great consternation of the Thessalians who had serious beef with both Phocis and Boeotia (Buck 1972), Thebes was pardoned for the unfortunate misunderstanding at Thermopylae and accepted in the Imperial world as a true and trustworthy ally along with most of Boeotia. Of course, the hardcore nationalists of Thespiae and the Atticizers of Plataea were excluded. The Thebans indeed became cordial allies to Xerxes; any obscurities due to Thermopylae were resolved and they proved their endorsement to the Persian cause time and again.

War with the God(s)

Reaching Thebes, the Imperial army was approaching menacingly Attica (Her VIII.34) as there was no actual point of interception due to the multitude of passes from Boeotia to Attica and to the proximity of the fleet, which could turn any Greek position from the sea. Before entering Attica, and possibly before even reaching Thebes, a task force, as described earlier, had been dispatched to a western campaign: The abortive Persian raid to Delphi, might have not been merely a plundering operation, as usually thought (Her VIII.35,2 & Diod XI.14,2). Plunder was within the scope, as it was performed time and again, but perhaps *not* the main objective. While ravaging Phocis, another shrine of Apollo had been plundered and torched, at Abae (Her VIII.33), instilling fear and despair to the faithful and driving home the fact that Xerxes was at war with the Greek Gods too (Green 1970). This policy of torching every temple in enemy territory was too disproportionate to the events of Sardis during the opening moves of the Ionic Revolt and was stemming from Xerxes' ardent Mazdaic Zoroastrianism (Burn 1962; Abdi 2007) as expressed in the *Daiva Inscription* (XPh 4; Klotz 2015) and despite efforts of modern scholars to exonerate him (Abdi 2007; Kuhrt 1997). The *Daiva Inscription* may well refer to Athens, which was officially an Imperial realm after its spontaneous offer of Earth and Water in 509–506 BC.

This fact of religious savageness is usually left unexplored by advocates of mythoplasy concerning the attempt against Delphi (de Souza 2003; Green 1970) who feel that Xerxes would not have provoked the feelings of his subjects, citing Datis' treatment of Delos (Her VI.97) as an example of tolerance towards major religious centres, especially if the omens and prophecies of the latter discouraged resistance against the empire. Of course, Datis was not Xerxes, Delos was not in a hostile region, and after all, Datis' practice led to the embarrassment, to say the least, of Marathon. With Xerxes, a staunch Zoroastrian, gloves were off (Burn 1962) and the Greek gods may well have accounted for some *Daiva* demons, to be purged by fire (XPh 4). A most mundane fact, obviously known to Xerces, was that the confederates had declared the God of Delphi as the patron of the resistance and swore to consecrate 10 per cent of the lands of the medizing states to the Delphic sanctuary (Diod XI.3,3). In effect, Apollo had declared against the empire and Ahura Mazda; as a consequence, he was marked as a Daiva and his sanctuaries had to be cleansed by fire and his worshipers enslaved or chastised.

Herodotus states that at Panopeus the invading army divided in two and the larger part continued into Boeotia and then Attica under Xerxes, while the other part moved towards Delphi (Her VIII.35). Diodorus' story is a bit different, having Xerxes dispatching his small expeditionary force to Delphi as soon as he had been in Doris (Diod XI.14,2) and himself spending some time in Boeotia (Diod XI.14,2), in Thebes no doubt, expecting news (and loot) from his expeditionary contingent before advancing further.

Thus the two parts of the Achaemenid army were unequal, but by how much? Perhaps not vastly, although the only source supplying a figure gives the strength of the task force at a mere 4,000 men (Justin II.12), a non-standard strength for Achaemenid armies and units and accounting to half a baivarabam – and this understrength. Still, its size is compatible with a pillaging, foraging and devastation detachment fanning out from the main path. But if Justin has it wrong, if the decimals are in this case wrong and 40,000 are to be read, it was not a group or some units dispatched, it must have been a hefty part of the army, a significant force able to conduct operations, not just a raid. This, according to previous practice means following anew two itineraries, with two separate objectives. The second force, moving westwards *through*, and not *to*, Delphi, intended to cross to Peloponnese in Achaia, thus outmanoeuvring the Greek army at Isthmus, as had happened at Tempe and eventually at Thermopylae.

Actually, one does not have to use the 'decimal theory' in any way which is after all nothing but a play with numbers, and a very arbitrary one at that. A small task force could do fine: torch the centre of the Greek religion, loot it and, during the awe and desperation, negotiate the uncomfortable passes to emerge at the north shore of the

Gulf of Corinth, leading friends to declare in Peloponnese, enemies to reconsider or to despair, while presenting Sparta with a new, NW front (nobody would know how many Persians were emerging or landing) and paralyzing all resistance, much as had happened at Tempe. This aspect would justify Xerxes standing fast and waiting for news at Thebes, as reported by Diodorus (XI.14,2). He intended to see whether the Peloponnesian army would divert NW, thus allowing him a choice between a fast advance from Thebes S-SW to the north shore of the Gulf of Corinth in Kreusis, and S-SE, directly to Megara to try to burst through Isthmus should the latter was left undefended due to the emerging threat at the west.

The miracles at Delphi (Her VIII.36–8; Diod XI.14,3–4), which, coupled to local resistance – possibly responsible for some of the said miracles (Grundy (1901) – demoralized and pushed back the raiders to the main body of the army (Her VIII.38), and did more than save the temple. They boosted the faltering Greek spirit for resistance, checked the Imperial propaganda for invincibility and a superior patron god and actually won the campaign for Greece. This contingent, had it overrun and razed Delphi, as ordered (Diod XI.14,2), would have wrecked the Greek morale to shreds, showing divine impotence against the eastern invader immediately after a major battle lost (Diod XI.16,2). Furthermore, it would have emerged to the north shore of the Gulf of Corinth, at Crissa, easily occupying the coastal towns westwards, reaching Naupactus and commandeering vessels to cross to Peloponnese at Rio, a replay of the invasion of the Dorians (Paus X.48,10), with no Greek fleet there to counter, nor any hostile coastal state in NW Peloponnese to resist a landing as had happened in Marathon. Vessels found by the Phocian and Delphian and Plataean refugees to evacuate them to Peloponnese (Her VIII.36,2; Diod XI.14,5) show that a Persian crossing of the Corinthian Gulf was achievable. This prospect coming to null, Xerxes eventually would have had to opt either for an assault at Isthmus by land, without the benefit of a fake move to disorient the confederates, or for a naval victory to be able to cross by sea to Eastern Peloponnese, where Argos, bitterly hostile to Sparta (Her VII.149), offered a ready-made, safe bridgehead (Grundy 1901).

Thermopylae and Delphi won the war for the Greeks long before rams and oars got blooded in Salamis. The terrible carnage at Thermopylae had taken a toll in Xerxes' psyche (Diod XI.11,5) and he decided not to seek land battle against massive Greek Hoplite infantry in straits, especially if augmented by defensive works. His back door operation was meant either as a viable alternative or as a feint. In the latter case, it was intended to keep/throw the Allies off balance and allow the invasion of Peloponnese before any reliable defence build-up in Isthmus or to have the defence disintegrate. This did not work.

Thus Xerxes went conventionally and consecutively in the pursuit of his targets, in a serial manner. He turned his attention to Athens, invading most probably from the main road, Thebes – Eleusis, although columns might have used some other passes over the range of Mount Cithaeron. Other choices of itineraries were possible, but the route chosen offered the best combination of security for the whole army, the least warning for the Greek high command and easy access to Attica for the main body of the army. The direct assault to Athens was meant to achieve a rather easy objective with the highest symbolic meaning and weight, an excellent propaganda strike against the enemy in the wake of the slaying of a King, and thus a good boost for the morale of his own troops. The lustre and shine of the empire were re-established, while the Greeks might be enticed out in the open to defend the city that was most prominent in the anti-Persian struggle. Or, terrorized and stunned by the burning of the city to ashes, they would be unnerved, leading the muster at Isthmus to spontaneous dissolution. That did not work, either.

Eventually, Xerxes did make a feigned land attack, although towards a well-guarded and fully defended Isthmus (Her VIII.75,1), hoping to capitalize on the blackened psyche of the Allies so as to have their navy dislodged from the straits of Salamis. This failed as well and ultimately he played the naval card at that spot (Her VIII.69,2) and at an inopportune moment. The time for naval operations in Greek waters was running out and autumn gales might at any time exact even heavier casualties from his fleet than before, off Pelion (Her. VII.190) and destroy the amphibious prospects altogether. The amphibious dimension of the invasion plan had worked perfectly well in northern Greece (Her VII.122–3) and immediately after Thermopylae. It resulted in subjugating by seaborne operations (infantry landings and cavalry encroachments) all remaining Euboea, securing the submissive Boeotian coast and the thin landmass north of Lake Copais and reducing the whole coast of Attica from Oropus, south of Euripus to Phaleron, just before entering the Salamis straits (Her VIII.66,1; Diod XI.14,5). The psychological warfare of Themistocles developed during these operations, by inscribing at watering spots all kinds of arguments inducing the Greek squadrons of the Imperial fleet to mutiny (Her VIII.22). This would have grown the natural distrust of the Phoenicians (but NOT of the Persians-Her VII.52) against such fellow vassals to absurdity, as was proven during the action in Salamis (Her VIII.90,1).

Once this amphibious card was burnt, or rather sunk, at Salamis, Xerxes never contemplated that a ground assault against Isthmus would turn the tide and retreated his royal person to Persia (Her VIII.115), to prepare for possible retaliatory invasions, or rebellions and revolts at home. He left a much decreased, but fully capable occupation army in Thessaly (Her VIII.113), way back north of Thermopylae, to re-establish the imperium to the areas he had to evacuate in anger. The invasion of Peloponnese was not forthcoming in that year, nor that of the rest of Europe. History proved him right.

Chapter 9

Facing the Tribunal of the Ages

The outcome of Thermopylae has raised heated discussions throughout the ages, regarding the voluntary sacrifice of Leonidas' task group and venturing to pinpoint the reasons and factors that led to its demise. The latter are usually identified as issues of leadership, generalship and command and control, deteriorated by factors of high strategy and facts of policy functioning far behind the lines, at the remote rear (Burn 1962).

The denial of some historians to understand the issue of sacrifice has been identified almost a century ago (Delbruck 1920) and it is a matter of mental inability to extend beyond a rationalistic but egotistic view of the duty as understood by a hired soldier. The Spartans, though, were professionals *and* a national army, fighting for honour and glory. Every bit, or more, heroic than the heroes of Homer, they advanced a culture based on the warrior ethos that found admirers and imitators. Modern historians are neither, but for centuries the most prominent military organizations had no problem whatsoever to comprehend and understand the Spartan priorities and determination; not very unlike the US stand in Los Alamos, despite the Americans being the invaders at that instance.

If the Spartan mentality is understood and accepted, one is faced with easier paths. The Spartans went to Thermopylae to conquer or die; hence the funeral rites and the selection of troops. The former might have been intended to appease the breaking of the taboo; but the latter, not being explainable under this light, establishes the intention to die there should it be deemed preferable, the decision being the prerogative of the War King. They were ready for Death, which seemed most likely, but were indeed hoping for Victory. They went there to fight to the death, intending to win but determined that should they perish, the subsequent defence might have an opportunity to derail the invasion. The *hows* have been discussed in this chapter but are also scrutinized in the next chapters.

Of course, this reading was never brought to the Allies' attention, or not at its full and logical conclusion. The drafted and mobilized confederates had no similar warrior code and were unenthusiastic at the very least. Only a campaign of pure, celebrated optimism (Her VII.203,2) would steady their hearts and minds; and Leonidas proved a master on this subject (Her VII.203,2; Diod XI.4,6; Plut De Her Mal 31). Once resistance became futile, Leonidas perfectly understood that to turn a defeat into a galvanizing sacrifice he had to produce an example and inspire, among other things, remorse and guilt to his confederate comrades who were spared and left to fight another day and would lead their native armies as revered veterans. The case of Aristodemos (Her VII.231), which is examined in detail later, shows the brutal efficiency of the recipe, although this was another, much lighter case of 'wrongfully surviving'.

Under this light, some things should be re-evaluated. Leonidas and perhaps his colleagues who commanded the elements of the expeditionary task force knew the size of the Imperial host through the report of the spies dispatched to Sardis (Her VII.146). If anything, these reports might have been exaggerated by the willful Imperial co-operation in the framework of Psychological Operations (Lazenby 1993). Thus, what he and the rest of his army observed when the Imperial host arrived, dragging as a gigantic serpent before their eyes at the north shore of the Oreos Channel, cannot have been *worse* than the estimations; it was though extremely unnerving as a sight and awe-inspiring. Knowing is one thing; seeing is another. Definitely, many of the troops and of the commanders must have been awe-stricken and panicked (Her VII.207).

Once Leonidas was able to steady them so as not to retreat or, rather, desert, he needed a better, sustainable solution to keep them there in good spirits. He did his best move; he asked for reinforcements and that must have placated their despair (Her VII.207). The thing is that he *could not* have done so. There were no grounds to ask for reinforcements at that point. He was up against exactly what he knew from the very beginning. Holding his position was not a matter of numbers. To commit reinforcements, Sparta and the League needed to know that their defensive plans, methods, tactics and techniques were working and to have the Imperials fully committed, so as to forfeit their operational mobility which allowed them to threaten the Greek forces with flanking and outmanoeuvring in general. Additionally, it was a thing of timing for reasons of logistics: if the follow-on army emerged too early, the supplies might run low – a very good reason for a minimal initial dispatch of troops (Matthew 2013b), before the successful raid to the plain of Malis solved the issue of supplies once and for all for the army of Leonidas.

Leonidas was expected to send detailed intelligence about the enemy, both qualitative and quantitative, along with his situation report: how many natives had joined the defenders, their morale, whether the circumstances were advantageous for a holding action, as these had been defined before the dispatch of his army. He also had to provide a temporal switch: if the preparations of scorched earth were implemented and the defence plan worked, he had to authorize the dispatch of the main army so that the latter would come at the right time; not too early and definitely not too late. There were quite some options for the proper use of that army: to reinforce and eventually relieve the first installment of defenders must have been the original proposition.

The sealing of Anopaia was another, most urgent one, which became evident only by the awareness obtained *in situ*. Understandably the locals who were not medizing had forgotten to mention it when the Allies were making an autopsy, before launching the campaign. With the Tempe aborted once such circumventing itineraries were discovered, reluctance to man another 'turnable' pass was expected from the southerners and thus such knowledge was withheld by the locals.

But a third option was also there: to bring the whole, or the greater proportion, of the relief army from the Doris itinerary, which meant it could position itself at the Imperial rear virtually undetected. If this surprise was timed properly with the effects of hunger, thirst and possibly disease (conditional on keeping the Imperial fleet away from the coast of Malis) the Allies might have another Marathon in a gigantic scale with a decisive battle at their moment of choice and with many advantages. After all, cavalry mounts suffer more from lack of fodder and water and turn inoperable under heat. This prospect, correctly identified by Matthews (2013b) was not the only one. Simply denying entrance into southern Greece, in a most passive manner, would eventually beat the Imperial invasion. Supplies, hygiene and morale were problems that would undermine the Imperial army if kept where it was for one or two months, for the autumn to enter fully. The fleet would have to retire and the spent occupied territories, denuded of provisions, would be on the verge of rebellion. The Greeks did not need to win. They were content not to lose, to win non-decisive, defensive battles so as to keep the Imperials out.

The above considerations are enough to nullify any argument that the fall of Thermopylae was due to the reluctance of the confederates to commit more forces (Burn 1962); the position fell due to lack of vigilance (Delbruck 1920) and, in reality, the factual reluctance to commit actually saved forces. Any reinforcements would be primarily directed to the battlefield at the Middle Gate, as the actual threat, battle-wise, would have been the attrition of the Allied forces. Leonidas' rotation was supposed to keep the Persians for some more days in terms of exhaustion. The casualty rate looked negligible but was not: in two days a minimum of 1,000 Hoplites must have been killed, allowing for 3,000 Hoplites and retainers for the last day (Her VIII.25,2); a 2,000 figure instead of 1,000 is more plausible.

Furthermore, a relief army, even if dispatched at once, upon receipt of Leonidas' request, would have been there when everything had been over; the Athenians were estimating that such an army was in Boeotia when the news of the defeat arrived (Her VIII.40,2). The timeframes are very restrictive. If Leonidas had dispatched a rider, or a runner of the quality of Phidippedes (Her VI.106) who covered the distance from Athens to Sparta in less than 48 hours back in 490 BC, his dispatch from Thermopylae to Sparta, where the Spartan army must have been assembling at the end of the feast of Karneia, would be four days at the very least, assuming a relay at Isthmus without any stalling. If everything was happening automatically, the Spartan army would take at least two days to reach Isthmus; on the third day, they had reached Athens in 490 BC (Her VI.120). The Allied contingents from Peloponnese would have assembled at Isthmus as well, as happened indeed under Cleombrotus some days after (Her VIII.71,1) and the next year under Pausanias (Her IX.15). To reach Thermopylae it was at least another two days. This sums at eight days after the dispatch. From the moment Xerxes appeared, opposite the Greek forces, till the securing of the straits for the Imperials it was a mere eight days (Her VII.210).

Leonidas, as presented by Herodotus, must have sent a dispatch on the second or the third day of the silent confrontation, when the endless snake of the Imperial host was marching the south Achaean coastal road at the north shore of the Oreos channel, just opposite Thermopylae, causing despair to some of his units and troopers. Thus, with the most permissive scenario, the relief army would have been two or three days away when Leonidas passed to Immortality, corroborating the Athenian estimates for it being in Boeotia (Her VIII.40,2). Any notion that the delay in sending an army to Leonidas resulted in his demise is unsubstantiated. Not least of all arguments, Herodotus, an Atticizer, says plainly that nobody thought so fast a defeat would ensue (Her VII.206,2). The collapse of the Greek defence had nothing to do with the availability of troops. It was the result of the Phocian inadequacy and that is all.

Could Leonidas have played this hand any better? Not really. In qualitative terms, much fuss has been made about stiffening the Phocians by tasking some Spartan councilors or officers to enforce discipline. The second was out of the question; the Phocians were confederates and the difference between confederates or allies and vassals is exactly the formers' prerogative to serve under their own leaders and chains of command. The Phocians were *not* loyal subjects of the British Crown to suffer foreign officers. Even the Imperials had some semblance of this kind of autonomy and dignity, as Herodotus mentions that their vassals and subjects had been allowed the use of their own officers in parallel with the standard Imperial organization and chain of command (Her VII.81). It was not yet the time of Gylippus for the Spartans (Thuc VI.93,2). After all, it was Leonidas who asked for the help of Phocians, not the other way round. He had to persuade the Allies and respect their sensitivities; he did so, to quite an effect, even at Thebes (Plut De Her Mal 31). When the Phocians volunteered to guard the Anopaia path, they did not file a request, leaving an option for a negative answer; practically they demanded this assignment and probably this was a condition for their participation.

Given that the other Greeks showed no real ineptitude of any kind, but for the occasional panic at the very first sight of the enemy, which was then remedied, one could not have foreseen that the Phocians would behave so miserably. Herodotus, an Atticizer, tries his best to exonerate them (Her VII.218,3) as they were at his time staunch allies of Athens; but in describing the pillaging and devastation of Phocis more extensively than that of Athens (Her VIII.32–5 vs VIII.50–54) he might, just might, be insinuating a degree of Poetic Justice, while of course underlying their sacrifices for the common cause.

In quantitative terms, the issue is even clearer. The Phocians were 1,000 shields in an army of some 7,000. Posting such a percentage away from the main defensive effort was bad tactics but a necessity, as mentioned above. It was bad tactics because the attrition, in all its forms, would have been the quintessential issue of the defensive effort should all had developed according to plan. Even if Leonidas had double or triple the number of men, he would have never spared another Hoplite up there, while at the gates storms of arrows and human waves were launched to swallow his phalanxes. Why should he send more men? The enemy had no idea about the path and there was no reason to believe that he would. Even if Xerxes was to learn, the 1,000 Hoplites at the selected position could hold a far more numerous force for quite some time and cause grave casualties. Even if the Imperials were resilient, capable and numerous enough to actually dislodge the Phocians by attrition, there would have been plenty of time to report to Leonidas once the engagement was imminent so as to send reinforcements in earnest.

Earlier it has been proposed that Leonidas had no reason to believe the Anopaia path would have been revealed to the Persians. This is partially right, as many locals would try to get rid of the oriental pestilence by facilitating its move southwards, especially after the loss of their crops by Leonidas' raid. The prospect of hefty rewards must not be underestimated too; it was the *motto* of the Persian throne (DB 63). With all his many vices, the Great King was never ungrateful.

The issue is that the Persians had to rely on local knowledge and expertise; when they became dispirited enough from the negligible results of the frontal assaults to seek advice, it might have been a tad late. One thing is certain: contrary to many modern scholarly views (Holland 2005; Bradford 1980; Burn 1962; Green 1970), the Persians, a mountainous people, were *not* experts in mountain warfare. In the heart of their own empire, they were never capable of disposing of bandit tribes, so they were paying them off with gifts for 'protection' and were drawing from their manpower for unknown missions (Kuhrt 2014). Their troops, with light kit and ranged weapons, were *not* supposed to fight on broken terrain. Their mobility, in infantry and cavalry, was better exploited on level ground, where they had two more, extremely important, advantages, which were simply lost on broken ground:

Exonerating selfishness through incompetence

Herodotus writes and presents in ominous times, when Athens and Sparta are already at loggerheads, although not yet entangled in the deadly Great Peloponnesian War. The Phocians are allies of Athens (Thuc I.107,2) and Thessalians are traitorous enemies (Thuc I.107,7). Thus, he remains very considerate towards the former. The little plateau along the Anopaia Pass entrusted to the Phocians, due to their own request – and naturally so, as they were a volunteer contingent with top morale and good knowledge of the whereabouts (Bradford 1980) – offers an inroad to Phocis, seated at the middle of the Alpenoi – Phocis road, a real junction of mountain passes (Burn 1962; Hammond 1996) as already mentioned. To these volunteers this approach to their homeland was much more important than any access to the rear of Leonidas, as it had already been used in the past by the Thessalians, their arch-enemies, to invade (Her VII.215).

By being positioned just west of this junction (Green 1970) the Phocian contingent shut the Anopaia path before the crossroads and thus protected both the rear of the defenders of Thermopylae to the north and the approach to the Phocian motherland to the south, which was explicitly the dual strategic mission of the Phocian contribution (Her VII.217,2). At the ominous moment and taken by surprise, they did not make a last stand under panic, as suggested (Green 1970; Bradford 1980) but formed their phalanx where it could interdict the invaders should they turn towards Phocis, which had been their main objective within a dual mission package. This was a perfectly legitimate and understandable fear, as the possibility that Phocis would be made an example of by an Imperial punitive raid *during* the main phase of the battle was not out of question. The Gauls proved the sagacity of such considerations some 200 years later by doing exactly that (Paus X.22,2–3).

The Phocians did not deliberate on the matter: at the moment of truth, they simply followed their instinct and training (in that order) and deployed to protect their motherland. Only under this light the absurd notion of the Persian task force not engaging them while they kept holding their ultimate position with determination against insurmountable odds (Her VII.218,3) becomes understandable. The Phocians did not compromise their primary mission, the defence of their homeland, by engaging off their previous, commanding position. The hill on which they assembled must have been selected as their last stand had they had to do so, after at least two, probably six and possibly even more days of inspecting the surroundings. And the Persians, seeing them out of position and defending another branch of the crossroads, simply bypassed them to fulfill their own primary mission as well (Her VII.218,3) as their lack of missile weapons and their meagre number made them unimpressive once out of the way.

The numerical advantage, which needs ample room to come into play, and the effect of their formation, which allows the synergy of the strengths of their kit. In formation, the arrow shower would eliminate *en masse* any enemy. On broken ground, it would revert to isolated shots, against enemies covered and possibly armoured; only the surging effect of massive fire would have been decisive, but this needed firing in formation. Thus the Persians were NOT particularly good at mountain warfare or, at least, not so much as to seek it preferentially.

One might note that the Greeks, also the spawn of a mountainous country, were not any good either. The Hoplite was purposed for level ground, where the collective protection and action multiplied the effect of the weaponry, stamina, nerve and guts to a metal juggernaut. This propensity for level ground was recognized by friends and enemies alike (Her VII.9). Still, as both opponents, and dissimilar opponents at that, preferred the same type of ground, the Greeks, after the traumatic experience of the Ionian Revolt decided that level ground was more to their enemies' advantage than to theirs. And since Marathon, they kept avoiding exposure on level ground but for the very briefest of times, to deliver a decisive charge. The campaign of Plataea is an excellent example of such concerns of the Allies and their management by manipulating space and time.

Part III

The Naval Standoff at Artemisium

Chapter 10

Intentions and Positions

As mentioned previously, it has been proposed that the main Greek defensive effort was not in Thermopylae, but in Artemisium (Delbruck 1920; Ray 2009; Shepherd 2010). The Decree of Troezen (Jameson 1960) is worded in a manner that makes it clear (Hale 2009). It is the quintessence of the naval policy of Themistocles, opposite to the Tempe expedition (Her VII.173), where, if Herodotus is taken at face value, the action would have been on dry land (Holland 2005). This proposal is contested, the position of Thermopylae was picked first and that of Cape Artemisium (Diod XI.12,4; Her VII.177), at the NE corner of the great island of Euboea, subsequently. Additionally, a Spartan King was leading the land army (Her VII.204), NOT the fleet, which was assigned to a Spartan commoner (Her VIII.42,2), a clear clue on the relative importance of the two (Lazenby 1993).

But things are a bit more complicated. Instead of comparing different army strengths, such as among Tempe, Thermopylae and Plataea, it is better to compare army and navy strengths in one campaign. The land position was selected first because there were fewer choices if it was to intercept or at least contain the invader on land while the major and decisive Allied arm, the navy, was to draw blood (Tarn 1908; Delbruck 1920).

In Thermopylae, maybe 4,000 Hoplites from the south had been deployed (Her VII.202 & Diod. XI.4,5), perhaps augmented to double that by local forces (ibid) and probably supported by an equal number of stewards (Her IX.29), a total of less than 20,000. The almost 300 triremes deployed to Artemisium (Her VIII.2) were worth more than 60,000 men, three times as many. They were to confront an enemy of four times this number (a more favourable imbalance compared to the land hosts) who were lacking cohesion and any true Persian nucleus in the basic sea-fighting component, which were the crews (Hale 2009). The Allied supreme naval commander or, rather, the Chief Admiral, was Eurybiadas, a Spartan (Her VIII.2), but, as had been the case with the *Polemarch* Euainetos at Tempe (Her VII.173), not of any royal bloodline (Her VIII.42).

Despite the meagre numbers of the Spartan fleet (Her VIII.1), a Spartan had been appointed Chief Admiral for one very simple reason: no other Greek, least of all the Dorians (Aegina, Corinth, Sicyon, Megara) who supplied most of the

Table 10.1. The fleet of the Allies at the first battle of Artemisium.

STATES	Triremes	Pentekonters
Athens	127	
Corinth	40	
Megara	20	
Chalkis	20	
Aegina	18	
Sicyon	12	
Sparta	10	
Epidauros	8	
Eretria	7	
Troezen	5	
Styra	2	
Ceos	2	2
Locris		7
SUM	271	9

fleet when one excludes Athens (**Table 10.1**), had any trust in the Athenians (Her VIII.2), especially the redoubtable Themistocles who was leading them. And perhaps rightly so; throughout the war, the contacts of Athenians of some renown with the Persians leave a stale taste in the mouth of the reader, even of the censored story presented by Herodotus to an Athenian audience. Tthe remark that Themistocles intended to deprive all other Greeks of their fleets by burning the Allied vessels in their mooring (Plut Vit Them 20), which was considered immoral but beneficial by none other than Aristides the Just (Plut Vit Aris 22,2), speaks vividly of the Athenian moral standing and the reasons for the widespread Greek mistrust. This mistrust was developing in a racial context as well, given the (Asian) Ionian gimmicks during their ultimately failed revolt (Hale 2009) and the current whole-hearted embracing of the cause of Xerxes.

The realism of the Athenians is astounding, though: they knew they had the most, even perhaps the best ships (Her VIII.1 & VIII.42), but they also knew they had not even the pretence of an army against Xerxes and that by making a concession (Her VIII.3) they could double the available fleet numbers (Grundy 1901) and thus the possibility of being spared from an invasion by containing the invader to the north. The Spartan admiral may have come from a city contributing only ten ships (Her VIII.1), but was respected, had trained long and hard in the Art of War and the science of command and was able to guide the distrustful crew with a pretence of harmony and with undeniable dexterity in tactics; not by knowledge of naval peculiars, but by expedient and expert opinion on issues like timing, adaptability, concerted action, psychology and morale, surprise, security and, of course, by a measure of discipline. As with the rebel fleet at Lade the admiral of a minor sea power could manage politics amongst the major sea-powers which have competing if not opposing interests and thus qualified for Chief Admiral.

The reason for the selection of this particular Spartan lies perhaps with his clear understanding of the Persian campaigning method, due to Spartan professionalism. And Eurybiadas must have been the man to interface Themistocles with Leonidas, both playing the same card of logistics. Once stripping a region of provisions, the Persian army had to draw supplies from their supply bases and the land routes could not accommodate the volume and rate of consumption – especially of liquids. Thus, a rendezvous with the fleet, laden with provisions from Therma, would be essential; more so if the progress to the next fertile and lush area was checked, as was the Greek plan, first at the narrows at Tempe and then at Thermopylae. In the case of Tempe, Xerxes used another, alternative land route (Her VII.128) and in Thermopylae he was bound to do the same, although after some major complications. But at sea, things were different.

Foreplay

Xerxes had started from Therma towards Thessaly with his (main) army, while the fleet remained in vacation mood. The joint staff of the Imperial forces had mostly accurate knowledge of the shores, itineraries, distances and landscape and were able to project the times of sailing and of negotiating ground so as to meet simultaneously, more or less, to the next rendezvous point. Such might have been Alus, the western coast in the large Gulf of Pagassai (**Map 3.1**), where the Greek fleet had called at during the abortive expedition to Tempe (Her VIII.173). But the definite convergence was at the coastal Malian plain (**Map 3.2**), due west of the NW edge of the island of Euboea.

Xerxes had decided not to invade Thessaly by the coastal road from Macedon, the one the Greeks had intended to deny, as they considered it the obvious choice. He apparently found it very pernicious ground, easy to block or litter with ambuscades (Bradford 1980). Thus, emerging through the mountains and keeping out of contact with his fleet, Xerxes was outmanoeuvring his opponents but remaining within a window of vulnerability. Speed was of the essence, which precluded any notion of sidetracking towards present-day Volos and the Pelion peninsula of Magnesia, leaving the sailing of his fleet unsupported. But the subjugation of this area, which had been coerced into submission in advance (Her VII.132), at least ostensibly (Her VII.191), would have been a mission well-suited to his naval contingents. Sporting a staggering 50,000-strong marine arm consisting of the boarders of the ships-of-war; 40 marines on each of the 1,200–1,300 triremes (Her VII.184–5) the fleet could tackle the arm of Magnesia as it did with the promontories of Chalcidice.

Of these, 50,000 an important proportion must have been cavalry. Aeschylus (Persai 302 & 315) made a point of cavalry officers and commanders, who are a good choice for boarders due to their honed balance skills, good armour, and ranged weaponry (especially javelins, but bows as well). From pre-history to the Middle Ages and beyond such weapons have been vindicated. (Rados 1915). The 30 Iranian marines on each of the 1,200–1,300 vessels (Her VII.184) sum to a total of 36–39,000, while the fleet was operating 850 horse-transports (Diod XI.3,9). Had these been similar to Athenian ones of later date, of 30 steeds apiece (Morrison & Coates 2000; Nelopoulos 1999), 25,500 mounts were with the fleet, providing a rough estimation of the number of the Imperial boarders coming from the cavalry arm – roughly half the total number.

The Persian invasion plan was different from the approach plan. The navy was sailing close to the enemy coast and subjugating it with its powerful marine forces. The army was moving inland, occupying a swathe beyond the reach of the naval power projection. The two were to keep contact but meet only sparingly, in designated rendezvous points: the basic issue in the Persian campaign had been water, and Xerxes' land route from Therma to Thessaly and from there to Malis was apprehensive of this particular issue. The same issue kept the fleet away from the army, so as not to share the limited water supplies. They should stay apart, meet briefly and punctually and keep moving.

The Persian schedule must have been rather intolerant in temporal terms and Xerxes had chosen the approach with the least prospect for resistance. Thus, he descended through the Pierian mountains (Her VII.131 & 173) making a road in the process, so as to outmanoeuvre any Greek holding force. Herodotus says this force had been long withdrawn from Tempe, but it is plausible that the Greeks retreated once the flanking itinerary of Xerxes' army and his monstrous fleet created a gigantic pincer movement. In any case, thanks to rather accurate information from the clan Aleuadae of Larissa, that is Xerxes' local proxies in Thessaly – and ardent Medizers – no real delays were expected; and one must remember that delays in some cases are more ominous than actual casualties.

The Allied considerations

The Greek choice shows clearly an interceptive posture, interconnected with the army at Thermopylae and endowed with a very elaborate system of communications, surveillance and early warning (Lazenby 1993; Green 1970; Burn 1962). This system included two fast vessels as liaisons, one available to each expeditionary branch (Her VIII.21,1) so as to keep fleet and army aware of each other; and naval observatories. The latter were both advanced, in Sciathos (Her VII.183), and in-depth, on the peaks of the Euboean mountains, probably Dirfys (Her VII.192), forming a well-laid plan that was leaving little to chance. These arrangements show a definite lack of 'innocence' and amateurism as some scholars suggest (Ferrill 1966; Lazenby 1993; Rey 2011).

The selected spot for the base of the Allied fleet was controlling the exit of the Sciathos-Sepias strait (Lazenby 1993), but this was inconsequential, as the Imperials could simply bypass it from the east, especially if the Allies tried to deny the strait (**Map 3.2**). On the other hand, from this base site, the Allies could keep a keen eye to the southward options of the Persian fleet. The open sea east of Euboea would suggest a fast descend to the Greek rear at the eastern shores of Attica or even in the Saronic Gulf: at Isthmus proper or at the peninsula of Argos, the Argolid. This would have been a true amphibious blitzkrieg in operational scale, bypassing the land and sea defensive positions of the Allies. The western route, through the straits of Trikeri (between the elbow of the peninsula of Magnesia and the eastern half of the northern shore of Euboea) and then of Oreos, would bring the Imperial vessels to their rendezvous with Xerxes at Malis.

It may be true that the Greeks would rather fight in confined waters, although they may not have realized it as yet (Lazenby 1993) since the initial engagement was provoked by the Allies in the open sea; when this proved not to be a smart choice, there were alternatives. Further to the west, near Histiaia, at the western part of the northern Euboean shore, better confines could be found, at the channel of Oreos, which is roughly a continuation of that of Trikeri, but narrower (**Map 3.2**). The Greek fleet did not move west, even when it was partially bypassed by the Imperials and it became clear that it had to opt for narrow and shallow spots. This was probably because Cape Artemisium offered the prospect of defending Euboea from massive landings (Hignett 1963; Fields 2007). If such were carried out at the beach of Artemisium proper, a landward assault to any Greek anchorage situated at a more westward position (Shepherd 2010) would be possible. And the selection of Artemisium was offering the Persian admirals an irresistible bait: the whole expeditionary portion of the – possibly negligible – Greek fleet.

For the Greek cause to prosper, the Persians should be kept out, to the east of Cape Sepias; or, at the very least, their transports and merchantmen. Had the Greeks been able to intercept the Persian fleet north-east of Euboea, they would kill several birds with one stone. They would keep the Imperials out of Euboea, protecting the Island proper, its considerable livestock and human resources and, additionally, forestalling a wide amphibious flanking of Thermopylae through Euboea-Straits of Euripus-Locris. They would also keep the Persian fleet detached from the army, as this was one of the two waypoints where these two branches could be detached (the other being Attica proper, with Cape Sounion), rendering it vulnerable to surprise actions and special warfare. It should always be remembered that the separation of the two Persian branches was not only possible in terms of space, but in terms of time as well. The separation would considerably hurt the Persian Army logistics, as the Malian plain was scorched (probably by Leonidas, as mentioned in Polyaenus I.32,3) and fodder was scarce for the cavalry.

Last, but not least, ideally, the Greeks would also deny plentiful watering, rest for the crews and the seaborne horses and would expose the gigantic Imperial fleet to the summer tempests by contesting the entry of the Persian Fleet in the straits and thus to the security of the Gulf of Pagassai. The reliance on the weather was a deliberate and focal strategy, as it is traced to the Oracle of Delphi proper (Her VII.178). With hindsight, there has been some success with this strategy, but not total; a possible rendezvous at Alus, south of Pagassai, was missed by the Persian fleet and the next, at the shore of the scorched Malian plain (Pol I.32,3), became vital for the Persian Army. The latter had arrived there in time, while the navy was delayed by weather and intercepted by the foe, causing an emergency if not a derailment of the logistics of the land army.

The naval invasion: Act One

The Persian fleet was ordered to sail a full 11 days after the army moved (Her VII.183). Within these 11 days, rather than on the 11th, a vanguard of 10 extra fast ships (Her VII.179), probably the lower tactical naval echelon, was sent to conduct a scouting mission. They were selected for their speed; thus, they might have been a special unit, possibly part of an elite body of the fleet, understood as brigading the fastest ships of different contingents (Aesch Persai 341–3) rather than a standard unit of one naval contingent.

Herodotus' wording implies that their mission was to identify a reef at the strait between Sciathos and the Magnesian coast, which was brought to their attention by a native (Her VII.183,3) and mark it with a pillar for the main body of the fleet (Her VII.183). The massive stream of vessels needed very clear headings to avoid confusion and congestion in straits. While three of the ships of the vanguard did the marking, the rest must have provided security but would have done some reconnaissance as well, especially regarding shores, water availability, landmarks and everything else needed by the main fleet to sail south safely, find refuge and water for the night and keep their heading. Alternatively, it may be understood by Herodotus' wording that three vessels were lost to the reef (Holland 2005) and the others marked it subsequently for further, future use by the fleet; in such a case, the intended objective was reconnaissance pure and simple. A very probable mission by itself is surveying the coasts and selecting shores for the fleet to call at (Green 1970).

While the Imperial scouts were sailing south, they fell on a Greek patrol flight of three ships based at Sciathos (Her VII.179). There is no way this had happened at night, as occasionally suggested (Holland 2005); this would not have allowed any detailed observation of the coastline of Magnesia, an issue focal for the forthcoming operations. The island hosted a naval observatory established by the Allied Greeks (Her VII.183), to provide early warning. Some scholars (Lazenby 1993) suppose that its mission was rather to determine as early as possible the strategic intent of the Imperial fleet. The latter could opt for the eastern route, east of Sciathos, which implied sailing east of Euboea, for an obvious descent through the Carystus-Andros straits to Attica. Both sides of this strait were in Imperial hands (Burn 1962) and were attacked by the confederates the day after the Allied victory at Salamis (Her VIII.111,1 & 112,2). Andros was a staunch medizer state (Her VIII.111) and Carystus had been subjugated since 490 BC by Datis (Her VI.99,2). This route would lead the Imperials straight to the eastern waters of Attica if Cape Caphereus, the southernmost tip of Euboea, did not turn patriotic. The operational prospect was then for massive landings in south Attica where the silver mines were situated and then a gallop northwards, to unhinge any possible land defence of Attica facing north. Alternatively, the Imperial fleet could go for an entry in the Saronic Gulf, either to assault the nominally defended west Attica and the rest of the Saronic Gulf states, Corinth included; or, to continue south, to the friendly Argolid. This must have been a very good reason for the reserve squadrons of the Allies, perhaps coming in belatedly from western Greece as they had to turn the treacherous Cape Maleus south-east of Sparta, to stay with the home squadrons of the campaigning states at the ports of Troezen or Aegina, as a precaution against such a manoeuvre (Burn 1962).

The other option for the Imperials, much more conservative, was to steer west, either to realize a massive landing at northern Euboea or to follow the straits of Trikeri to join Xerxes at Alus, in the Gulf of Pagassai. A still better option would be to follow the straits of Oreos, the continuation or extension of these of Trikeri, to call at the apex of the Gulf of Malis.

The whole idea had some merit; there is no reason not to pass west of Sciathos and then descend to the east of Euboea. The other way round was not a valid option, as it would mean a detour. But the observers posted at the highlands of Euboea (Her VII.192) were surely deployed exactly to stare and survey the open seas (Lazenby 1993) and thus Sciathos observatory was meant to give the heads-up for the approach of the enemy, possibly a rough estimation on numbers and the shores of call.

The Imperial flight emerged victorious from the skirmish, taking as prizes two ships and chasing the third to the shallows of Tempe, where the crew landed and made good their escape by land (Her VII.180–2). One prisoner was sacrificed as first-fruits of victory by the Phoenicians (Her VII.180) and the most gallant one was kept alive in their flagship and treated with the utmost respect for his bravery and determination by the Persian boarders who had subdued him only after almost hacking him to pieces (Her VII.181–2).

This whole episode has many intriguing issues. The Greek naval observatory was at Sciathos, but the Athenian vessel, which shirked the Imperial assault, was ditched much to the north, at the site of Tempe, at the mouth of river Penius (Her VII.182). Thus, when did the opponents see each other, and where? The Greek scouts were all together, as a team, or delegated each to a sector and the enemy overtook them piecemeal? If the former proposal is the case, as is the usual practice – but NOT the usual opinion for the last 2,500 years – where did the skirmish take place? Its geometry is intriguing, since the refuge of the Athenian vessel is much to the north, deep behind enemy lines on land. Thus, did the skirmish happen that much to the north and the Athenians simply made a fast race aground? Or the event took place near Sciathos and the Athenians circled the island or took any other fanciful action to appear behind their opponents and disengage, possibly because the Phoenicians were on a tight schedule for their mission?

It is not clear whether the Imperial flight of scouts returned triumphant before the main fleet made waves or met it *en route*. One thing was certain: the confederate naval observatory at Sciathos, seeing no friendly vessel returning, or witnessing two taken and one running and never returning, would have signalled the total loss of the flight to the anchorage at Cape Artemisium.

In any case, it took at least one sailing day for the Imperial fleet to reach the east coast of Magnesia (Her VII.183) and cast anchor for the night, probably by using the Mediterranean system of interwoven casts and cables, obviously hoping to negotiate Cape Sepias the next day and enter the Trikeri straits, either to reach Alus north-west within the Gulf of Pagassai or to proceed west through the Strait of Oreos to the Malian coast. The Mediterranean system allowed the accommodation of large fleets at relatively narrow and shallow sandy beaches. A row of ships was resting ashore, the next was cabled in checkerboard formation to them by prow and casting anchors astern, and the next rows were doing the same, being cabled to pairs of the preceding row. The scheme was in eight rows at this instance (Her VII.188,1), taking just 1,500m of beach for the 1,200 warships.

To arrange the vessels in eight lines for mooring, a line-by-line arrangement is implied, with the first vessels occupying all the length of the shore and the others forming successive lines (Her VII.188,1). Thus, ships of the same squadron would have been in the same line, one next to the other. Should something befall one line, because it was more exposed, or if a diver was to cut their cables, these vessels would suffer all together (Her VII.188,3).

Alternatively, in a file-by-file arrangement, where the vessels are arranged practically serially, there are some practical complications. The depth of a file is homogenous and vessels of the same squadron are practically forming a square block. If one such file is compromised, by nature, accident or enemy action all vessels might be destroyed in a file, with the possible exception of the first, dragged to the sand. This would explain the survival of a single ship out of a state contribution of 12 Cypriot vessels (Her VII.195).

The observatory in Sciathos must have reported the huge size of the Persian navy and the result of the engagement between the reconnaissance flights. According to Herodotus, this brought about the spontaneous flight of the Greek fleet (Her VII.182) posted at Cape Artemisium.

A most windy and wet intermission

The retreat of the Greek fleet was considerable, in spatial terms. They went all the way west through the channels of Trikeri and Oreos, rounded the Lichas promontory (**Map 10.1**) and then continued southeast, deep into the northern Gulf

Map 10.1

of Euboea and possibly all the way to the narrowest point, the strait of Euripus, in the vicinity of Chalcis (Her VII.183,1). Herodotus gives a detailed account of the Greek fleet, 271 triremes and 9 pentekonters (**Table 10.1**), a total of 280 vessels (Her VIII.2), hardly a quarter of the Persian ships of the line.

These are facts, both the numbers and the move. The reasoning, though, might be an issue. The observatory at Sciathos would have been able to look for signs of weather and send a warning. The narrow northern Gulf of Euboea, stretching from north-west to south-east, if hit perpendicularly by winds coming from the north-east (i.e. the Hellespont), presented little width to develop high waves. Thus, the Allied fleet was safe from an oncoming gale; even more so if it was beached at the Euboean coast, towards the direction of the weather. This explains perfectly why the Greek fleet went so far south, near Chalcis, to the narrowest point of the straits. Some scholars refuse to accept such a lengthy retreat, pointing to the protection offered by the mountains of northern Euboea once a fleet simply rounds Histiaia and Oreos, to stay at Aidipsos (**Map 10.1**), in stark contrast to the area near Chalcis, which is afforded little protection from north-east winds by mountains (Grundy, 1901).

The Greek retreat was executed before making contact with the Imperial fleet; thus it could not have been a bait to lure it into an ambush. Additionally, it left Euboea exposed to Imperial landings at Artemisium proper, while the defence of the island was a priority objective served by the deployment of the confederate fleet at that particular spot (Her VIII.4,2). Thus, the only remaining valid reason for the Allied fleet to retire was to seek refuge from the incoming tempest; and Chalcis offered much better accommodation for ships and crews.

The Magnesian shores, on the other hand, where the Persian fleet beached for the night, were quite exposed and the gale, a 'Hellespontias' due to its north-east direction, struck hard. It was raging for three days, wreaking havoc (Her VII.188; Diod XI.12,3); a cardinal issue that maximized the damage was the, rarely spoken of, cutting of anchors and cables by the diver Skyllias and his daughter Hydna from the city of Scione in Macedon (Paus X.19,2), who were conscripted (voluntarily or not) as divers in the King's service. Afterwards, they salvaged sunken treasures for the Persians, possibly pocketing a hefty piece of them on top of the regular payment by their employer (Her VIII.8,1). The Imperial fleet had some 300–400 ships-of-the-line lost and suffered much more massive loss of lighter and transport and cargo vessels (Diod XI.12,3; Her VII.190–1), as these were more susceptible to storms and/or less well anchored. There is no wonder Skyllias and Hydna were honoured with statues at Delphi after the war (Paus X.19,2). Offering such honours to private individuals cannot have happened due to rumours, which means that scepticism on the fact is unwarranted.

The Confederates had promptly resumed, after the gale, their interceptive position at Cape Artemisium (Her VII.192). The notion of 'promptly' is debatable, the Greeks were in position to intercept the Persian fleet which set sail the fourth day from the onset of the storm. This timeline fits perfectly with the duration of Xerxes' inactivity in front of Thermopylae.

By the second day of the storm, the outposts positioned in the highlands of Euboea (Her VII.192) would have informed the Greek Admirals of the magnitude of the Persian disaster, possibly as a relay from the observatory at Sciathos. The Greeks might have contemplated engaging the surviving and roughly handled Persian ships as they were to emerge between Sciathos and Magnesia and turning west to negotiate Cape Sepias; after the battering they took they were not likely to try any long-range legs east of Euboea. The Greek intention must have been to intercept or to contain within the Gulf of Pagassai, or even, if possible, to destroy the battered royal fleet, but in any case to keep it away (i) of Malis in an effort to expedite the starvation of the Imperial army and (ii) from Euripus so as not to turn Leonidas' position by sea, nor to cut the Allied fleet off its home ports and bases. To deny the opportunity for deep naval raids towards Messene or Argos, the soft front and back yards of Sparta, were also instrumental for the success of the Allies' strategy, but it seemed to have been taken care of by Boreas, the north wind whom Athenians considered family (Her VII.189).

Still, the Persian navy was so massive that it entered the Trikeri straits uncontested. This is definite proof that neither the straits were narrow enough for the numbers involved, nor the Greeks had any intention of deploying perpendicularly and fending off the straits. One of their primary objectives was still to protect Euboea and their ambition would have been to keep an advantageous flanking position and launch at the side of the Persian columns as the latter entered the Trikeri straits. There was no intent, or possibility, for the Imperials to bypass the Greek fleet by posting some squadrons to fend it off while the rest would be passing by; this was a recipe for disaster, as the numbers involved would result in equal, or at least comparable, terms (Green 1970). But much more important, leaving the Greek fleet to their rear meant that the transportation of the supplies would be a one-off operation. Once unloaded, the merchantmen would not be able to return to Therma and haul a new load. And the provisioning of the army required a regular stream of supplies. With the Greek fleet at Artemisium, these trips would be suicidal.

The emerging Imperial columns were so massive, that one of the Greek flanks would have been exposed to a flank attack had their fleet moved to form a battle line and charge the side of the enemy columns (**Figure 10.1**). As a result, the Greeks stood down, possibly after some persuasion not to flee and were delighted to see the Persians not bypassing them and sailing for Malis but hitting the beach almost across from their own position, at Aphetae (Her VIII.4; Diod XI.12,3). Whether Aphetae was just across from their own position, or at the turn of the promontory, at Trikeri, the mouth of the Gulf of Pagassai (Grundy 1901), is still a matter of controversy (**Map 3.2**). Had it been the latter case, the anchorage was situated a short, unimpeded and uncontested distance from Alus, allowing easy communication with the Army without compromising its watering resources, had the rendezvous been implemented. Although such a meeting would be very natural, and Xerxes' more than usually lax proceedings through the area (Her VII.197) suggest such intentions, it remains purely conjectural and not supported by the time factors of Herodotus' account, which, however, is notoriously untrustworthy (Grundy 1901), especially, but not exclusively, for this campaign.

Preparing for battle

Once the Imperial fleet was able to make waves, it turned Cape Sepias and called at its next anchorage to recuperate, at Aphetae in Magnesia. While approaching, the Persians had spotted the Greek position and perhaps had a measure of the Greek fleet. Such intelligence must have been provided, of course, from the Phoenician scouts as well. They could engage right away, and possibly hold off the Greek fleet in a frontal action while the rest of the fleet, especially the transports, made their way to Malis – in theory. But they were battered enough by the storm, in need of water, some rest and generally a break. Moreover, they would rather trap and capture the entire Greek fleet than simply deliver a crushing blow. Thus, as they approached, a task force of two squadrons of 100 vessels each was diverted off Sciathos, to the East, so as to disappear from enemy sight, and then to steer south, around Cape Caphereus of southern Euboea and up the Euboean Gulf, to cut off Euripus for any Greek retreat (Herd VIII.7; Diod XI.12,3).

A strategic masterpiece, competently conceived. The capture of the crews of the two piquet triremes of the Greeks (Her VII.180–1) would have furnished first-rate intelligence on the numbers, position and morale of the Greek fleet. Thus, the Persian plans had been devised beforehand and respective orders were issued. The tempest introduced some uncertainties, but once sailing south was resumed, the Persians spotted the Greeks (Her VIII.6), made sure they were still, or again, at Artemisium and set in action their preconceived, existing plans. The encircling task force might have set off *before* the fleet made sail for Aphetae, to optimize schedules and times of arrival, based exactly on such intelligence from the scouts; but then the position of the Greek fleet would not have been known with any certainty.

Herodotus reports that once the Imperials had called at Aphetae, Skyllias deserted unnoticed and brought word of the specifics of the disaster to the Greek fleet (Her VIII.8,3); a most important and believable report, given that the Imperial admiralty took a tally of the seaworthy vessels at Aphetae, the destination base (Her VIII.7,2), *not* at the starting anchorages; thus the captured/deserting squadron of Sandoces (Her VII.194) might have offered some crude estimates but not solid and accurate data. The claim of Skyllias that he swam undersea from the Persian to the Greek anchorage, a distance of 80 stades/ roughly 7 nautical miles (Her VIII.8,2) is perfectly plausible. Nobody maintained that he did so in one breath, nor without the use of equipment. As an experienced diver, he might have improvised a system for adjusting his buoyancy and for supplying air while submerged (a weighted belt of pouched stones and reed snorkel with leather mouthpiece are easily coming to mind), both secrets of the trade that he would have been most unwilling to share with others. Additionally, Herodotus maintains that the Greeks were tipped off for the dispatch of the encircling squadron by Skyllias, not before; which is weird, as this would have been the exact event for the outpost at Sciathos to notice and relay. Had it not been so, did the events unfold as Herodotus has them? It is most likely that the task force was dispatched at a moment's notice, implementing a contingency plan formulated by the intelligence provided by the scouting Phoenician flight of ships on the whereabouts of the Allied fleet (Her VIII.6,1). For executing this plan the 'go' orders must have been intended to be issued *en route*, once the Greeks were spotted and confirmed at their established position at Artemisium (ibid) by the vanguard and before the Imperials approached close enough for the enemy to notice a not-so-small task force going in the wrong direction.

This issue is indeed important: many modern scholars, starting from a clear-cut denial for the numbers of the imperial fleet (i.e. Bradford 1980; Green 1970; Hignett 1963; Burn 1962) consider the produced strength of this flanking force exaggerated (i.e. Grundy, 1901). The latter source, though, understands well that to attempt such a wide envelopment against the Allied fleet of 270 triremes (this number is not challenged), one must have a most comfortable numerical advantage. The enveloping force, venturing by day and night in unknown waters, far from the coast as it was striving to remain elusive for as long as possible, had to be powerful. The enemy force was likely to fight viciously to reopen a retreat path, perhaps in relatively open waters, probably near Oreos, and enemy patrols and squadrons were to be expected to emerge and engage when the task force would be turning up-channel. To discourage them, and defeat them should the need be and accomplish the mission, the enveloping force had to be quite large and, transporting a marine element, able to execute an opposed landing (though not heavily opposed), assault and secure both sides of the straits of Euripus. The rest of the fleet should have remained proportionately large, AFTER the gale, for the Imperial admiralty not to consider this endeavour unduly risky, as it did for the proposal of Demaratus some days later, after the conclusion of this phase of the campaign (Her VII.236,2). The 8,000 marines of the 200 vessels were more than the armies of most city-states of the alliance and only Chalcis was presumed hostile in theatre.

The massive size of the encircling task force, 2/3 of the entire Greek fleet, meant not a holding force but a decisive one, executing a wide envelopment manoeuvre so familiar to the Persian naval staff; they were to try the same at Salamis (de Souza 2003) and with as many ships. But this approach was standard for the Persian high command in general, as they were constantly trying to envelop their opponent, at both tactical and operational levels. Thermopylae, possibly Tempe (but, importantly, not Plataea) and the envisaged co-operation of fleet and army were all examples of the pin-and-flank routine, even if one does not count the similar effort in Marathon, as it is not solidly substantiated. Thus, it is highly possible that once the Persians spotted the Greek fleet at Artemisium, they stopped thinking about getting to the Malian shore, to Xerxes' camp (Her VIII.6). More by standing orders than by instinct, they would have considered the utter destruction of the enemy fleet a mission of the highest priority and *opted* for Aphetae, where they could engage at short notice and give chase promptly. It was a stupid thing to do, although the poor shape of the fleet after the gale might have been a heavily weighting factor. The Persian admirals did by themselves what the Greeks wanted to make them do but did not dare to endeavour: they stopped short of joining the army and Xerxes, accepting the certainty of a delay and a temporary inconvenience for the army against the prospect of acclaiming Sea Dominance. It is conceivable that they relayed such proceedings to Xerxes overland, and this might be the reason Xerxes decided to force the issue at Thermopylae. He knew his fleet would take at least two or three days to wrap up the situation as the circumnavigation would take at least one day and possibly up to two.

Schemes and plans

Still, the Greeks had taken measures. The Persian practices were by now perfectly known. The inscription at Behistun, known throughout the empire by leaflets read by heralds, declared the decisive battle of extermination as the centrepiece of the empire's policy (DB 25, 33, 35, 36). This, coupled with a vigorous system of rewards and punishments (DB 63) created a profile of an enemy lavishly equipped and supported, competently handled, crudely managed, lacking cohesion and intellectuality and thus easy to trap and ambush. The approach was vindicated in Scythia, Marathon and even during the Ionian Revolt. Wily Themistocles and Eurybiadas, the latter being one of the Spartans (a people renowned for tricks and cunning) were the perfect leadership. It is likely that the Greeks had an operational plan in case winds and waves would not oblige. And once more this plan would probably take advantage of the Persian compulsion to exterminate an enemy by giving chase (DB 32).

The straits were perhaps six nautical miles wide (Her VIII.8,2), meaning 50 Greek vessels per mile, that is something like one ship per 30 metres or more. With a functional width (oars extended) of more than 10 metres (Fields 2007), it was not the place to block a much more numerous fleet by deploying perpendicularly, especially with the one northern shore controlled by the enemy and possibly bristling with hostile bows. The Greek idea would be to anchor both flanks at their shore and attack at the side any Persian column trying to bypass them and reach Malis (Green 1970) – an intention made obvious by their advanced position. Bypassing the Greek anchorages in both Artemisium and Salamis was do-able in theory (Lazenby 1993) but the Persians were thus exposing their flanks. They should at least detail some vessels to protect them from the Greek ships should the latter attack. Though, the concept of holding forces was employed for extermination setups, not for slipping from an inferior enemy, as disengagements were always risky and not particularly glorious. This was neither appropriate for the Imperial dignity nor acceptable for the ego and stance of the admirals, and, possibly, for the Phoenician arrogance as well. Leaving almost 300 galleys behind them meant, moreover, that the Imperials forfeited any plan of securing their maritime rear and establishing maritime traffic for logistics.

The plan set in Salamis was to be very similar, a fact indicating it was the preferred strategy for the Greek fleet (Sidebotham 1982). This is usually attributed to Themistocles, but one must remember that the Masters of Deception were the Spartans and baits were their motto, both in Thermopylae and at Plataea. There are some recurring factors. An intrinsic correlation of the width of the strait, the number of the Persian fleet columns comfortably allowed in, ready to turn at right angles to receive the Greek attack and the distance the Greek fleet could afford while attacking without presenting its flank to subsequent Persian squadrons, in the van or the tail of the column, should be understood. This issue emerged anew in Salamis. Thus, an enemy of perhaps double the number of the Greek vessels, sailing in one or two columns, to provide mutual support, could be dealt with by the Allied navy. But a size of triple or four times their number at line-ahead would make the plan void as the hanging Greek flanks would be assaulted *en masse* and in-depth once exposed by their advance (**Figure 10.1**). This may have been an excellent reason for some Greek commanders and admirals to show reluctance to engage.

An interception point further to the west, at Oreos, deep in the straits might have been envisioned (Diod XI.12,4). Ambushing at Lichas, the turn of the shoreline

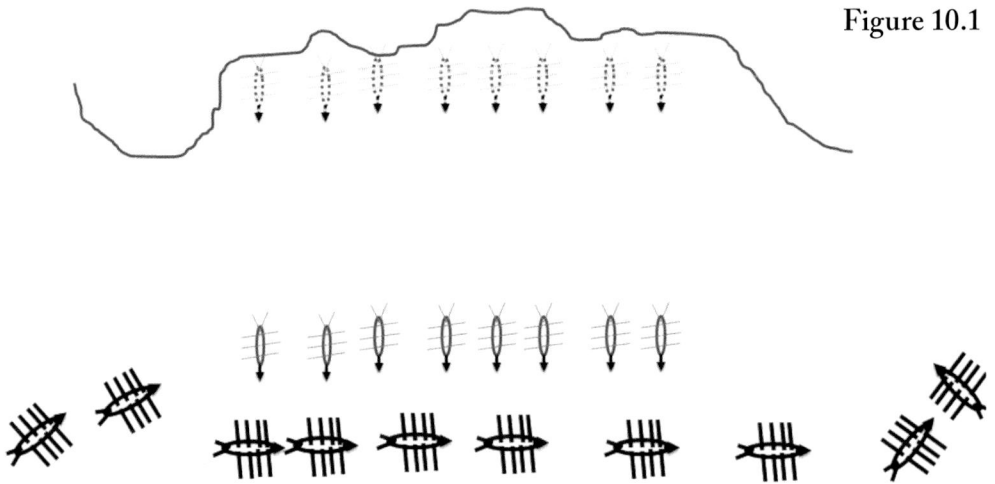

Figure 10.1

of Euboea, the Greeks might cause enough damage and havoc right before the Imperial ships were to call at the coast of Malis. But that was a risky business. The Imperial fleet, once in the straits of Trikeri, could always land powerful amphibious forces at Euboea to raid any Greek base camp and perhaps even get by land to Euripus (Green 1970). This undermined the defence at Thermopylae while also presenting the distinct possibility of a coastal base for archery, likely to cripple the retreating Greek vessels, or set them ablaze, as it was to do with the improvised wooden fortifications of the Acropolis of Athens some weeks later. This was an excellent reason, among many, for the choice of Artemisium by the Greeks. They must have originally intended to lure the Persians in, at a chase, which would tacitly and subtly deny time or aptitude for amphibious operations by the Imperial boarders. At a chase, the Greek trap could spring with minimal risk for Euboea. And perhaps the Greek captains, who were reportedly (Her VIII.4,1) quickly preparing to sail away, Chief Admiral Eurybiadas amongst them, intended exactly that, to implement a plan set beforehand, before the benevolent intervention of Boreas, the god of the North Wind, as a strategy to defeat the arrogant and magnificent armada by concentrating on their leading elements and decapitating it. It was Epaminondas in prospect and a new interpretation of Marathon.

The Allies thus might have resorted to performing (literally) a new retreat in order to implement this previous plan, as the tempest did less damage to the Persians than expected by the Greeks; and less than needed to change the balance. In plain sight, early in the morning, the Greek fleet could move west and away as the weary and battered fleet of the King of Kings was sailing into position just across the strait. The Persian instincts, as well as their standing orders, would make them give chase; and when at the promontory of Lichas, or even before, at the deep straits of Oreos, the Greeks would reverse to attack. Does the plan seem familiar, in its naval implementation? Does it read like Salamis (Holland 2005; Green 1970)? Same plan, same staff, same conditions, same fleets.

There is another subtle but very important issue. Herodotus casually says that the Greeks were watching the Imperial squadrons hitting the beach and anchoring in great numbers, and that the beaches were full of troops (Her VIII.4). This is much more important than usually (not) believed. The Persian admirals, when calling at the shores of Magnesia, during the first tempest, had to make an improvised fort with the timber of the wrecked ships, to guard against any possible hostiles while ashore (Her VII.191), as they had no intelligence from Imperial headquarters on the disposition of the natives. The locals had medized beforehand (Her VII.132,1; Diod XI.3,2) but the bitter experience of Mardonius (Her VI.45,1) had resulted in due caution and precautions. The issue of sneak attacks against fleets still beached or anchored recurs, not only in the naval history of Classical Greece, as in Aegospotami (Xen Hell II.1,28) but during the Persian Wars. Both Herodotus and Diodorus attest for such plans of the Allied Admiralty in Artemisium, although in different phases, indicating different sources. Herodotus narrates such an attack at the second dusk, against a Cilician contingent (Her VIII.14), while Diodorus relates such a plan for the initial engagement (Diod XI.12,5). Despite the presence of numerous troops (probably marines) deployed ashore, which made such endeavours much riskier, the Greeks at the end had at least partial success with this concept.

This, most likely, has been the reason for the commotion reported by Herodotus (Her VIII.4). His Athenian source, possibly favouring Aristides, discredits at once Adeimandos, the Corinthian, Eurybiadas, the Spartan, and Themistocles the Wily, for taking bribes (Her VIII.4–5); the former two for being cowards as well (Green 1970; Grundy 1901). Thus, for the bitter Athenian source, the two Dorians allegedly wanted to fall back all the way to the south and expose Leonidas' flank, with both Spartan and Corinthian troops under his command! But eventually, they agreed not to do so due to bribes (Her VIII.5). The latter, an Athenian and thus morally superior and a man of valour, does not intend to withdraw, but welcomes a bribe nonetheless (Her VIII.4). In Plutarch, the direct accusation of Aristides to Themistocles for 'greasy hands' (Plut Vit Arist 24) was the cause of their undying hatred.

The Euboean folk, not privy to the plans of the Greek naval command, once seeing a commotion at the the naval camp and given the previous retreat to Chalcis, correctly thought that a new, maybe definite retreat was imminent and bribed for some time to evacuate (Her VIII.4). Themistocles simply took the money but changed neither intent nor conduct – and quite possibly passed a commission to some colleagues.

Of course, this rounding of edges is denied to the two Dorians when the natives first approached the Admiral. The vileness against the Spartan is deep but unfounded. Retreating meant exposing his King's flank and Eurybiadas could have never done so. The Spartans were notorious for taking bribes, but this was true at the time of Herodotus (or, rather, *since* the days of Herodotus); this was not so for the days of Artemisium, at least not yet. Herodotus' own account on the conduct of Cleomenes I when Aristagoras tried to bribe him (Her V.51,2) should be remembered. And Cleomenes I was a maverick king, rather unscrupulous, who had been accused of bribery in the case of Argos, whose power he destroyed utterly by using debatable practices, verging on both crime and irreverence, if not outright sacrilege (Her VI.75,3 & 79,1 & VI.80).

It was, though, a straight slander. Both Adeimandos and Eurybiadas were not the scoundrels the Athenians wanted to vilify to eternity. In Plutarch (Vit Them 7) the Spartan admiral is presented as saying constantly that the Persians were undefeated at sea. It is an insinuation that he is afraid, or rather unwilling to engage. Then, what exactly is he doing there with all these ships? Not showing the flag; his fleet is too unimpressive for that. Moreover, Eurybiadas was a Spartan, not an idiot and should have known well that if anywhere, it had been at sea that the Persians had *not* been invincible. Regarding 'Xerxes' undefeated armada' (Green 1970), it was undefeated indeed, and also unengaged, but for the skirmish off Sciathos. Before that, the Persians won only one major naval action against Greek fleets, off Lade, where 1/3 of the Greek vessels defected (Her VI.14,2–3 & VI.8,1). On the other hand, the only clear-cut Greek victory during the Ionian Revolt occurred at sea, near Cyprus, probably in 497 BC (Her V.112,1). There the rebel fleet, anywhere between 200 triremes – the task force sailing against Naxos in 500 BC (Her V.31,4 & V.32) – and 350 (its strength at Lade, Her VI.8,2) had been victorious against a Phoenician fleet. The latter's strength could be anywhere up to 300, the strength of its expeditionary contingent under Xerxes (Her VII.89), with possible reinforcements from the fleet of Cilicia, up to 100 triremes, the strength of its expeditionary contingent under Xerxes (Her VII.91), meaning a maximum of 400 vessels.

Adeimandos, on the other hand, was not a mere admiral, commanding an unimpressive 40 triremes (Her VIII.1), a suspiciously low figure for the city-state who lent 20 ships to Athens some years before at a token cost of five daily wages per ship (Thuc I.41,2; Her VI.89). He was the admiral of the city-state where the headquarters of the League was seated, the city which designed the first trireme and which was contributing the second largest naval contingent.

Both men, by nurture conservative, understood a need to revert to the original plan of baiting and ambushing by feint retreat as the Persian fleet appeared to be an overmatch. This exposed the strategically but not tactically-sensitive southern flank through Euboea and nobody liked it, but the two Peloponnesians must have thought there was no other workable option. Attacking in mid-morning was too risky with the numbers involved. Themistocles disagreed (Diod XI.12,5). He must have formed a plan for dusk attacks and have possessed better information on the status of the Persian fleet, its real size, casualties and particulars. After all, the Greek spies at Sardis had witnessed first-hand only the Imperial land army, as the fleet mustered at Cyme (Green 1970) and, in any case, the Imperial fleet had not been fully assembled yet; this must have been concluded at Doriscus (Her VII.59 & VII.100). But this does not mean he had not a better grasp of the intentions of the Imperial admiralty. Among his vital pieces of intelligence, the dispatch of the flanking task force, a knowledge attributed to Skyllias but possibly corroborated by the outpost at Sciathos, should have been instrumental. This development undermined the ambush plan at Oreos, as the Imperials would emerge at the rear of the Greek fleet, and sat well with the propensity of the Imperial admiralty to stay put at Aphetae for some time to recuperate.

The intelligence leading Themistocles to a different interpretation of the situation, which was rather speedily adopted by the two senior Dorian admirals, might be linked to the capture of the Imperial squadron of 15 vessels (Her VII.184), along with the report of Skyllias and the possible relays from Sciathos. Herodotus narrates some very interesting details, implying a close source of his on the matter, but fails to mention who this was. The Greek fleet captured these vessels. Yes. But which part/squadron of the Greek fleet did so is not mentioned. It is impossible for all 271 – or rather 268 – vessels to have taken part in the capture of 15. Is Herodotus downplaying their extremely important feat for some clandestine reason? Or was it not the Athenians, and thus Herodotus' source neglects to be specific?

The Imperial squadron was 15-ships strong and made a fatal error in identifying the designated anchorage; or did it? They saw, at dusk, a naval encampment, had no idea that the Greeks were in the vicinity and had lost track of previous squadrons turning right to the entrance of the straits – an argument for Aphetae being at the entrance of the Gulf (Grundy 1901), and not anywhere along the arm extending west of Cape Sepias. As the squadrons in front of them were eventually beyond their field of view, the 15 stragglers went straight for the anchorage they saw. After all, although under the command of a Persian official (Her VII.194) this was NOT a squadron, but an assembly of survivors of wrecked squadrons. Assembled ad hoc for the cruise to Aphetae or Pagassai, there was the Commander, Sandoces, a Persian from the north-west coast of Asia Minor (Cyme) and with bad blood with the ruling dynasty (Her VII.194). It may be important that he was the governor of the city where the Imperial navy had mustered (Diod XI.2,3). Additionally, there was in this squadron a petty ruler of Caria in south-west Asia Minor, and a Cypriot Admiral and kinsman to a petty king of one of the cities of the island, who had lost

11 out of his 12 vessels to the gale (Her VII.195). Actually, at least two of the three dignitaries, Sandoces and the Cypriot, would have expected harsh treatment by the King for inefficiency and misconduct once in his presence. The perfect scenery for a defection. Thus, the arguments based on the supposition of an honest mistake of navigation, the position of the Persian anchorage included, may have been invalid. Herodotus briefly mentions the questioning and dispatching of the prisoners to the Allied headquarters at the Isthmus (Her VII.195). He is not disclosing how they were sent there, by sea or overland. If the Persians were to win, the prisoners would be able to report some navigational error, communications breakdown and problems with identification; if the Greeks were to win, they would be treated to safety, which was not a given under Xerxes' rule for some of them.

Herodotus says nothing of their final fate; perhaps an indication of a second-grade 'witness protection programme', compared to the land installments for deserters and defectors like the Greek captains of Imperial ships (Her VIII.11). He also says nothing about how all these people were ferried to headquarters. The squadron was 15-strong (Her VII.194); even with the Greek quota for triremes, which Herodotus takes as universal, this means some 3,000 prisoner mariners of whom 450 were crack Iranian marines (Her VII.184), beefing up the native marine units.

The Greek outpost in Sciathos was a vital vantage point that would have NEVER been abandoned, contrary to the suggestion of Connolly, 1981. It probably took heed of both the size of the Persian fleet, despite the storm, and the encircling manoeuvre, and passed the word, as mentioned earlier. How this relay was achieved is a valid question, possibly by beacons, which have a limited data content and may account for some erratic relay. Reflecting the sunlight, for example on a metal shield, as with the notorious signal from Athens during the Marathon campaign (Her VI.115), is another possibility.

The observers posted in the highlands of Euboea (Her VII. 192) would also have seen the Imperial flanking force and would have provided updates for its progress. Cape Caphereus is notorious for its wickedly rough weather, and the Persian naval intelligence must have been accurate in terms of geography, due to the mission of Democides, but was lacking in data concerning the weather, especially seasonal tides. Most mainland Greek defectors/traitors were with the Army and the Persian admirals would pay by default little attention to anyone but the haughty Phoenicians. Sailing east of Euboea at that season was not a wise decision and some home fleet squadrons were left behind by the Greeks (Her VIII.42,1), for such an eventuality. After all, Artemisium was an expedition, so one should understand a 2/3 rule for the expeditionary forces. True to this estimate, the Athenians had deployed almost 120 out of 180 ships and the Spartans 10 out of 16, both acceptable approximations of the 2/3 rule. Thus, 1/3 of the Greek fleet (estimated at 130 vessels by the above mentioned rule) was left behind, available and in position to engage the flanking force. This implies that the Imperials were excellently informed (by their captured PoWs) and purposefully sent such a powerful contingent to circumnavigate Euboea.

It is likely that the first instinct of the Greek admiralty would have been to retreat south and trap the encircling task force between the home fleet(s) stationed south-south-east of the Saronic Gulf and the expeditionary Allied fleet bearing down on Euripus (Her VIII.9), with both coasts being friendly to the Greeks, despite the highly inconvenient lack of a mass missile arm that would have turned the confined waters into a death zone. Assessing the time better, another plan developed: first a sudden blow to the main Persian fleet, considering itself safe due to its very numbers and thus lax in vigilance and feverish to regroup and become ready for the next day's toil. A victorious result would discourage any thought of aggressive deployment of the main Persian fleet while the Greeks would be absent, making sail at night for Euripus (*ibid*).

The first part of the Greek plan went perfectly, as described later. The second was aborted; a new storm, now from east-south-east, not only made impossible a Greek night endeavour to Euripus, but also took care of the encircling force for them. The following morning, home fleet reinforcements (Her VIII.14) arrived along with news (but not necessarily *bringing the* news) that the encircling task force was no more. It is tempting to assume, but cannot be solidly established, that the reinforcements were the heralds of the new round of divine assistance. Shipwrecked to the inhospitable east coast of Euboea (Her VIII.13), any surviving Imperial galleys would have drifted back north due to the south-east wind and no longer presented any danger.

Chapter 11

Methods, Means and Tactics

Apart from an extensive and systematic, but rather discrete pertaining of military intelligence in the facts and features of the Greek campaign, which is hardly ever appreciated by historians (i.e. Lazenby 1993; contrary Burns 1962), a tactical and operational dimension should be explored, interfaced with known technical attributes and hard facts. The military intelligence examples, such as the spies sent at Sardis (Her VII.145), the naval outpost in Sciathos (Her VII.182), naval observatories in Euboea (Her VII. 192), outposts at heights over Thermopylae (Her VII.219,1), liaison ships connecting the expeditionary forces stationed at Thermopylae and Artemisium (Her VIII.21) and officers operating behind enemy lines (Her VII.232) should rather indicate a Spartan hand; whenever an instigator is named, the Spartans appear.

The tactical disposition always depends on the environment; that is geography, weather, season (it includes many other attributes, on top of the weather) and time of the day. The choice of the environment depends on one's assets and liabilities and the opponent and lies with the side that has the initiative, even if instantaneously only. Doctrine, training, size/numbers, tactics and weapons and platforms define both antagonists.

Fleet strengths, organizations and chains of command

The numbers and sizes of the ships are the most important issues. The number of a fleet allows tactical dispositions and dictates logistics, such as basing, communications and supplies. For the numbers of the Greeks, there is no scepticism. For the numbers of the Persians, contemporary scholarship has frequently proved sceptical (Tarn 1908; Hignett 1963; Shepherd 2010), but with few if any solid arguments and an abundance of adjectives and adverbs. Diodorus (Diod XI.3,7–8) and Herodotus (Her VII.89) provide the same total (**Table 12.3**), but with slight differences in contingents (Her VII.89–95; Diod XI.3,7–8), which implies different sources and thus a reliable cross-examination. The numbers of ships are easy to count (Lazenby 1993) and, regarding the Persian fleet, by no means enormous: the royal fleet is just double the standard number given for the Scythian expedition (Her IV.87), Lade (Her VI.9,1) and Marathon (Her VI.95,2); the latter two being theatre actions of local significance without the presence of the King. Given that Athens proper could field 200 ships and man 180 (Her VIII.1 & VIII.14; Plut Them 14) at the time and that the figure rose to 300 battle-ready at the beginning of the Peloponnesian War (Thuc II.13,8), any notion that the King of Kings at the zenith of the Persian power could not (or would not) assemble 4–6 times the figure, which depends largely on human and currency resources, is unpersuasive.

The chain-of-command and organization of the two fleets are seldom substantiated: the naval engagement off Sciathos (Her VII.179) shows that the Imperial fleet used flights of 10 vessels; the Allied fleet might have used sub-flights of three, as in said skirmish, and this is supported by the report of 127 Athenian triremes to Artemisium (Her VIII.1) to be supplemented by 53 (Her VIII.14). The three vessels, which would have made both numbers round, might have been somehow engaged and no substitute could be found to round things up. Furthermore, 120 instead of 127 or 130 Athenian vessels would have been the obvious deployment at Artemisium as it would have satisfied the 2/3 expeditionary rule. The Decree of Troezen provided for 100 vessels and a reserve of the other 100, obviously drawing from a total of 200 vessels (Jameson 1960). Just 80 Athenian-manned and the 20 manned by the Chalcidians – an exact match to the manpower represented by the Athenian settlers at Chalcis (Her V.77,2) – would have satisfied the vote; but the Athenians overdid it. Sending all their fleet to Artemisium means that they turned the expeditionary quota to full levy. There is no indication of how and why this had happened; but it offers an explanation for their belief that the Peloponnesians had already done the same and thus they had good reasons to expect that the full levy of the Peloponnesian army was in Boeotia (Her VIII.40,2). This justifies their feeling of betrayal, at least up to a point.

The Allies had state fleets that dispatched contingents to the Allied expeditionary fleet. A weird number for squadron strength, the 30, appears for the Allies (Aesch Persai 339–40). This is quite a surprise as many Allied fleets and Allied contingents to the confederate fleet (Her VIII.1 & VIII.43–46) were not divisible by 30, and the same was true with the 50-strong fleet of Athens before Themistocles; one vessel furnished by each attic Naucraria (Poll Onom VIII.108; Tarn 1908). Further down the chain of command, a flight of 10 for the Allies should be assumed, with one flagship and three sub-flights. For the Imperials, the squadron of 15 vessels under Sandoces (Her VII.194), even an ad hoc one, rather implies sub-flights of five vessels. This agrees with the standard decimal system, supplemented by a subordinate binary one in each echelon.

The Allied fleet had one Chief Admiral, Eurybiadas, functioning as Commander-in-Chief, and a Board of Admirals from the different contributing states, each commanding his state's contingent and being answerable to its government and civic body. Decision-making must have lain with the Board; once a decision was reached, the Chief Admiral issued executive orders and the Board functioned as a General Staff (Shepherd 2010).

Although many see Themistocles as the real commanding authority (Diod XI.12,4; Holland 2005; Shepherd 2010), this must be rejected outright (Rados 1915); the Allies had not decreed unanimously against an Athenian Chief Admiral (Her VIII.2), despite the 200 Athenian ships, only to obey him under some pretext. This is pro-Athenian propaganda. But as the commander of the largest contingent, Themistocles carried a most important opinion in the Board of Admirals, weighing much more than any other or, perhaps, all the others together. He might also have been Chief of Operations (and this would be a far more plausible interpretation of Diod XI.12,4), as Eurybiadas might have been a good tactician (at the very best), but his lack of seamanship made him incapable of understanding the actual practicalities of a tactical plan, such as currents, depths, winds, crew endurance etc.

Although the Athenians were the largest contingent by far and (most of) their vessels were brand-new and built for speed and agility (Plut Vit Cim 12,2), they had no previous experience nor any record to date. Thus, when Herodotus remarks that the topic of small talk in both fleets had been the Athenians (Her VIII.10), the event should be taken with a pinch of salt. Had the Athenians been considered a worthy opponent, the Imperials would not brag about who would be the first to assault and capture an Athenian vessel, to get a reward from the King of Kings (ibid), but who would capture an Athenian vessel, period – or sink it. The prospect of capture initially shows the preferred assault option of the Imperials, but also that they thought less of the Athenians than usual (Her VIII.10). After all, the Ionians probably had not forgotten their treason and desertion after the battle of Ephesus, in 499 BC (Her V.103) and everybody thought of them as arrogant newcomers in the arena of sea-fights with massive fleets.

The chain-of-command of the Imperial fleet is more complicated. Its admiralty was made of four men, all Persians, practically District Admirals; Herodotus reports they were heading specific contingents, though he provides such information for only two (Her VII.97). The Imperial fleet of 1207 ships divided by 4 admirals means 4 District Naval Commands of 300 ships, more or less. Usual Expeditionary Fleets, as in Scythia, Marathon or Lade, were merges of two such commands for a usual strength of 600 vessels (Her IV.87 & VI.95,2 & VI.9,1). In Xerxes' invasion there is no sign of the existence of such an echelon, to have the Imperial fleet divided into two Expeditionary Fleets, each of two District Naval Commands. Alternatively, it is conceivable that the Imperial fleet is *always* made up of 4 District Naval Commands, no matter its ceiling; the latter is defined by the mobilization level. Thus for the campaigns against Scythia (circa 515 BC) and Athens (490 BC),

Darius might have mobilized all his naval districts but to a lesser degree, to an output of 600 vessels, while Xerxes doubled the quota. Contrarily, for the campaign against the Ionians, only the available District Naval Commands had been mobilized, since Ionia was in rebellion. As a result the ceiling of the Imperial fleet depended both on the districts mobilized and on the degree of the mobilization.

The possibility of additional District Naval Commands (Tarn 1908) is somewhat appealing, but unsubstantiated. The standard Imperial decimal system is perfectly satisfied with a grand total of 10 top-echelon slots, 6 for the Army and 4 for the Navy (the Army being the principal and national branch) while 5 District Naval commands would tip this fine balance.

Each of the District Naval Commands is made up of ethnic/local contingents, in strict territorial format (Tarn 1908) and divided further to standard squadrons of 100 vessels and flights of 10 vessels as noted before, possibly with some echelon in between (50 or 30 vessels). Echelons based on 5 (sub-flights of 5 ships, half-squadrons of 50) would be in perfect harmony with the land army structure, with a binary division of each successive decimal echelon. Any assembly of echelons, usually over squadron level, comprise task forces of variable size, as the 200 ships sent against Samos under Megabates and Aristagoras (Her V.32), or the 200 ones sent round Euboea (Her VIII.7,1; Diod XI.12,3); incidentally, this corroborates the secondary, binary structure model already mentioned. Decimal echelons are not only divided into two subgroups, but also grouped by twos.

In Mycale, in 479 BC, Herodotus assigns 300 Persian ships to a triumvirate of admirals (Her IX.130), implying 100 per command, and lack of a District Admiral, as the one in charge of the District Naval Command of Ionia had perished at Salamis (Her VIII.89 and VII.97) and might have not been officially replaced as yet; obviously the most senior of the three commanders was Acting District Admiral.

Strangely, Herodotus does not provide the name of the District Admiral of the Phoenician fleet and even weirder is that he considers High Admiral the commander of the Egyptian contingent, Achaemenes (Her VII.236), brother of Xerxes and one of the 4 District Admirals. Neither his ships (possibly enhanced by another contingent to reach the 300 prescribed for a District Naval Command) nor the capabilities or the dependability and past service record of his subjects qualify for this honour and responsibility. It might have been the pro-Egyptian bias of Herodotus (possibly due to his Egyptian sources) or a clear case of Achaemenid nepotism.

Diodorus' candidate for High Admiral (Diod XI.12,2) is Megabates, without any notion of collective admiralty and joint command. The name is wrong, belonging to either the father or a son of Megabazus. He was one of the four District Admirals (Her VII.97) and is a much better candidate for High Admiral. He was possibly the grandson of the notorious general of Darius who subjugated Thrace (Her V.2 & V.10) and son of Megabates, the commander of the Imperial army who attacked Naxos to no avail in 500 BC with Aristagoras (Her V.32), himself a cousin of Xerxes (ibid). Assigning to him the admiralty of the Phoenician District Naval Command, a homogenous and superb force (Her VII.96) seems logical, but his kin is based for two generations at Dascylium (Her VI.33,3 & IV.144,3); from this area come 160 vessels, 60 Aeolian and 100 Hellespontine (Her VII.95) having nothing to do with Phoenicia. On the other hand, his excellent knowledge of the area and his family being implicated in the dig of the Athos channel (Her VII.22,2), the annexation of Macedon (Her V.21,2) and the Imperial project in Europe ever since the failure of the Scythian campaign make him uniquely eligible to command the best Naval District and lead the invasion fleet. The naval contingents of his satrapy would be under the direct command of a lesser family member or associate; (as was the case with Masistes, satrap of Bactria, who was Marshal and so his brother Hystaspes led the army contingent of the satrapy. The same would be the case with the land forces of the satrapy, as it was furnishing both sea and land elements. The separation of contributions was applicable at the city level rather than the satrapy level; the satrapy of Egypt furnished the Ethiopian and Libyan army units and the Egyptian fleet.

A very important fact is that there was no Admiral-in-Chief, as was Eurybiadas in the case of the Greeks, no matter how loosely and conditionally. The same goes for the land army; no one of the six Marshals was assigned supreme commander. Achaemenes, according to Herodotus, and Megabates/Megabazus according to Diodorus are High Admirals and *acting* Admirals-in-Chief; the notion of decisions taken by the Persian *Admirals*-plural (Her VIII.15,1 & 107,1) suggests exactly this lack of one head, the Chief Admiral. This is due to the presence of Xerxes, who was *Karana*, that is Supreme Commander, as he commanded the proceedings, the preparations and the conduct of the fight (Her VIII.107,1), an arrangement proven fatal at Salamis. Due to distance he had delegated authority to his admirals but had not forfeited it.

The account of Diodorus of the battle of Salamis, which mentions Cyprian, Cilician, Lycian and Pamphylian ships (Diod XI.19) trying to enter the fray in the wake of the Phoenicians, may be indicative of another District Naval Command, following that of Phoenicia, preceding the one of Ionia, comprised of the vessels of the above mentioned areas, with a notional strength of 330 vessels (Her VII.90–2) and attributable by default to Prexaspes, the fourth District Admiral. Additionally, the order is the one found in Herodotus VII.889–92 (Lazenby 1993); except the Egyptians who were guarding the north-west pass. This most probably indicates an actual order of seniority within the Imperial fleet but this order may not have been linear; Phoenicia was no 1, but whether Ionia, Caria etc. preceded or followed Cyprus, Cilicia etc. and the seniority of the Naval District of Egypt, under the King's brother, cannot be deduced.

In effect, the Persian Imperial default would have dictated organizing standardized divisions in the naval sector as well, to create four naval commands of 300 vessels (Her VII.97), by brigading together different contingents. This approach would readily brigade the Egyptians with the Cilicians, as the sum would be 300 vessels. That would leave the Carian contingent to be brigaded with Cypriots, Lycians and Pamphylians (Her VII.89–95).

Still, managerial and command difficulties due to strength differences in District Naval Commands would be counterbalanced by an improved cohesion offered by relaxing the standardization and promoting the local and kin issues when brigading fleets and squadrons. Keeping the Carians with the Greeks would swell this naval district to 360-odd, and the Cilicians being with their neighbours would result in a naval district of 350 vessels, leaving the Egyptian fleet alone and the naval district understrength (Her VII.89–95). This could be amended later on, by adding all later musters to this command (Her VII.185,1), possibly while at Therma. This approach would undermine the cohesion of only one Naval Command, and since Ariabignes is mentioned as the Admiral of the Ionian and Carian fleet (Her VII.97), the second arrangement most probably had been opted for and put into effect. But the massive casualties off Sepias (Her VII.190,1) must have resulted in reshuffling and the newcomers would be re-delegated to make good some of the casualties. Such action would have been postponed until the rendezvous with the army at Alus or Pagassai, where major reform and corrective actions would be possible in safety, but the Greek attacks off Artemisium hindered such intentions till after the conclusion of the engagements.

Vessels, Crews, Marines and Methods of Engagement

The vessels

The main warship in the Persian wars was the trireme. It is unclear when it became standard in Greek fleets, as it had been invented three centuries earlier in Corinth (Thuc I.13,2–3), but the preferred warship remained for most of that time the 50-oar 'pentekonter' (Thuc I.14,1–2) *and* an elusive 'long ship' mentioned by Thucydides in juxtaposition with the pentekonter (ibid). It might have been a bireme; such designs are seen in Greek pottery and are smarter, lower and much more elegant than the Phoenician model but never referred to in classical-era texts recounting naval battles.

Truth be told, one trireme was very expensive to build and operate. It had to be light and thus was not adequately watertight, nor protected from rotting,

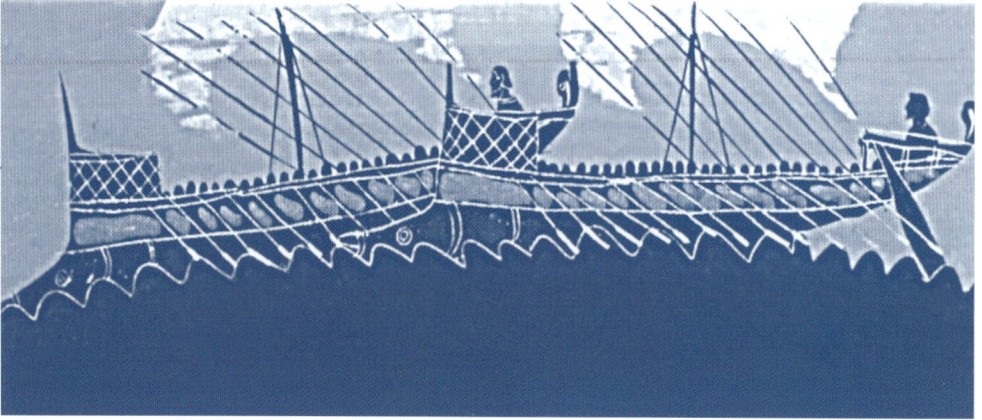

Fig. 11.1. Greek Pentekonters.

compared to pentekonters. The planking of the latter may have been treated with lead for water-tightness, anti-rotting and mechanical strength during beaching. The trireme absorbed manpower enough for a bit less than four pentekonters in terms of rowers and social reasons might have previously frustrated investments into trireme fleets; at least until Samian rebels in triremes bruised the pentekonters of the navy of their tyrant Polycrates (Her III.44,2–45,2), showing the power of the trireme (Hale 2009). Conceivably, the pentekonter navy was in essence private (Haas 1985), much like the English fleets under Elizabeth and the Christian fleets of the sixteenth century participating in the Mediterranean War against the Ottomans. In this context, the shipwrights' tradition of Corinth may be seen in a more modern sense: expensive, export designs were developed for filthy-rich users,

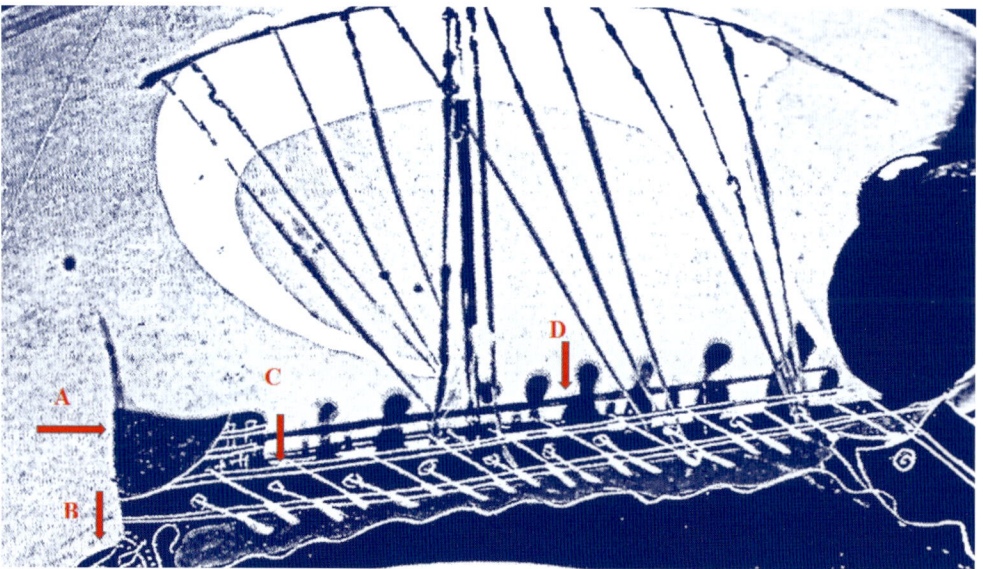

Fig. 11.2. Greek Bireme.

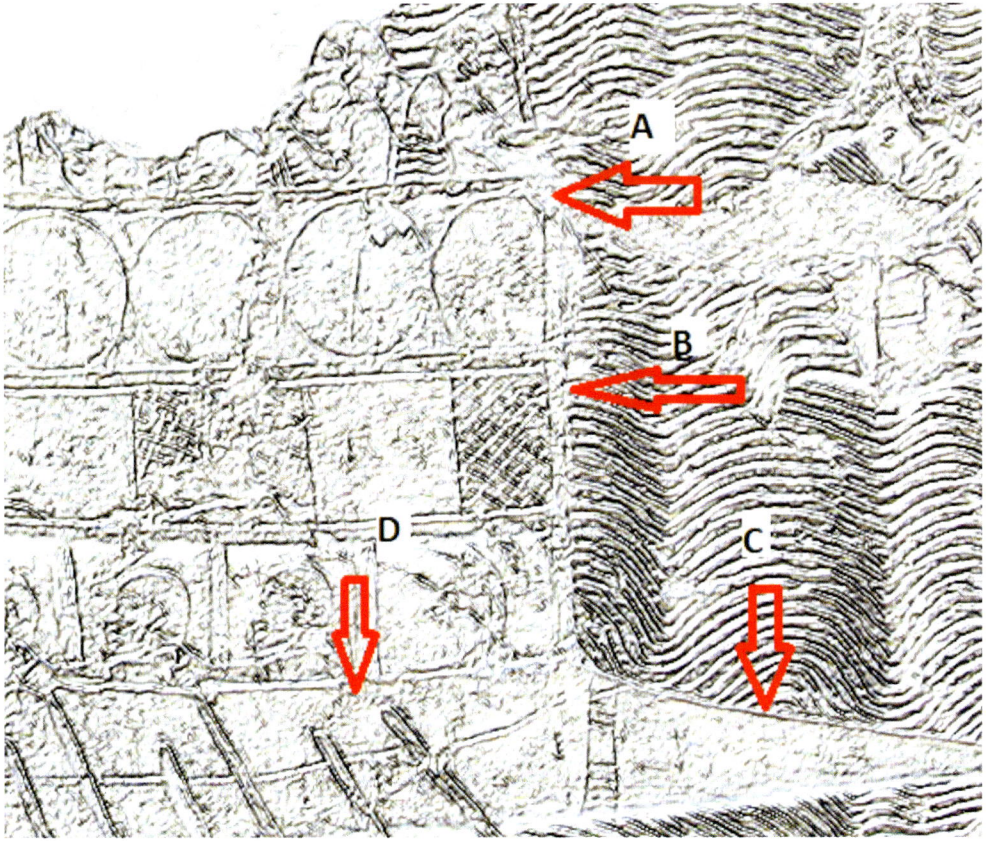

Fig. 11.3. Phoenician Bireme.

Fig. 11.4. Greek Trireme.

usually suggesting regimes of tyrants (Thuc I,13,3) with its own colonies, as the ones in Sicily (Thuc I.14,2) enjoying priority in deliveries and perhaps lower prices and some kind of offsets.

In this line of thought, it is a matter of conjecture whether the Athenians built 100 (Plut Vit Them 4) or 200 triremes (Her VII.142–3) in two to four short years. The lower figure (Tarn 1908) allows for at least 50 more triremes built under the revamped but practically ancient Athenian system of the Naucraria (Haas 1985) and another 50 unaccounted for but possibly insinuated as a continuation of the original programme due to the eminence of the threat (Her VII.144). The version speaking of 200 new triremes obviously considers the previously operated vessels obsolete, possibly pentekonters, and written off in due time, as the Athenians had difficulty to man even the 200 new vessels, which required 40,000 rowers and 2,000 marines. These were conscripted from a citizen body estimated at 30,000 one generation earlier (Her V.97,2) but possibly already expanded, plus a more massive body of Metoics/resident aliens attracted by the development of Piraeus. Additionally, when the need became dire, underage males, under 18, may row pretty well (Tarn 1908) and earn the subsidy to support a poor family.

The number 200 must be preferred for newbuilds; with 100 newbuilds there could have been no Athenian fleet of 180–200 triremes, as their previous navy was 50-strong. The legacy, obsolete hulls might have been allocated to secondary roles. One might have been a Home Fleet for the protection of home shores when the expeditionary fleet was away; another might have been the supply of vessels to close allies to man (Green 1970), such as the Plataeans and the Chalcidians. Still, there is no mention or insinuation of reserve squadrons over the 180 manned vessels for the Athenian navy nor any indication for ships delegated entirely to Plataeans, most unfamiliar with the sea (Her VIII.1,1), contrary to the reporting of vessels supplied to the Chalcidians (Her VIII.1,2). In such a context, using these older vessels as replacements for casualties might be a valid guess, as it explains the miracle of the Athenian fleet being, in Salamis, of the same strength as the fleet of Artemisium; though additional, not necessarily exclusive, proposals, have been suggested and are discussed later.

In some cases, Herodotus might have mistaken ships of the line in general for triremes. He does not do so for the Second Persian War, where he mentions separately triremes and pentekonters, or for events of the mid-sixth century – the early days of Polycrates of Samos (Her III.39, 3) and the migration of the Phocaeans (Her I.164). But between the Persian ascendancy in Asia Minor and Marathon, there might have been some confusion and uncertainty.

According to Herodotus, the triremes were used by all implicated parties. It is not self-evident that the Phoenicians made the jump from pentekonters

(**Figure 11.1**) to triremes; it is almost certain that the evolution had gone through the bireme, a type also used by the Greeks and shown on pottery (**Figure 11.2**). The extremely awkward and high-decked galleys seen at the bas relief from the Palace of Sennacherib at Nineveh (**Figure 11.3**) are biremes: they feature a very high troop platform/Upper Deck (**A**); almost vertical prow profile (**B**); pointed ram (**C**) and two banks of oars (**D**). One may compare the corresponding figures of a Greek bireme (**Figure 11.2 D, A, B, C** respectively).

Any notion that these Phoenician galleys *might* be triremes because there *could* be a third row, somehow not illustrated by the artist (Fields 2007) is absurd, unsubstantiated and meant to bolster the perhaps prejudiced reference of Clement of Alexandria (an ardent Christian bishop with inclination to forced indoctrination and profoundly anti-Greek) that the trireme was a Phoenician invention (Clem Strom I.16,76). This is the sole indication currently referenced for a Phoenician origin of the trireme, as there is no representation in Phoenician art. It still seems to be accepted by some scholars (i.e. Lazenby 1993; Fields 2007) to the point of creating a consensus on the subject (Rees 2018) with no shred of evidence.

There are at least two separate source lines on the evolution of the trireme, for the Greek one (**Figure 11.4**): Thucydides' (mainly but not exclusively in Thuc I.13) and Plutarch's. The former focuses on the Athenian navy and the disputing of its thalassocracy (maritime empire) by the Corinthians (mid- to late-fifth century BC). Plutarch, on the other hand, focuses on early Athenian triremes in the Lives of Themistocles and Cimon (early to mid-fifth century BC). Plutarch's testimony, although far later in temporal terms, is much more explicit. He specifically says that the Athenian triremes of the era of Themistocles were smaller than the Imperial ones (Plut Vit Them 14) and that the Athenian triremes of the Persian Wars were smaller, not so stoutly built and without the planking armour and high troop-carrying capacity of the later model developed under the oversight of Cimon (Plut Vit Cimon 12,2).

This 'armoured' trireme of Plutarch's should be identified with the Lenormant relief (**Photo 11.1**), which shows a superstructure of planking and supports. The planking protected the rowers from the sun and incoming high-arc missiles while accommodating many troops for assault, boarding and firing (shooting) from a height; it was a convergent evolution towards the biremes in the Palace of Nineveh. Even more to the point, the description fits well with the trireme 'Olympias'. The latter is an interesting but clearly miscarried effort to rebuild a trireme (Morrison & Coates 1986), as it has nothing smart, elegant or light and looks more like a hybrid of the trireme and sturdy medieval designs, such as the *Caravel*. This awkward design can only be the upper, sea-deck of Cimon's new, armoured triremes (Thuc I.14,3; Plut Vit Cimon 12,2). Actually, 'Olympias' (**Photo 11.2**) resembles the Korean

Photo 11.1. Processed image of the Lenormant relief. The red arrow shows the supports of the sea deck planking (yellow arrow).

Geobukseon (turtle ships) of the fifteenth century (Bryan 2013) or the converted flat-tops of the Second World War; the latter were aircraft carriers built by converting hulls intended for other ship types, such as battleships, cruisers or commercial/cargo vessels, with the Japanese *Soho* being a perfect example (Brown 1977).

In the first years of the Peloponnesian war, the 100 triremes of an Athenian task force carried in one case 1,000 Hoplites and 400 archers, a 10+4 composition per ship (Thuc II.23,2), exactly as many as the decree of Troezen sanctioned. In another case, a similar armada carried 4,000 Hoplites and 300 cavalry (Thuc II.56,2), meaning 10 horse transports (modified older triremes) for mounts and riders and 90 line vessels for 4,000 Hoplites, some 45 Hoplites per vessel. Still, it was these bigger, stouter triremes which had been so manoeuvrable and fast that, when governed by competent helmsmen and powered by disciplined oarsmen, gained the sea dominance. The lighter ones, of the Persian War, designed for speed and agility, may have been neither bigger, nor higher than the Imperial ones, despite concerted efforts with no arguments or weak ones to support such a case (Rees 2018 and Lazenby 1993 respectively). There is not one such ancient source cited in the modern scholarship; not one case of a Greek trireme being mentioned as higher or larger or longer by any measure. The Greek word 'heavier' used by Herodotus, for anyone who ever has been aboard a wooden craft, is NOT tantamount to larger size nor to construction mass; it *may* imply each, or both, or something else.

Moreover, it is not certain that all triremes of the same era were the same in design, as occasionally maintained (i.e. by Rees 2018) or in anything else. The design of the fast and massively produced Athenian ones might have originated in Ionian, probably Milesian or Samian shipyards, with refugee shipwrights finding a prospect of livelihood in Athens, possibly but not necessarily through

Photo 11.2. The HN trireme Olympias as reconstructed during the 80s. Its sea deck offers protection from sun, rain, droplets/sea spray and high-arc missile fire; it allows troop movement from prow to stern so as to repel enemy boarding along the full length of the hull, affords a higher level for missile fire and fits well with the description of the triremes as redesigned by Cimon after the defensive phase of the Persian Wars. (Photo: **Hellenic Navy**, retrieved 7 Jul 2020 @ https://www.hellenicnavy.gr/en/history-tradition/ships-museum-exhibits/trireme-olympias.html)

intermediaries in Western Greece. This might explain the very detailed knowledge of the Greeks, both Themistocles and Eurybiadas, on the specifics of the Persian naval practices which resulted in staging massive surprises, especially in Artemisium. The Persians and their proxies had never – or only seldom – fought with a Greek fleet from the mainland, much less with an Athenian one, as it did not exist before Xerxes' invasion.

At the times of the great friendship and understanding between Athens and Corinth (Her VI.89), poised to sap or obliterate the Aeginiteans, staunch commercial competitors of the latter, a Corinthian connection for the Athenian fleet might have occurred. After all, the shipbuilding programme of Athens was officially directed against Aegina (Her VII.144,1) and this probably qualified for Corinthian support and help. In such a case, the triremes of the Allied Greek states could have been identical or similar, stemming from the same Corinthian pedigree of early eighth-century BC; Thucydides, who hated the Corinthians as did every Athenian of his age, would have jumped at any other lineage projected for the advent of the trireme, as the supposed Phoenician one; but he reluctantly accepts the Corinthian line and in detail, too (Thuc I.13,2–3). Depending on the interpretation of the Greek wording, the above passage may well be attributing the design of the trireme to them, NOT just the construction of the first Greek triremes as occasionally proposed (Fields 2007).

But the Imperial ships are another issue altogether. The story of the ships being built by the King and manned by the subjects (Diod XI.3,7; Her V.95,1) supports a standardized design, especially for the contingents that were less current to such endeavours, as were the Egyptians. In years past, contingents and fleets might have been conscripted provisionally from naval subject states, as in the case of Cambyses (Her III.19) and Otanes, the latter commandeering vessels from the friendly tyrant of Lesbos (Her V.26). But the preparation of the invasion most probably allowed, favoured or even dictated, standardized ships.

Still, this could not have been universal. Different shipwrights, or rather shipwright guilds of different areas use and develop different standards (Hale 2009). It is not the quality of construction, or of the crews that made the Phoenician vessels renowned. Nelopoulos (1999) proposes that the Phoenician vessels were not triremes but biremes, better for seakeeping due to higher beam-to-length ratio (Wood 2013), evolved from the ones shown in the bas relief of the Palace of Sennacherib in Nineveh. Plutarch clearly implies in successive passages that the Phoenician ships are excessively big, large and high (Plut Vit Them 14) but modern scholarship (i.e. Rados 1915) scorns him, probably as being affected by different Roman traditions and stereotypes. Still, the arguments and events as presented by Plutarch are fully compatible with the narration of Herodotus, who had no such bias (Diodorus might have had) and with common sense: the Imperial vessels had boarding parties of 30 central Asian troops, PLUS any marines from their national contingents (Her VII.184). The latter were at least 10 men, the lowest unit in the Imperial army, but this is the low limit; there could have been more, at least in some contingents.

The Athenian vessels had only 18 marines (Plut Vit Them 14). The Hoplite element amongst them, 14 in Salamis as recounted by Plutarch (ibid) despite just 10 provided for by the Decree of Troezen, are most probably the 20–30 age-class selected for agility, speed, endurance, reflexes and strength. It is the same age-class who made *the* Run at Marathon and, well-versed in Hoplitodromos, practised the Ekdromi (Sekunda 1986; Sekunda 2000; Kambouris 2022). Should the Imperial vessels have double the boarders AND be faster (Her VIII.10), it is logical that they were bigger, with more rowers (Morrison & Coates 2000).

Herodotus also mentions a Sidonian galley amounting to a 'royal ship/flagship' (Her VII.100 & 128) and there is no way Xerxes, his 'golden' tent and his security detail, plus any other officials and consultants, had been accommodated in the confines of a Greek-type trireme as we see them in the representations and estimating them by their hangars. A perfect reason for the Imperial ships to be larger than the Allied ones is the prestige factor. It is inherent in any empire, but the Persian Empire *adored* size, quantity and luxury. Quality was never neglected: Xerxes, or his staff, had the whole fleet beached at Doriscus, the keels cleaned, the hulls dried out, maintained and becoming watertight (Her VII.59; Morisson & Coates 2000). At the same time, the Greeks were needlessly patrolling in the Gulf of Pagassai, (Her VII.173,1) to intercept any possible Persian landing at the rear of their expeditionary army which had landed at Alus and advanced to Tempe Pass, to dig in (Her VII.173,1–2). The Greek fleet from that point could deny landings in the Gulf, especially near Pagassai and Alus, and possibly to Malis, which would cut off their army at Tempe. As Green (1970) noticed, the landing at Alus instead of Pagassai seems to imply that the former was safer ground, controlled by a non-medizing faction, possibly the ruling clan of Pharsalus. This clan became renowned for its support for Alexander the Great (Arr Anab III.11,10). Pagassai, at the territory of the third major city, Pherrai, was aligned with Larissa in Medizm. This operational plan seems intended to counter any Persian Marathon-type, autonomous amphibious operation *through* the Aegean. The Greek spies dispatched to Sardis (Her VII.16,1) had never set eyes on the Persian fleet (Green 1970) and the Greeks had no *actual* idea of its size and its intentions, at least not until it was tallied at Doriscus (Her VII.59,3), from where it assumed a coastal path along the land route (Her VII.121,2), making clear that its mission would be, at least primarily, to shadow the advance of the army and not to embark on independent, blue-sea operations.

Contrary to some suggestions (i.e. Fields 2007), drying and making the planking watertight is a time-consuming procedure and the Allies never had enough time to do it before or during the expeditionary season, as they had to be on high alert for any enemy motion with a scant intelligence margin. The time elapsed between the Greeks stationing their vessels, for example in Salamis, and the engagement was insufficient for such work. Thus, their vessels, even the newest ones, were waterlogged and slow, although at least the brand new Athenian ones were built for speed and manoeuvrability, more so than the later Athenian triremes designed under Cimon (Plut Vit Cimon 12.2), which were actually renowned for their speed and nimbleness (Aristoph Birds 108).

This is a very good explanation of the ambiguous statement of Herodotus (Her VIII.60) that the Greek ships were 'heavier' than the Persian ones (*all* the Imperial ships, not some or certain of them). This should be understood as 'slower', since manoeuvrability depends on the technical excellence of the captains and the kind of manoeuvre. Additionally, the next year, before Mycale, the vessels of the same Persian fleet (except for the Phoenicians) are mentioned as worse sailers than the known quantity of the Greek fleet (Her IX.90). There is no way this virtue is attributable either to sailors or any systemic parameters, such as design and quality of construction, as these cannot be inverted in a year for the very same fleets, crews and vessels. It must have been the water-tightness, which the Greeks had all winter to improve while the Imperials could not, as the fleet was in bad shape, partially neglected and on alert as the means to keep Ionia at peace and shy of any new rebellion (Her VIII.130).

Crew conscription and sustenance

And then there are the crews. The rowers had to be experienced and in good condition to be efficient and persistent, which means endurance is needed as much as strength. But the key issue was the synchronization and co-ordination. This required mass training in realistic conditions. Deck crew (*Hyperesia*) were minimal and probably professionals, or reservists from merchantmen, but the rowers (*Heretai*) were mostly lower-income, like the Athenian *Thetes*-citizens (Plut Vit Them 4,3) or foreign professionals (Xen Hell I.5,4) and would need sustenance. A fleet of triremes was expensive to build; the Athenians were able to build it due to the discovery of new veins at their silver mines (Plut Vit Them 4). But they were every bit as, if not even more, expensive to operate. Heavy taxation to the tune of extortion (actually protection money) was the trick during the next decades that enabled the Athenians (Plut Vit Arist 24) to man fleets. At the time, Themistocles followed or rather initiated the policy of extortion and receiving bribes to keep his fleet running after Salamis (Her VIII.111–112; Plut Vit Them 21), since the generous offers of the Athenian Aristocracy of the Areios Pagos council, which made the sea-battle possible (Arist Ath Pol XXIII.1; Plut Vit Them 10), were obviously exhausted. Herodotus mentions only the first source of sustenance; the second had been targeted and exterminated as a political body by Pericles and his associate, Ephialtes, shortly after the Persian War (Arist Ath Pol 24,1–2; Plut Vit Per 7). The vital donations of Areios Pagos might have been partly given under compulsion; the confiscation of large sums by the authorities during the first evacuation of the city (Plut Vit Them 10) would not have skipped the Aristocrats and might have been at the heart of the financial ruin of many well-to-do citizens who, out of bitterness, organized a coup and treason just before the battle of Plataea (Plut Vit Arist 13).

In times past, the sustenance of a crew and the maintenance of a ship was the task of a Naucraria; by 480 BC Herodotus seems to imply a nascent application of the semi-private concept of *trierarchia*; we hear explicitly of two Athenian ship commanders who were paying their crews by themselves and fighting as ship commanders. One is Architeles, who lacked the cash to pay his crew at Artemisium and thus wished to withdraw (Plut Vit Them 8); the other is Cleinias, a millionaire who sailed in a trireme fully manned and equipped at his own expense (Her VIII.17). The account of Aristotle (Ath Pol 22,7) for the funding arrangements for building the Athenian triremes supports such a notion, but Herodotus perhaps sees fit to silence the established practice *but* for the bloodline of Pericles.

There are two intriguing issues regarding the conscripted Athenian fleet, which monopolizes our interest as there are regrettably few sources and information on other Allied fleets. The one is the Plataeans; the other, the Chalcidians. The former are Boeotians, but Herodotus has explained already how they came to belong to the Athenian state (Her VI.108). They had always been true to their commitment, in Marathon (Her VI.108,1) and now with the fleet (Her VIII.1). Still, one must not make an issue out of nothing. They were vassals to the Athenian state, if not something less, as some scholars seem to think (Badian 1993) and *of course* they assembled to fight at Marathon; they were not allies, nor help, but part of the beleaguered state. It was the same in 480 BC; liking it or not, knowing how or not, they followed the rest of the Athenians – many of them not at all seafaring stock, especially the rural population of the central highlands – and manned the fleet. No wonders, nor heroes there.

The latter is a similar case. They are not Chalcidians; after a brief, victorious war the Athenians divided among themselves the land of the landowners of Chalcis; 4,000 Athenians received lots (Her V.77,2) and became eligible for Hoplite service. This colony some 20 years later sent a 4,000-strong contingent to Eretria and then to Marathon (Her VI.100,1 & 101,1). At the time of Artemisium, being part of the Athenian state, the Athenian landowners in Chalcis were manning the fleet, as did the whole of the male Athenian citizenry (Plut Vit Them 4) and Metoics (Jameson 1960) and, less probably, slaves as well. The exact figures regarding these troops and sailors are challenging; from a total of 4,000 able-bodied men who received lots and thus became Hoplites, the sum went to Eretria and Marathon twenty years later. Still, after ten more years, they obviously furnished 4,000–4,200 men, the minimum required for the manning of 20 triremes, crew and marines (Jameson 1960). It is more than probable that the 20 vessels reported by Herodotus was not a random number but their set contribution to be manned under a standing mobilization plan. Without assuming a thoroughly organized mobilization and training plan going at least two years back, when a considerable number of new triremes would have been delivered, while more were pending, the excellent performance in discipline and cohesion demonstrated by the Athenian fleet cannot be explained.

Sailing crews' status and comparison:
The competence of the crews is quintessential for the correct selection and effective execution of tactics and the implementation of operations and strategy. The massive

rowing effort indicates a subtle need for perfect timing and concurrency to avoid damage to the oars, to achieve maximum acceleration and perform about-turns. The need for human energy and endurance is much more obvious and such physically competent rowing bodies (*heretika* – singular *heretikon*) allow better exploitation of open space and calm waters.

But seafaring and seaworthiness goes further. In operational terms, navigation and weather-worthiness are paramount; the Imperial fleet, although NOT the Phoenician squadrons, was found wanting in both. In a tactical and technical context, the steering with temporal and positional accuracy was, is, and will always be, paramount and it makes the difference in straits and shallows (Delbruck 1920). The intimate knowledge of distance, currents, depths and gusts of wind, the seasonal and daily or hourly differentiation and intensity are also factors of seaworthiness, valuable for action in confined waters. In all these factors there is not one instance of the invaders, ANY of the invaders, being better performers than the Greeks.

As a matter of fact, in previous engagements and confrontations the Imperial squadrons and fleets had unimpressive performance and showed no superiority of any kind compared to Greek navies. Thus there is no ground for conjecturing any Phoenician naval superiority in terms of deck crews and captains. There is no record of high seas sailing; nocturnal operations ended in disaster, weather perception was poor at the very least and the naval tradition and experience factor is overestimated, especially by historians biased by the Roman stereotype, which was based on the notorious Roman discomfort with the sea element. Still, that did not impede them from conquering in most naval battles and, ultimately, winning the sea war against the Carthaginians.

A reality check is most illuminating and telling: Herodotus' Artemisia says that the Greeks are far better at sea than the Imperial fleet – *not* than the Persians proper. This is true at the time of Herodotus' public performance, with the Athenian thalassocracy. But this by no means proves it was not so during/before the Persian Wars. It is a common belief that the Phoenicians negotiated vast and tricky seas and did that by sailing mid-sea, not by coastal routes and did so for quite some time to accumulate experience and tradition, contrary to the Greeks.

Even the Athenians, though, whose fleet was new-built, had practised intensive seafaring for more than a century. By Solon, they started exporting goods to Italy, and Themistocles massively increased this direction in the Athenian economy (Green 1970). The poisonous exchanges of the latter with the Corinthian Adeimandos show only a bitter actual antagonism of trade interests between two former friends and allies (Her VI.89); selling war galleys for five days' wages each (ibid) is speaking for itself for previous times of cordiality.

But the Athenians were half the fleet. The other Greeks were negotiating the Black Sea, where Phoenicians never ventured; they also sailed to the East, Central and West Mediterranean. To reach Massilia and the other colonies in the West Mediterranean, coastal sailing would not do. From southern Italy to the southern French coast and the Mediterranean Spanish coast, there were only hostiles: the Etruscan coast, and the Carthaginian outposts in Corsica and Sardinia. How thus were the Greeks sailing and trading in the west (the Atlantic coasts included) if not by mid-seas navigation?

In terms of seamanship, there is absolutely no indication for Phoenician – or Imperial, in general – superiority, as often suggested (Rados 1915, Fields 2007, Shepherd 2010). Rowers' stamina and endurance is another issue and their performance in battle, after repeated prolonged challenges both in Artemisium (gales, daily travel and then surprise attack) and in Salamis (all day and night standing by at the oar before day-long engagement) is commendable; as it is for the whole of the Imperial fleet. The advantage in open seas shows no superior seamanship; simply more and faster ships, possibly with higher rowing stamina and efficiency. But agility and manoeuvrability and in general dexterity is shown in closed and confined waters, and the more numerous and most recently built Greek contingent, the Athenian, comprised vessels built for agility by Themistocles' deliberation (Plut Vit Cimon 12.2; Morrison & Coates 2000).

There are some scholars, especially modern ones, who consider the Egyptians similarly a superior seafaring contingent. Till the time of Xerxes, the Egyptians by themselves had only twice built a fleet, under Sesostris (Her II.102) possibly Senusret III of the twelfth dynasty and under Necos II (Her II.159), which is very understandable as there is no suitable timber in Egypt; timber had to be imported from Lebanon. If Egypt had anything to do with seafaring, the Egyptian name for the sea would not have been the Great Green (Ward 2012), as some miles out of *any* coast, the sea in the Mediterranean is blue. Nor would they have tolerated the trade city of Naucratis, nor foreigners in their ports implementing the transport part of the Egyptian sea trade (Her II 178).

Inefficiency in terms of seaworthiness should be presumed in the ranks of Xerxes' Greeks – especially the Ionians. Their effective trade reservists being exterminated in the Ionian Revolt but for the Samians, their commerce was decaying even before the revolt; a fact possibly fostering the revolt proper. There is no need to assume any difference under Xerxes; thus rowers and deck crews had the qualities and skills acquired under training and practice for the mobilizations against Egypt and Greece, practically less than a 6-year effort, which is not negligible but has nothing to do with the insinuated long seafaring experience of days past.

Tactics, fighting style and weaponry

At the time there were two fully-developed ways of sea battle, which were not mutually exclusive; they could be combined or expanded and modified. The first method was the boarding, the second was the ramming. Boarding could be inferred in Egyptian accounts of naval battles (or, rather, riverine battles) and definitively by Thucydides, who considers it the 'Old Way' (Thuc I.49,1–3). A spinoff, defined as the use of troops aboard armed with standard land battle weaponry, was the assault with massive archery and possibly with other ranged weapons either from the shore or from a vessel carrying enough missile troops to create a barrage (Humble 1980). The victim, ideally incapacitated from a standoff distance, was made susceptible to ramming, or an easy prey for boarders. This had been the Egyptian choice in the riverside battle of the Delta of the twelfth century BC, where Rameses III prevailed against the Sea Peoples as commemorated in the Medinet Habu reliefs. Arrows, as used by the Imperials against Acropolis after the fall of Athens (Her VIII.52) have not been mentioned in such capacity, but they were a plausible risk and an excellent reason never to venture to battle on sail, or even with sails onboard (Xen Hell II.1,29; Thuc VII.24,2). Javelins were less an issue than arrows, but an issue nevertheless (Her VIII.90; Thuc I.49,1), especially when there was a dynamic advantage (as when cast from higher Imperial decks) and in any case, the Imperials were much better prepared for this kind of fight.

The four archers onboard Athenian vessels (Plut Vit Them 14) were almost certainly Cretan mercenaries (Rados 1915), by the account of Ctesias (Llewellyn-Jones & Robson 2009). The notion against such pedigree (Pritchard 2018) because the Cretans decided not to assist the mainlanders against the Persians (Her VII.169 & 171) is ill-substantiated, as this reluctance refers to the Cretan city-states and by no means to individuals. Moreover, the timeframe of the commission might have been more permissive (Rados 1915), i.e. if taking effect before the embassies, the oracles and the rejection of overtures by the cities (Her VII.169). Mercenaries could have been hired from Crete and there was not one notion of vetoing or any reasoning for doing so by the Cretan states. Additionally, since archery needs practice for many years and the Athenians had neither time nor any propensity to encourage such developments, native archery at the time is not a believable alternative to the Cretan hypothesis, while the silence of the Decree of Troezen (Jameson 1960) on the subject of their conscription is telling. The Athenian triremes were manned according to the conscription catalogues, which were for rowers and Hoplites. Although the serving archers could have been recorded *somewhere*, for payroll purposes if nothing else, there is no indication or insinuation that the archers were on the conscription catalogues and thus Athenians in any sense.

On top of that, although Peisistratus, a supporter of the eastern/Black Sea trade (he promoted the Athenian control in the Hellespont), had probably used Scythian archers since the second half of the sixth century, after the demise of his line the straits to Euxine were in Persian hands. The communication of Athens with the Euxine had died out, and with it the import of grain. This was a valid reason for the western policy of Themistocles, evident by the names of his daughters (Plut Vit Them 32,3; Lazenby 1993); for example in naming a daughter 'Italy' Themistocles made his westward policy more than evident. As mentioned earlier, this shift predictably brought friction with Corinth. Thirty years after the fall of the Peisistratids, Scythian archers serving aboard the Athenian fleet (Shepherd 2010) is a gross historical error. The whole Skudra region of the Persian Empire and its vassals were keeping apart the recruiters and the source. Scythian archers were reintroduced during the mid-fifth century (Aeschin 2.172–3; Andoc 3.4–5).

Many, or all, of the 30 Iranian marines (Her VII. 184) were armed with the bow, although not exclusively, especially if they were cavalrymen and the notion of cavalry armed with both bow and javelin stands (Her VII.61,1 & 84). Compared to this force, the four archers onboard each Greek trireme was a joke, or rather a token archery force having only one realistic purpose: to snipe against enemy *hyperesia*, the Greek word for non-rower crew members, such as helmsmen, commanders and captains. Their objective then was to decapitate the command chain in control of both the boarders and the rowers, disrupt the sailing routine of an enemy vessel and expose it to assault by ramming rather than boarding.

Ramming: the choice of the brawler
Ramming aimed at sinking the enemy vessel by crashing onto it, prow first, so as the bronze-encased waterline ram would tear a breach in the enemy planking (Fields 2007); and, ideally, then backing to go for another target and allow the breach to flood. Rams might be identified within the context of the Ship Procession Fresco at Akrotiri, Santorini, in Minoan context before the first millennium BC and half

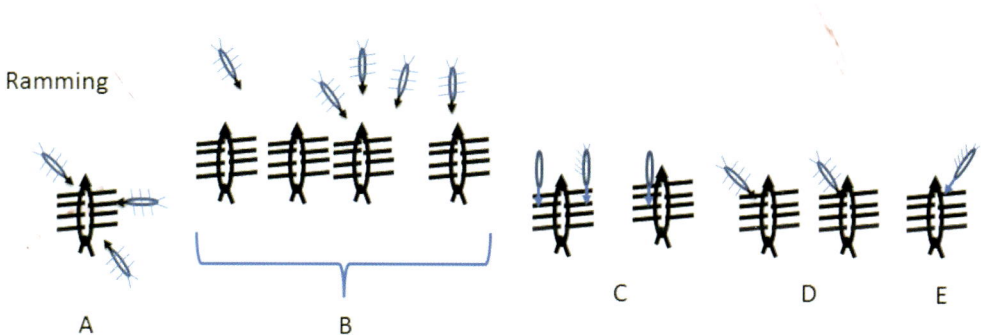

Fig. 11.5.

a millennium later in the land-locked Nineveh, in the bas relief of the Palace of Sennacherib, in Phoenician context (**Figure 11.3**) as already mentioned.

Ramming was most effective when delivered at the side, with the stern being the second choice (**Figure 11.5A**). A head-on ramming (**Figure 11.5B**) might entangle ships and then boarding might incur (Plut Vit Them 14), or the most fragile ship might shatter and possibly sink, but definitely be out of action (Thuc VII.34,5). Even if a vessel were not sunk after a ram attack (Fields 2007), it would be incapacitated by hull damage (Her VIII.90). But this was not necessarily so. A ram attack might hit but not penetrate, depending on kinetics, velocity, angle of impact and solidity of ram and target (Fields 2007). Two lines of enemy vessels in contact may ram, then reverse and then pick up speed to ram again, similar to battering rams. In these cases the surging effect would be important as the speed developed in this palindromic move may be insufficient. A threshold may have been 10 knots (Fields 2007), especially against stouter vessels and at non-ideal angles. This grinding business needed stamina and endurance, resulted in front-quarter ramming and favoured stouter designs with superior acceleration, not necessarily higher top speed. A struggle reminiscent of phalanx warfare, head-on ramming was taking a toll even from the winner and rams could be blunted or destroyed, thus disarming the vessel, as suffered by Greek pentekonters off Alalia (Her I.166).

Deployment was important: close order discouraged the opponent, presenting narrower arcs for ramming and aiming many more friendly rams to an enemy vessel. (**Figure 11.5B**). Too compact a formation, though, would jam the oars of nearby vessels and shorten the front line, thus denying the necessary margin for *Periplous'* own vessels and presenting respective opportunities to the enemy.

There is no real reason to follow the misconception of modern scholars (Shepherd 2010; Lazenby 1993) that ramming was a novel tactic, which is due to a literal interpretation of the Thucydidean account of the battle of Sybota (Thuc I.49,1–3), where boarding and missile-fire were the offensive methods of choice for both antagonists. The prominent rams of eighth and seventh century BC Phoenician biremes in the bas relief from the Palace of Sennacherib at Nineveh (**Figure 11.3**) are occasionally explained as cutwaters, which they are not, as they are very pointed. But Herodotus' account of the naval engagement of the Greeks against the Carthaginians and Etruscans off Alalia (Her I.166) clearly proves that ramming had been the main offensive tactic then and there, with pentekonters and thus at least ever since as the triremes were much better suited to it. Accordingly, the notion that since the trireme had been an eastern invention – which it was not, at least not by any coherent argument – the Greeks, who adopted it, were not as proficient in ramming (Lazenby 1993) does not stand, as the ram was not exclusive to the triremes, as noted above.

There is also a disagreement about the fate of a rammed ship: if both vessels remained entangled, they might sink together, but the usual result would have been a boarders' fight (Plut Vit Them 14). If all went smoothly and the victor reversed and retracted his ram, the breach would flood the victim. And then what? In Herodotus there is only an implication (Her VIII.96 and VIII.18); in Thucydides, it is clearly stated that rammed triremes even in open water were not sinking but towed (Thuc I. 50). The idea formed is that triremes, or at least some triremes, probably from specific manufacturers and implementing a certain design and set of specifications, after being rammed and abandoned, were too light to sink (Fields 2007); they drifted, half-sunk, and were possibly salvaged and reused with minor repairs. Still, Aeschylus narrates of the sinking of the Persian ships (Persai 415–20); Herodotus directly mentions one Imperial and one Athenian vessel that sank in Salamis (Her VIII.90 and VIII.87 respectively), both after ramming by Imperial ships, but the former sank with all hands on board.

A version of ramming was the attack against the oarage, which left the attacker unscathed (**Figure 11.5C, D**). Either by the ram or by the hull (**Figure 11.5C**), a fast and close passing by, with own oars retracted (Shepherd 2010) or folded parallel to the hull (Rados 1915) could shear off an enemy's row(s) of oars (Warry 1980; Montagu 2000). This would severely impair the target's mobility and expose it to any attack, ramming or boarding. A good skipper might even pass by, holding a course parallel to the enemy vessel but with the attitude of his trireme angled to the enemy. In this way, the ram and prow destroy or, at least, compromise the enemy oarage without need to retract one's own (**Figure 11.5D**) and thus retained speed and control of the vessel throughout the attack, while dealing a mobility kill.

Another dimension of collision dynamics is the destruction, or rather the degradation of outriggers, which severely compromised the mobility of a trireme. In this contest, a higher ship has a distinctive advantage as almost any colliding angle, short of receiving a clear, 90-degree ramming, leads to its hull smashing the lower vessel's outrigger (**Figure 11.5E**). A similar confusing situation might develop when one vessel goes parallel and close to the other to sear off its oars (Lazenby 1987). The more solidly built ship may smash the outrigger of the enemy, except when the height difference is considerable. In this case, the outriggers may pass one over the other and the taller vessel needs some slight lateral motion of its steering oars to smash the outrigger of the lower vessel. This dynamic analysis must be taken into consideration when one reads the account of Herodotus for the final battle of Artemisium, where half the Athenian ships are considered incapacitated for further action (Her VIII.18), but they easily sailed home at night and, obviously after being repaired, fought at Salamis.

Manoeuvring supreme

In this context, an agile and fast vessel would go for the vulnerable and exposed flanks of the enemy formation (*Periplous*) to deliver a mortal blow with impunity, with the least possibility of being boarded or entangled or to lose the ram (**Figure 11.6**). This was the standard Athenian tactic during their thalassocracy (Fields 2007, Montagu 2000, Whitehead 1987).

Thus, when one fleet reaches a flanking position it seizes the initiative and practically wins the battle. It is understandable that to assume a flanking position, a fleet must be either larger, to deploy into a longer line, or have faster, more agile vessels able to manoeuvre to the flanks of the enemy ships before being smashed head-on by a denser enemy line which would engage vessels with numerical superiority (**Figure 11.7**). In the latter case, backing water would help to stall the head-on decision until

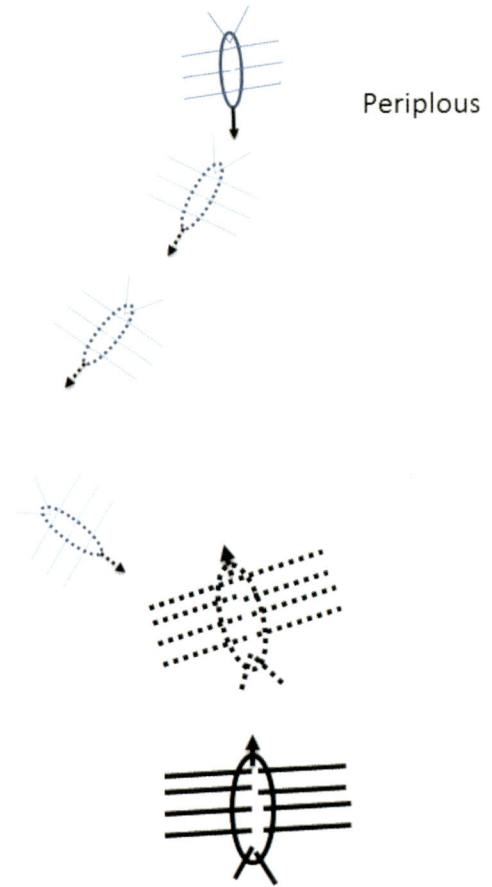

Periplous

Fig. 11.6.

Envelopment by
A: fastest vessels
B: Larger fleet

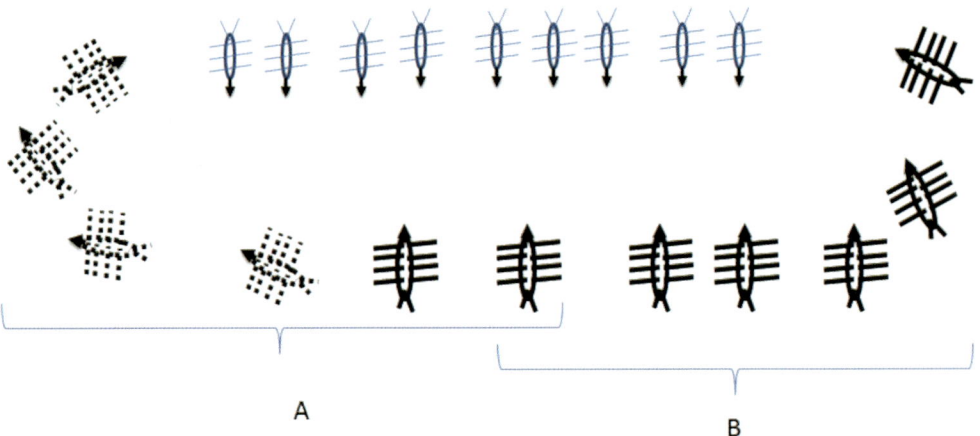

A

B

Fig. 11.7.

the flanking took effect, as happened in Marathon, in a land interpretation. Open water is advantageous for flanking in any practicable case (Whitehead 1987) and more so in a numerical imbalance, as by definition a more extended line had better options to envelope the enemy and bear upon each successive vessel from the side (Her VIII.16). Thus, open water would allow the fewer but faster ships to manoeuvre to flanking position, using their speed to overcompensate their smaller number (**Figure 11.7**). Additionally, in open water, the battle lines tend to be longer, with greater spaces between ships, and there the more agile ships may infiltrate and, turning faster, seize an angular advantage in a series

The Circle

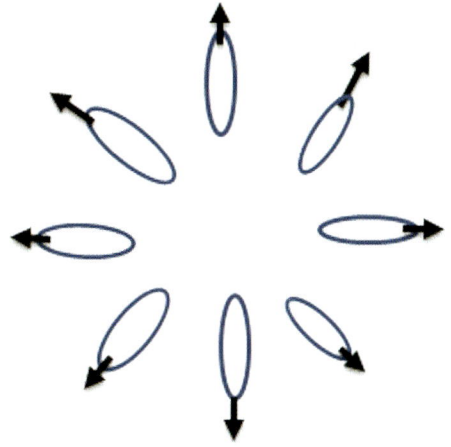

Fig. 11.8.

Diekplous

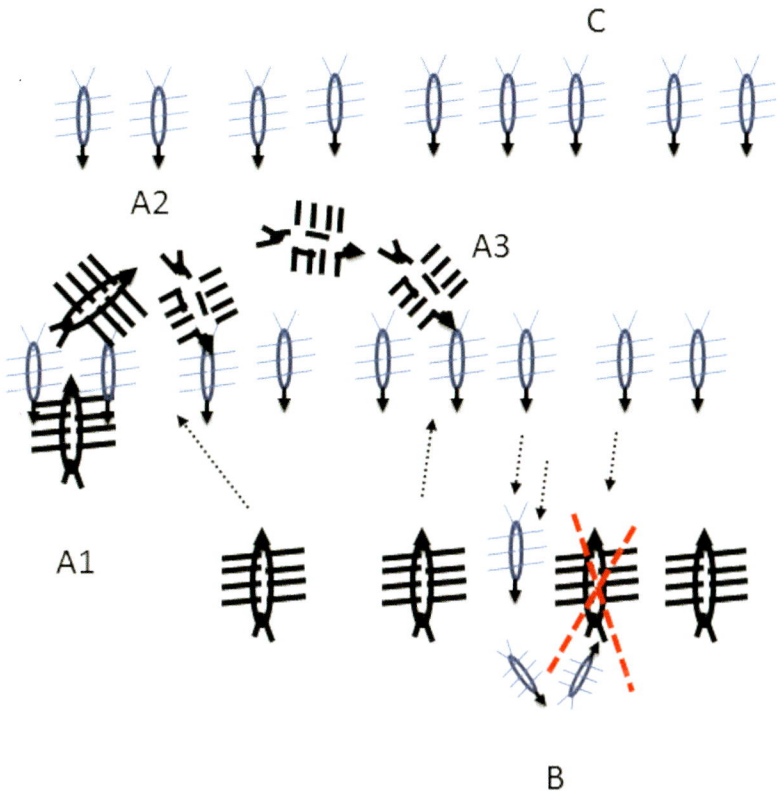

Fig. 11.9.

of ship duels so as to ram the side of the enemy vessels, most probably at an angle; the latter action may have been the paradigm for the *Periplous* (**Figure 11.6**) and demanded excellent steering and highly drilled rowers (Whitehead 1987).

Similar to land armies, fleets extended to achieve envelopment. This is why off Artemisium (see below) the Greeks formed a *Circle* (**Figure 11.8**) and Herodotus describes nothing other than a circle. If the Allies had formed a convex line (Shepherd 2010), even if the same numbers were engaged, the Imperials would have the same angular but longer linear distances and thus would take the flank of the smaller force faster. The Circle denies flanks and thus it is a natural defence for Periplous and flanking/envelopment; if tight enough, or if formed in a double format, as the Peloponnesian one at Naupactus (Thuc II.83,5–84,3) it denies Diekplous as well. Short of the Circle, anchoring the flanks on promontories or other land features (such as islets) and the demanding, bruising head-on ramming attack are the tactical answers to encirclement/flanking and Periplous. Or, at least, were, until the advent of Diekplous.

For the smaller force to be able to flank, a decisive mobility advantage was necessary, as already mentioned and vessel size did not matter. The paradigm is the naval battle of Naupactus where the faster and fewer vessels of Phormio tried to flank the Peloponnesian fleet (Thuc II.83,5–84,3). Speed was the most important issue, manoeuvrability the second. On the other hand, if one side had faster, more and bigger ships it would have an advantage in envelopment and Periplous due to the first two factors, and the size mattered in head-on brawling. If enough marines equalized the issue in terms of boarding and missile exchange, victory was almost a done thing. *Almost* a done thing, as the Imperials were to discover.

The equalizer

There was another tactical development to deliver smashing, ram attacks. It provided a definitive advantage to forces able to act independently and in packs, thus needed excellent training. But it allowed disastrous side and stern ramming without actual envelopment while still sparing boarding actions and high attrition of the rams. It was the *Diekplous* (Lazenby 1987; Fields 2007), most probably developed by Dionysius of Phocaea (Her VI.12,1) to counter larger numbers of enemy vessels carrying more boarders, or, definitely, more missile-armed boarders.

The Diekplous made fleet size irrelevant and vessel size as well. It allowed a smaller fleet to offer battle with flanks exposed or even encircled. It was about a swifter vessel acting independently and opportunistically (Lazenby 1987; Rankov 2017), not a column of vessels as some modern scholars suggest (i.e. Morrison & Coates 2000). It aimed at passing through the space between two enemy vessels line abreast, before they had the opportunity to either ram or entangle and board

(**Figure 11.9**). Preferably the darting action would ruin some of the opponents' oars (Rados 1915, Lazenby 1987) and, once clear behind the enemy line, a hard turn was required to bring the vessel to the ramming position against the stern or the side of its enemy's before they could reposition themselves to defend (Whitehead 1987). Crashing the rudder oars and/or having a killer or maiming shot at the Skipper or the Commander were also favourable outcomes.

The vessels enjoying the advantage were the most solidly built (**Figure 11.9A1**), *or* the swiftest (**Figure 11.9B**). The latter could dart between their opponents. The former might feign a head-on ramming and crash, at the last moment, by a slight turn, at the oars of the enemy, who would be trying to avoid the head-on collision with a stiffer prow. Heavy vessels could achieve a breakthrough but were difficult to turn *sharp* to the enemy; fast vessels darted through and turned. The vessel which accomplished a Diekplous did not have to about-turn, or even turn sharply (**Figure 11.9A2**). It could turn leisurely behind the enemy line and pick any vessel for a hind or flank attack (**Figure 11.9A3**). In a naval battle, some vessels being able to perform the Diekplous could destroy the entire enemy fleet, as the enemy vessels destroyed by the hind attack were to leave openings in their line for more friendly vessels to cut through and repeat the drill, or find opportunities for one-on-one Perilous, thus collapsing a whole line in a matter of minutes (**Figure 11.9B**).

Diekplous can be countered by head-on ramming, which favours heavier or rather stouter vessels. But the ultimate defence against Diekplous is a second line of ships behind the first (**Figure 11.9C**), to engage the enemy vessels as they emerge (Fields 2007; Montagu 2000; Warry 1980, Xen Hell I.6,28) – an interesting association to the alleged triple line of Persian ships in Salamis (Aesch Persai 365–6). Still, this disposition, if similar numbers are deployed, makes the front of the double-line fleet shorter and exposes it to standard flank attacks and Periplous.

Diekplous was taught by Dionysius to the rebel fleet before the battle of Lade (Her VI.12,1). Whether it had been used in Lade cannot be surmised, as he was relieved beforehand. Once the Ionians were defeated, it was expected that the Persians would have been made privy to all their secrets and ideas. The Phoenicians might have been too arrogant to adopt it, or they might not. Dionysius' escape to the west would have allowed the mainland traders there who developed dealings with the privateer (Her VI.17) to be taught. The Athenians were amongst the western adventurers, at the very least under Themistocles' policy (Lazenby 1993) and because of the closure of the eastern markets due to the Persians, especially of the cornfields of the Black Sea and Egypt. Other Greeks must have learnt Diekplous from survivors and refugees. All the Allies of 480 BC were concerned that the fleets of the subjugated Greeks (Ionians, Aeolians, Dorians etc.) might have adopted it; thus, both in Artemisium and Salamis, but especially in Artemisium (Her VIII.9) they took some necessary

The origin of rams

The first indication for rams comes from the fresco at Akrotiri, Santorini (Red solid arrow in the **Figure B-11.1**). It is a Minoan representation with many issues, some of them contradictory. The position of the helmsman seems unconventional, actually opposite from the ordinary. As evident from other representations, the bow of an ancient vessel was more or less vertical (see **Figure 11.1**) and the stern gently sloping upwards, with the helmsman in control of two steering oars. At an earlier date it was thought to have *one* steering oar, which gives less control and it is evidently a much plainer device than the later ones; but its position cannot be different. The helmsman must be at the stern. Moreover, there are structural and hydrodynamic reasons for the prow to be the vertical end and the stern the sloped. It has to do with the construction, which affords all rigidity and tolerance to the prow, and much less to the stern, which, additionally, by its sloping, makes landings easier both on the sand and by a pier. Only if one accepts that the helmsman at the fresco is situated at the prow of the vessel, not at the stern, the design makes sense and the projection may be considered for a ram.

Starting from the latter issue, it is either a ram or a cutwater. The second option is not very convincing as excellent naval designs had no such thing. The Viking *drakkars* and the *caravels* come first to mind. Thus, if it looks like a ram, it must have been a ram. The former issue though, is tricky. It might have been artistic licence to have the helmsman (and for all practical purposes, captain) in the wrong position, but this is dubious. The inhabitants were sea people and such inaccuracies would have caused most impolite remarks, something no real – and rich – patron would have taken lightly. Thus, it may invite some other explanation; for example, that the vessel had, for any reason, to reverse. In such a manoeuvre, the steering oar exercises much less control if it remains at the stern, for several reasons. Most important is its position in *front* of the propulsion centre. Thus, taking the steering oar, and carrying it to the other end of the vessel, seems the best approach for such a manoeuvre. The steering

Fig. B-11.1.

oar was not very efficient, but, being plain, it could be lifted and carried along the vessel. Many questions about the whys and hows of such a reverse sail emerge, but the whole thing makes sense in terms of steering a ship. Obviously, the pair of much larger, heavier and diversified steering oars of later designs (**Figure 11.1**) could not be lifted, carried and then put at the prow to enact such a solution in subsequent generations of vessels; still, their superior steering qualities and their operation in pairs allowed sufficient authority, even when the nature of the manoeuvre dictated their suboptimal use.

There are very few, if any, literary sources on Minoan sea power and technology. The earliest detailed ones concern the vessels of the Trojan War (Hom Il II.494–760), and although different ship sizes are mentioned, there is not *one* report on a naval fight, or of rams. The only weapon attested for a naval engagement is a very long spear – or, to be precise, a long, shafted weapon (Hom Il XV.678). Its conceivable uses remain speculative. It could be used against planking, to punch holes; or against ropes/sails, to shear and cut them, similarly to an improvised shafted weapon invented

Fig. B-11.2.

by a renowned *Oplomachos* (Close Quarter Battle expert) of Athens (Plat. Laches 7); or to kill key personnel on an enemy vessel, like the helmsman. Its reconstruction from archaeological findings suggesting a bident (although with a much shorter shaft than the one implied by Homer) can be seen in the **Figure B-11.2** (Copyrights: Association of Historical Studies 'KORYVANTES' – koryvantes.org).

precautions. The Circle (Her VIII.11,1) denied both space for Diekplous and suitable aspects for Periplous (**Figure 11.8**); the battle line formed for the engagements of the third day in Artemisium and in Salamis were too near the coast (Her VIII.16,1 & 84,1 respectively). Thus, they denied space behind the line of the Allies for enemy penetration and about-turning to ram from behind. And this is a fact, irrespective of the tactical intent, which might have been simply to fight at the shallows, where deeper Imperial vessels would be at a disadvantage.

The tactical options and preferences of the antagonists

There is considerable scholarly debate as to which method was preferred by the two opponents. The concept of bigger and stouter Greek ships (i.e. in Connolly 1981) leads to the Greeks opting for boarding (Fields 2007), but this is a usual contemporary interpretation of the 'heavier' ships as mentioned in Her VIII.60. There is nowhere any notion in the sources for bigger and/or stouter Greek ships; select incidents in Salamis imply exactly the opposite. Such is the whole sequence of the episode of the slaying of the Persian admiral Ariabignes (Her VIII.89 & 84; Plut Vit Them 14). At the same time the belief of better Phoenician and, in some cases, Egyptian seamanship (40 per cent of the Imperial fleet) leads to the conclusion that the Imperial fleet prefers ramming (Fields 2007), although maybe 35 per cent of its vessels are manned and sailed by the Greek vassals and all the Imperial vessels carried enhanced marine parties.

Better than analogies with other centuries (Rados 1915) and suppositions based on later events (both extremely helpful approaches), are the facts as reported from near-day sources. Thus, the Imperial fleet shows a preference for boarding:

- The initial skirmish of the 10 Phoenician ships with 3 Allied ones ended with boardings (Her VII.180–1) allowing the third Greek vessel to escape. Had the two first vessels been rammed and sunk or even incapacitated and left there for boarding and capture by the slower ships of the Phoenician flight, the fast sailers would have reached the third Greek vessel.
- Later, before the first engagement at Artemisium, Herodotus reports (Her VIII.10) that Imperial mariners were discussing and bragging about the prospects of *capture* – not the ramming/sinking – of Athenian ships to receive royal rewards.
- In Artemisium, the Egyptians *capture* 5 Greek triremes (Her VIII.17) and are acknowledged as the best Imperial fighters at that engagement.
- In Salamis Herodotus refers to a number of Greek vessels *captured* by Imperial captains (Her VIII.85) which led to very high rewards by the King of Kings.
- Only Greek vessels of the Imperial navy are recorded as *ramming* their opponents – or friendlies for that matter – in Salamis by Herodotus (Her VIII.90 & 87).

This picture fits perfectly with a flashback: in the battle of Lade, the outnumbered 1.2 to 2 Ionians (Her VI.8,2–9,1) take care not to be outflanked by the Imperials. Without the tricks and manoeuvres of the maverick Dionysius, (Her VI,12,1 and VI.12,4), they resort to a compact formation and the Chians load their vessels with 40 select Hoplites (Her VI.15,1) giving a hell of a fight to the Imperials and taking many enemy vessels (Her VI.15,2), the size of the marine parties of which is not disclosed. The Chians obviously disregarded the speed and manoeuvrability penalty, as they envisaged a static fight with boarding, intended to limit flanking exposure. The lesson is well-learnt by the Imperials and their triremes under Xerxes have 30 Persian, Median and Saka boarders on top of their native marines (Her VII.184). As the 10-troop squad (Dathabam) is the lowest unit in the Persian army, a minimum of 10 native marines must be accepted for a total of a 40-strong boarding party, equal to the ones of Chians. But this is a minimum and the Imperial boarding parties may have been even larger.

Of course, precaution against mutinies would advise *against* large native marine complements, so that any mutiny by the unarmed rowers would be easily suppressed by the Royal boarders. It must be stressed, however, that in two instances of successful Persian boardings, i.e. the feats performed by the Egyptians in Artemisium (Her VIII.17) and by Samothracians in Salamis (Her VIII.90), the credit is given to the weaponry of the native marines (Her VII.89 and VIII.90 respectively). This implies perhaps larger numbers and definitely more significant participation in the boarding action than usually admitted.

Thus, the Imperials were well-prepared for boardings in number and equipment of marines, performed well in this respect and, most importantly, intended to implement it. The Athenians had just 18 marines on board according to Plutarch (Vit Them 14) and as most Imperial boarders were top-class troops, probably cavalry, it cannot be surmised that they were a defence against Greek boarders. They had the numbers, the morale, a clear weapons advantage (in missile weapons) and probably the dynamic advantage of higher decks to shoot and jump from (Plut Vit Them 14). No commander with so many advantages plays them on the defensive. After all, the Persian ethnic contribution to the fleet, and thus their control and initiative upon the engagement, was the boarders' game. It is only natural that THIS was the main battle technique of their fleet, once they were aboard, filling its decks. After all, the beefed-up marine parties prescribed after Lade were taking quite a toll in terms of ships' speed and agility, which were quintessential for ramming action. The result of the battle of Artemisium, where the Allies had some staggering success in boarding actions as implied by Plutarch (Vit Them 8) was a major surprise for the Imperials, if it were not a result of a surprise attack against an unaware opponent.

A remark from a more careful reading of Herodotus' account implies that the Iranian/Central Asian units of 30 boarders (Her VII.184,2) as standard in Imperial war galleys, must have been Xerxes' innovation, at least regarding their integration into the vessel's armament. Native Persian troopers must have been on trireme decks at least since Darius' expedition to Samos under Otanes, circa 519 BC (Her III.141 & 144) and definitely against Lemnos and Imbros under Otanes, circa 512 BC (Her V.26) and Naxos under Aristagoras in 500 BC (Her V.32). The expedition against the revolt in Cyprus, circa 497 BC (Her V.108) might have had the land army of the Persians transported in transport ships or in the Phoenician galleys of their fleet. But in all these cases the troopers were meant for amphibious assault, not for a naval battle. The apex of this approach was the campaign of Datis and Artaphrenes (490 BC), where a major army was transported by sea to a considerable distance, in another theatre of war, without a shoreline to follow and without a supporting army moving along a shore. It was a true seaborne assault, with horse transports built for the first time (Her VI.48,2 & 95,1) and intended to carry a cavalry arm (Her VI.95,2 &101,1) while troops were carried on triremes (Her VI.95,2). But there was no naval engagement, nor any notion that the fleet was geared for such an eventuality.

With Xerxes, though, the Iranian troops of the fleet are the best boarders, intended to engage in naval encounters and amphibious operations, of course. The former assignment is amply shown during the skirmish off Sciathos, where the Persian boarders, not the natives (Phoenicians) tended the wounded prisoner-hero Pytheas (Her VII.181,2–3). These Iranian boarders must have been delegated and boarded in Doriscus; before touching there, the Imperial fleet had only the native marines on its decks.

Before Xerxes, as in Lade 494 BC (Her VI.14) and off Cyprus circa 497 BC (Her V.108 & 112), there is no indication that the boarders of the Imperial vessels who engaged in sea-fights were any other than the natives who were manning the ships. And this must be the case for some amphibious operations as well: the naval leg of Cambyses' invasion of Egypt, launched in mid-520s BC (Her III.13,1–2 & 14,5 & 44,2) and the naval campaign of re-submission of the rebellious coastline of Thrace from the Hellespont to the Bosporus after the battle of Lade in 494 BC (Her VI.6 & 28,1 & 33,2–3 & 34,1 & 41) are narrated without any single indication or hint of Iranian boarders on the Imperial vessels. Natives, and mostly Phoenicians, are explicitly mentioned.

Chapter 12

The Battles

The initial engagements

The first action was an evening sneak attack (Her VIII.9). According to the narration of Diodorus (XI.12,5–6), it was a surprise reminiscent of the one the Spartans were to implement some 80 years later at Aegospotami (Xen Hell II.1,28). This explains the large number of prizes (30) taken from the Imperials (Her VIII.11). Herodotus explicitly states that the Greeks wanted to test the Diekplous and battle potential, and the usual interpretation of the passage (Her VIII.9) is that they wanted to evaluate the *Imperial* capabilities and tactics and especially the Diekplous. But it is very probable that the passage, or at least its source, should be understood that the Greeks wished initially to explore whether the Imperials were using the Diekplous and, additionally, to rehearse in very real conditions, but in a limited context, their *own* methods of fighting against the Imperials. Prominent in this consideration had been the Diekplous, being both an innovation and the wildcard that would furnish an advantage against the Imperial superiority in numbers, speed, boarders and, most probably, ship size. And then, should the Imperials be using the Diekplous, it was the Circle.

The initiative on the subject must have been mostly, if not purely, Athenian; the new Athenian navy, a massive investment in all kinds of resources, must have been built with a tactical doctrine in mind at the very least, if not with an operational and a strategic one. The central concept must have been sea denial, not naval superiority or dominance. A defensive strategy implemented by offensive operations and occasionally tactics, assigning top priority to the interception of the enemy armadas as far away as possible, especially amphibious task forces. Such planning may have devolved to the abandonment of the city and the concentration of all resources and hopes on to the fleet (Her VII.144,3).

Along with the possibility of the expatriated Phocians teaching in the Far West the Diekplous to the rookie Athenians as the latter ventured into this part of the world seeking new markets, the design principles of the new Athenian vessels must have been highly affected by their intended tactics. The surging, with multiple vessels attacking a single enemy and the fighting at the shallows, due to their shallow draft, featured prominently, although the latter was applicable in defensive fights. This can be seen in Salamis, with the retreat to the shore when the Imperials turned to engage (Her VIII.84,1) and on the third day at Artemisium, when the Allies stayed put next to the shore (Her VIII.16,1). On the other hand, the hit-and-go, imperative approach to intercept larger, but heavily laden fleets of galleys set to land troops across the Aegean, required higher speed than the one achievable by the laden enemy vessels, which explains the specifications set by Themistocles. But their actual lack of maintenance degraded the capability of the design and, combined with the qualities of the Imperial vessels, as became obvious from the skirmish off Sciathos, made subsequent escape quite an issue and thus dictated dusk attacks (Her VIII.9 & 10,3 & 14,20) and the use of the Circle, when the enemy was catching up (Her VIII.11,1).

Still, the difference in numbers and competent Imperial SOPs allowed a prompt reaction, with Imperial squadrons emerging from different beaches and gulfs and a bitter fight, quelled by nightfall. To repel the Persian numbers, the Greeks formed the Circle, prows outward (Her VIII.11), a tactic to be tried some 50 years later against Phormio by Peloponnesians (Thuc II.83,5–84,3); but in this case, it was successful, as the Persians – despite their numerical superiority – could neither infiltrate and flank nor envelope or overrun the Greek ships. If the Diekplous had been applicable, this would have been at an early stage and might have worked miracles for the Allies. The successive arrival of Imperial squadrons from different beaches, possibly arrayed in columns to surge as rapidly as possible, would have made it utterly impracticable, even less so once the late squadrons deployed behind the first line of the Imperial vessels. Possibly this experience made the Persians present a multi-line formation in Salamis, with successive lines-abreast, to discourage the Diekplous, as they had the numbers required to do so without exposing their flanks to Periplous.

The different accounts of Herodotus and Diodorus do not allow a clear understanding of the taking of the 30 prizes by the Allies. Was it during the engagement with the Greek fleet formed in a circle, as Herodotus implies (VIII.11,1–2)? Or were they taken during the initial surprise and before the fighting evolved into the set-piece naval action (Diod XI.12,6) where the Circle features prominently? In any case, the identity of one high-ranking prisoner of war (Her VIII.11,2), a member of the Cypriot fleet, allows an assumption (Green 1970) that many of the ships taken as prizes were from the Cypriot fleet. One can extend the issue and conclude that as these ships were indeed hit severely by the storm (Her VII.195) and had taken horrendous casualties, they performed poorly. They might have been targeted implicitly, based on intelligence concerning both the poor state of the Cypriot contingent and its whereabouts, obtained either by Skyllias or/and by the captives taken with Sandoces (Her VII.194).

Within the mayhem and chaos, a Lemnian trireme deserted to the Greeks (Her VIII.11,3), obviously commanded and manned by Athenian settlers whose families had come to the island and settled therein when Miltiades conquered it (Burn 1962). This view is validated by the land grant by Athens to the trierarch Antidorus (Her VIII.11,3). The defection implies that Iranian boarders had not been detailed to the vessel, as there is no report of an attempt to neutralize them (Tarn 1908).

A second tempest, from the south-east this time, stunned the Imperials further, kept them awake and allowed a more focused Greek sneak attack at the next sunset (Her VIII.14). In this second tempest, neither fleet had casualties, but the wreckage and corpses of the morning engagement drifted to the Imperial anchorage, making sailing (or, rather, rowing) meddlesome and shredding the morale (Her VIII.12,1). This implies that the Persian anchorage was in a western direction from the area of the fighting and the Greek anchorage, but other factors may have been there and thus the conclusion is not very safe.

There was no question now of the Greek fleet going down the Euboean Gulf to intercept the Persian flanking task force, as the wind was opposite to their projected south-east course down-channel. But this same wind wreaked havoc on the very same flanking task force, throwing it to the east coast of Euboea, at a disputed (today) location called The Hollows, either to the southern third or to the middle of the eastern coastline of the island. The first view is supported by a look at the map; a rocky, convex area. The second by the existence of a small island of similar name, even in recent years.

The same gusts, when decreasing the next morning, helped the Athenian home fleet of 53 vessels, possibly kept to guard northern Saronic and southern Euboean gulfs – or simply belated in their outfit and manning (Lazenby 1993) – to arrive as reinforcements. They may just may have brought news on the latest Imperial disaster, either having witnessed the shipwreck or having been informed by friendly watchers in central and southern Euboea (Grundy 1901) by signal fires or runners. But they did swell the Athenian navy to full levy.

It has been suggested (Green 1970) that this Athenian flotilla may have been dispatched to shut Euripus, had it been notified. In such a case it is more conceivable to have it arriving at Artemisium early the next morning to bring the news of the Persian disaster. In this account, it is possible that some Persian vessels turned the southern tip of Euboea (Cape Caphereus) and found refuge in southern Euboea and Carystus (Bradford 1980), or even ventured north and were intercepted by the Athenians (Green 1970). Had such a thing happened, though, the Athenians would have publicized it and Herodotus would have mentioned it. If one dismisses the unlikely, that these 53 vessels went on up the *east* coast of Euboea and witnessed the disaster firsthand, to reach Artemisium from the south-east, the only valid scenario for them to have accurate intelligence on the Imperial task force is by the islanders or assigned watchers (Her VIII.183,1) running across the island to tip them off even as shouters from the shore. Grundy (1901) strives to resolve the issue more imaginatively, suggesting that the Persians did turn Cape Caphereus into the southern Euboean Gulf and were hit there by the gale, which, in his opinion, was from the south-west, not the south-east, locating thus Aphetae further east, very near Cape Sepias. Although the south-west wind in the Aegean (*Garbes*) at this time of the year occurs and may be destructive, once in the Gulf it has less momentum, and there is no place in shape or tradition to identify with the Hollows (Her VIII.13).

Although Grundy's view is indeed flawed, so are the other two, of Green and Bradford. There is a very troublesome issue: the exact whereabouts of these 53 vessels and the exact means they were ordered to position; pigeons and ravenry are not an option. The admiralty at the north, intending to intercept by the main fleet the flanking Imperial task force, seems to have no idea on the subject. It could be that a nice opportunity was presented to shut the Imperials between two divisions, the main fleet and the 53 vessels of the incoming attic flotilla, so as to annihilate a strong enemy task force. Unfortunately, the communications available at the time were not up to the task of allowing concerted, co-ordinated actions over such distances. Probably the 53 vessels were due at Artemisium anyway to join the fleet, but were late due to manning difficulties (Lazenby 1993), and happened to arrive at an opportune moment, possibly but not necessarily carrying the news (Grundy 1901).

These fresh ships were a welcome addition for the second sneak attack at dusk the very same day (Her VIII.1,2), while the Imperials were sleepless due to the second storm, which had been throwing shipwrecks and corpses in their midst all night long. They were also receiving bad news from their task force, possibly by some of its vessels (the rearguard or the stragglers) that had time to reverse course and escape back north, aided by the wind astern (Bradford 1980; Green 1970).

Whether the new Greek raid, which sank a Cilician detachment (Her VIII.1,2), targeted survivors of the flanking task force or some isolated squadron of the main fleet is difficult to tell. The size of the Persian fleet made the scattering of some squadrons to secondary, isolated shores unavoidable (Diod XI.12,5) and respective intelligence would have been available at the time, if not from Skyllias, by carefully watching the contours while proceeding to attack the previous afternoon. Still, Herodotus' wording reveals no numbers of captured ships, which implies a fast, opportunistic action at dusk, with unsure counting. The second-day raiding action was conceivably merged with the first-day engagement by Diodorus (XI.12,5–6) into a two-phase, one-day naval action and inverted in temporal terms, to make better sense in a single-day format.

Diodorus' account is in some cases more appealing: it recounts a startling attack by the Greeks, which resulted in a number of Imperial ships being sunk while at port or during the initial contact, before the Imperials could mobilize their numbers properly, turning the fight to a brawl more evenly contested (Diod XI,12,6). This fits well with the taking of 30 prizes as reported by Herodotus (VIII.11). But as the Imperials started coming onto them from different beaches and in great numbers, the smaller fleet, operating far from its anchorage, was encircled relatively near the enemy anchorage and could not go for the shallows, as the beaches were bristling with hostiles. This explains the circle formation mentioned by Herodotus (VIII.11) and the fact that they were near a coast explains how they were able to hold formation. Bitter fighting ensured, with the Greeks denying flanks, thus making ramming action easier for the smaller ships and the boarding action frontal, and in a small front per ship, utterly advantageous for the better-protected marines and boarders and not for the larger parties. When dusk became darkness, the Persians could not tell friend from foe apart in the congested space and would have to disengage for their anchorage, giving the Greeks, who had made quite some impression, a respite and the opportunity to fall back to Artemisium.

Diodorus' account has the two fleets engaging only once more (Diod XI.13,1–2), an open and extended action, after one more savage storm which hit the Imperials (Diod XI.13,1). It is a more logical string of events, as it explains how the startled Imperials were able to encircle the enemy fleet, despite its unexpected emergence; it also explains how the Greeks were able to occupy and then tow away enemy vessels intact, using, of course, boarding tactics (Plut Vit Them 8). This is a most improbable feat while fighting in a circle, whence the enemy would have more opportunities to re-board with fresh troops from other vessels and contest them. Additionally, this version does not make fools of the Imperial admiralty, taken twice unprepared and with its guard down by the same late-evening attack scheme, while compatible with the encircling attempt by the notorious 200-ship task force. In all, a better story; not necessarily the *actual* story.

The crucial engagement

The Greek command had played its cards correctly and scored some impressive success, invaluable in terms of morale. Who was the brain behind these operations? Themistocles is the obvious choice. Regarding the Circle, there can be little doubt. The formation needed drill and experience in a multi-ship context and only the Athenians had enough vessels to practise it beforehand and teach and share it with the rest of the Greek vessels. The dusk attacks could have been the product of Athenian boldness, aggressiveness and determination, evident throughout the works of Herodotus, Thucydides and even Xenophon. Still, the mark of the Lacedaimonian caution, manifest during all the operations of this war and throughout antiquity, with its most prominent moment the denial to hotly pursue Xerxes after Salamis, is also detectable in such practices, as it intends to lower any risks inherent in enterprising operations.

But the third day (by Herodotus VIII.15; by Diodorus XI.13,1–2 it was the second day) a full-blown morning action was fought by Imperial initiative. The Persians had a full day of rest according to Herodotus, except for the hapless Cilicians. Diodorus' timeline is more permissive, as it does not suggest any specific time lapses, although it is usually taken to imply an immediate, second-day engagement.

The event might have been precipitated by the need of the Imperial army for supplies; Xerxes might have sent word to the fleet to break the deadlock as in the second day he had failed to make any impression to Leonidas (Burn 1962). Lazenby (1993) does not accept any dependence of the Persian land host on their fleet for supplies; only for operational support, to turn the enemy defence by sea. Be that as it may, the Imperials emerged from their anchorages first (Her VIII. 15) and deployed promptly while advancing fast. It was not an effort to fall on the unprepared Greeks, as their orderly deployment into assault formation, a long line-abreast, was time-consuming (Her VIII.16). It was a sound choice; the waters were not familiar near the Greek anchorage and nasty surprises were possible. Having the numbers meant they needed no unconventional advantages such as surprise, which come at a risk. They were simply taking the fight early into open waters, for a clear-cut and protracted struggle, where numbers and size would tell.

The Greeks follow a forestalling strategy, they have no reason to rush and when the Imperials emerge, they do not move until the last minute (Her VIII.16); they stay motionless in their anchorage, and ready to engage at will, should the Persians dash west to make contact with Xerxes. Scholars of previous times fully understood the advantages of a galley line-abreast along a friendly shore, especially if said shore was infested by friendly troops (Rados 1915); the lack of such armies does not radically change the rationale, which would have been familiar, if not SOP, for the admirals of both sides and as such even more applicable in Salamis (Rados 1915). The Allied ships emerged just in time to intercept the Imperials before being assaulted while into their very mooring, since the Imperial patience was growing thin by the Allied refusal to engage.

It is well understood that the Allied fleet was lined parallel to their coast, actually hugging it, wings denied and anchored on projections of dry land (**Figure 12.1**) to forestall both Periplous and simple flanking to the more numerous Imperials.

Being very close to the coast, the Allies collapsed any space behind their vessels, thus making Diekplous impossible as well (Lazenby 1993; Hale 2009). Any notion of putting out to physically shut the straits (Burn 1963; Green, 1970; Shepherd 2010) by deploying at right-angles to both shores, even further to the west, near Oreos, where the straits are much narrower, would have been purely suicidal. The Trikeri channel is 8 km wide (Lazenby 1993; Bradford 1980), meaning that the 330 Allied vessels would be at 24 metres each, of which 15 are the width of a trireme with oars extended (Bradford 1980; Lazenby 1987), meaning a gilded invitation for Diekplous as there is enough space for a trireme between any two. The Imperials may come at successive lines-abreast, or in a denser, one-line formation, to sweep opposition aside. They would also deploy archers to the northern shore, under their army's control, to shoot the Greek vessel forming the left wing. But such theory mostly stumbles on the fact that in this way the anchorage at Artemisium goes to the Imperials and the door to conquer Euboea with 30 boarders per trireme plus cavalry is left wide open. This means an emerging threat along all Euboean shores to the south by massive archery and especially at Euripus (Green 1970), as discussed previously (**Map 3.2**).

The Greeks sailed, or rather rowed out in high spirits but practically having no other option. The match at Thermopylae made imperative an Imperial naval breakthrough, thus if they declined battle, the Persian fleet would simply either turn and sail west, forgetting all previous considerations or attack them while still in their anchorage, although not at anchor. The Persians' bellicose instincts and possible directives did not allow the former course of action; the latter option would rectify previous reverses and avoid the exposure of a flank, along with all other considerations.

Green (1970) accepts the importance of the arrogance and dignity of the Persian admiralty in different cases, but not as a catalyst for a major action. It may be a short-sighted view. The Persians inspired awe and only extreme aggressiveness may hammer such aura. Standing orders, pride, confidence, morale and the strict punishments delivered instantly in the slightest case of defeatism or pacifism, as clearly insinuated by Herodotus in his account of the naval staff meeting before Salamis (Her VIII.69,1) would have dictated aggression on every occasion, especially in advantageous terms. Taking a respite to restore vessels and troops to battle-worthiness was acceptable, but preferably if combined with a ruse to net the opponent, as by encircling or envelopment. The Persians occasionally showed caution, as did Datis for days in Marathon (Her VI.110), Xerxes in Thermopylae (Her VII.210,1) and Mardonius in Plataea (Her IX.39,1) but the presence of the King in the environs stimulated his subjects, Persians and others, to boldness, courage and aggression (Her VIII.69,2 & 86). As with the Athenians, and contrary to the Spartans, caution was not the motto of the Persian war ethics.

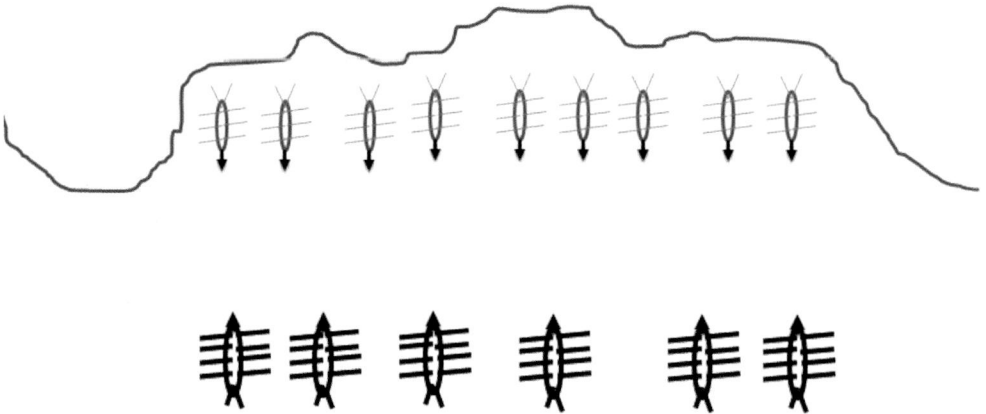

Fig. 12.1.

Thus, the Greeks emerged slowly and tardily – after the Persians took a crescent formation (Her VIII.16) and showed their hand – and deployed in a convex formation, as near to the shore as possible (Bradford 1980; Lazenby 1993), in shallow waters, which posed a disadvantage for the Imperial vessels and denied any attempt for Diekplous. Both of the Allied flanks were anchored at their own shore (**Figure 12.1**) to avoid Periplous and encirclement or envelopment (Hale 2009).

Despite the difference in numbers, the initiative lying with the Imperials and the determination of the Persian commanders, the Greeks held. This illustrates perfectly why the Imperial admirals had no intention to partially engage, with a portion of their fleet, the Allied vessels, while the rest of their vessels would sail for Xerxes, as suggested by Shepherd (2010); neither in this case nor in Salamis, as suggested by Lazenby (1993). They may have been ignorant of the dire straits of the Army, having lost the crops of the plain of Malis; most probably they were not, they would have been able to establish a (land) communication with the Army from the west side of the gulf, similar to the Greek practice (Green 1970). But in any case, simple caution and standard generalship would advise against such risks, especially after two murderous gales and two reverses by an unforeseen and aggressive enemy – who, by the way, they were instructed to exterminate, not just brush aside. It must be remembered that if the Allied navy was destroyed, the campaign was practically over and the empire victorious, given that the Army stayed in good shape.

The battle, as the Greeks once more took good care not to be exposed, would have devolved to head-on ramming and boarding (Plut Vit Them 8). This brutal brawl was punishing for the smaller Greek ships; they suffered damage rendering them unserviceable (Her VIII.18). Few, if any, were sunk (Lazenby 1993) and the loss of ships reported (Her VIII.16,3) must refer to vessels taken by boarders.

The fight took all day, until dusk. The Greeks were victorious. It was not an extermination battle. They had fought a defensive battle and kept their position. The Persian fleet did not break through (Her VIII.15–16). In this battle, the Greeks had achieved their objectives. They held their position and drove the enemy back. This is an uncontested victory (Her VIII.16–8; Plut Vit Them 8). A limited victory, yes; not decisive, yes; paid dearly in casualties, yes. But a victory. It is an interesting question to doubt this (Delbruck 1920; Tarn 1908). Herodotus (VIII.16 & 18) recounts a Greek victory, Plutarch (Vit Them 8) the same while he also recites some monuments built to commemorate the victory (scriptures and stele).

The Imperials do not act as victors. Their reluctance to pursue once the Greeks retired (Tarn 1908) is not the acid test on the subject. Being in possession of wrecks and dead bodies was a Greek formality of acknowledging victory, not necessarily followed by the Persians and thus of disputable importance in the wake of this battle (Her VIII.18); but the Greeks were in possession of both and they could claim victory. Additionally, the Persian command (not only Xerxes) is always portrayed as thoroughly dissatisfied with the conduct of the fleet (Her VIII.69,2), with one of its petty admirals, Artemisia, being a harsher critic than protocol allowed (Her VIII.68). The Imperial conduct in Salamis is described as much more valorous even though they were thoroughly beaten (Her VIII.86). How can the sum of all that be considered a draw? Although the control of the area of the battle, the wrecks and the dead bodies which defined the victor for the Greeks might not have been so for the oriental Imperials (but they were for their Greek vassals) the fact was that the Imperials had been intercepted and were not in possession of the Greek fleet or anchorage, nor able to break through (Green 1970). They retired to their anchorage, they did not continue west to Malis, despite having pinned the Allied fleet on an isolated beach.

The number of battered ships, although it meant few total losses and human casualties for the Allied fleet, also meant that the morrow might have been untenable. Weary crews had to spend the night fixing their damaged vessels, whenever possible, for a rematch next morning. In terms of operations, a high number of damaged vessels could be more destructive than a smaller number of sunk or captured ones if action is imminent. The Greek captains were most probably thinking of retreat (Her VIII.18). They had bled the Persian fleet, with the help of nature's elements, to a little less than 50 per cent and sapped its morale. They tested its resolve and prowess and found them wanting. If they escaped extermination by sheer attrition, they could win decisively on a later occasion. They needed time and space to bring their battered vessels to battle-readiness. The said battered vessels were not fully neutralized, nor incapacitated as sea platforms; they could sail perfectly safely to home waters. They could not fight, though (Her VIII.18).

Taking a break, the admirals were wondering what was going on in Thermopylae and how they should proceed to possibly evacuate the locals and perhaps the Leonidas' expeditionary force. The 300 or so Greek vessels, with 14–20 marines each, which was the boarding platoon in Athenian vessels in Salamis (Plut Vit Them 14), had plenty of room for at least 20–30 more in a transportation action along the littorals, with no need to fight or to flee. This is something like 6–7,000 men to be evacuated, or the sum of Leonidas, expeditionary force, including retainers but not the local contingents.

This line of thought leads to the most interesting question regarding the intentions of the opposing commanders and possibly to causative facts unknown to us. Why did the Persian admirals on the third day take so long to engage? It is inexplicable why they had to wait to fight until mid-day (Her VIII.15). All possible motivations would normally lead to an early onset of the engagement. More time to wear out their opponents, so as to achieve an extermination victory; the possibility for surprise (although slim); denying the enemy any chance to withdraw or relocate and generally, the seizing of the initiative. Stalling would be justified for reasons of timing. This might be an issue of expecting orders from a higher echelon or of letting an event develop and bring a desirable effect.

Accordingly, if the Imperials intended to keep the Allied fleet distracted so as to prevent them evacuating Leonidas expeditionary force, they would have initiated the fight early, to extend the naval engagement for the duration of the window of opportunity for the Greeks and thus to shut the said window. There could have been no notion of concerted action with the army that would have created a combined effect. Had they simply wished for a show of effectiveness in direct naval combat, they would have done the same. The only reason for waiting it out would have been to tip the Allied fleet on the fate of Leonidas and the collapse of the defence at Thermopylae, which would entice them to retire. But the Imperials had no wish to allow a Greek retreat, much less to engineer it.

The Imperial fleet must have been able to communicate somehow with its army as did the Greeks (Green 1970) and with means allowing high informational volume, that is *not* by beacons. The land route was wide open in the wake of Xerxes' advance and the fleet had many cavalrymen up to the task of being messengers or liaison officers, as did the Army, and the know-how of mounted couriers of the Royal Messengers was there, fully functional (Her VIII.98,1). On the other hand, the occupation of the northern shore along the straits allowed the establishment of a system of beacons, or any other visual signalling, to transmit single-word messages such as the signal for an attack. The only possible reason for the Imperial fleet being so late to engage the Greeks might have been a breakage in the chain of command. The nocturnal Spartan raid on Xerxes' camp that unsettled the whole host would justify the lack of *any* signal prompting action by the fleet. Such a signal must have been sent after things were settled in the Persian camp, a factor which delayed the holding action by land until midday. (Her VII.15). Thus, a combined action, meant to maximize efficiency and allow as few as possible of the enemy to retire safely (Green 1970), based on careful co-ordination of three elements (the flanking force might have signalled once it negotiated the top of the ridge) had been unsettled by the Spartan special operation, which intended to end the war in one stroke.

The fat lady sang

And then the lightning stroke in the Allied naval camp: Thermopylae had fallen, Leonidas was dead and the survivors of his expeditionary force headed southwards through terrain unsuitable for cavalry chase and with quite a head-start due to the bitterness of the fighting in the north. The navy had no one to extract from there. The possibility though of Persian archer masses storming to the narrows of Euripus, after the fall of Thermopylae, prompted the Greek fleet to a hasty night retreat (Her VIII.21; Diod XI.13,3), to deny the enemy any such thoughts.

It was a long shot; the Persian army was in bad shape and in desperate need of provisions and water and the coastal road was difficult and through the Locrian territory, with the natives having fought in Thermopylae (Her VII.203). Still, both Themistocles and the Spartans, a.k.a. Eurybiadas, were cautious and took to retreat immediately after feeding their crews. It was a perfectly ordered retreat by night, which means the Greeks were familiar with night sailing and near the coast at that, a very tricky operation. The sailing order may have reflected the battle order of the Allies; if so, in this case, the Athenians had the position of honour, on the right, and the Corinthians the second such, the left wing, possibly due to the numbers of vessels supplied. This being so or not, still, the best sailors, the Corinthians, led, the best fighters, the Athenians, by the testimony of three engagements, according to none other than Pindar, a Theban poet, brought up the rear (Her VIII.21,2), should any enemy vanguard have caught up. It was a pernicious issue. The Euripus strait could be negotiated by a pair of triremes abreast, at five minutes per pair, meaning more than 10 hours for the Allied fleet. This meant the fast vessels should have sailed with breakneck speed to cross early and the rest of the fleet would extend to cross at ease, without being jammed. That would offer great opportunities to any Imperial pursuing force, be that the fleet or the army (cavalry), to attack a bottled Greek fleet. Thus, timing must have been factored in any number of Persian possible and probable delays which would start to count since dawn, when the Allied naval base would be visible.

Except from salvaging whatever could be salvaged from the shipwrecks, the Allies, while retreating, took an opportunity to tease the Greek contingents of the Persian fleet into insubordination by leaving carved messages at the watering positions, instead of befouling them (Her VIII.22; Plut Vit Them 9). This sapped further the Imperial cohesion and morale and resulted, in Salamis, in wild accusations by the Phoenicians of an Ionian betrayal (Her VIII.90). The Phoenician slant practically backfired, while the effort of Themistocles paid little direct dividends, especially due to the boarding parties of Iranian troops, who kept watchful eyes. The time spent in this noble endeavour must have been calculated to coincide with the delay for the crossing of Euripus and thus the vessels assigned would have been the very last in the column, and the fastest, to make successive calls. These simple facts imply a rearguard position, as indeed reported by Herodotus, NOT a vanguard as proposed by some scholars (Green 1970).

The retreat of the Allies, in theory, made the execution of deep, independent moves of strategic importance once more a possible course of action for the Imperial navy. One such was the amphibious assault and occupation of Cythera, south of Laconia, as Demaratus suggests (Her VII.235–7). Still, the Greek Admiralty felt that it could take some risks. The Persians would not venture again east of Euboea; the Greeks could dictate any operational tempo from the southern Euboean Gulf, defending Euripus until the Imperial army arrived at the shore and the Imperial fleet needed to call at Malis. Thus, the most obvious Persian course of action would be west of Euboea, subduing the great Island and Locris, should the need be, and then the coast of Attica; and thus be exposed to the psychological tricks of Themistocles.

The Persian admirals were tipped off, in the deep of night, about the extraction of the Greek fleet (Her VIII.23) from a position becoming a trap. It was pure gold, and the bearer, a native of Histiaia, on the north Euboean coast, eyed a kingly reward; or some benevolence for his state, which was now deserted by the Allied fleet despite the bribery (Her VIII.4–5) and exposed to the Imperial wrath, due to its support for the Allies and since it represented the only readily achievable military target. If the Imperials gave chase, they might catch the Greeks, especially as the latter would choke at Euripus (Hale 2009) and leave the area alone in their haste.

The Imperial admirals did not believe the man; they were reluctant to negotiate, after so many disasters, unknown and potentially pernicious littoral waters in the dark and leave a protected anchorage during the night, exposing their already battered vessels to another sudden gale, or unknown reefs, shallows or any combination of the above. Moreover, even if they were bound to give chase, they had developed a healthy suspicion for Greek tricks and surprises: if they gave chase, they might be heading straight into an ambush, or be deprived of sleep and proper rest after a daily ordeal, finding themselves at a disadvantage in an engagement (Hale 2009), or both. Thus, bitter experience made them play safe and follow due procedures and not their instincts. They kept the man under custody while they sanctioned a reconnaissance mission (Her VIII.23).

This detailed narration says a lot: first and foremost, that the Persians do not feel like victors: after a hard engagement prow-to-prow, they were not thinking that the Greeks had any reason to retreat in haste. The other detail is that the Persians keep the unsolicited informer under custody until they can confirm the accuracy of his report, by dispatching reconnaissance vessels to check and safeguard against potential Greek foul play; possibly they sent the same flight they used off Sciathos. The report was proven true, and, no matter their actual condition and possible risks, they failed to give chase due to their caution, something very serious for their master and their war ethics. This string of facts and factors, coupled to the strategic objective of the Imperial fleet, to utterly annihilate the Allied navy, weighed heavily in Salamis in both Xerxes' and his admirals' decisions (Hale 2009). It must be remembered that this objective of total annihilation of the navy of the foe had not been attained at Lade, with some very unfortunate results; both immediate (the piratical spree of Dionysius and his flight off the Phoenician coasts) and long-term, as was the construction of the Athenian fleet and its tactical indoctrination.

At first light, the whole Imperial fleet in battle order, to avoid surprises, advanced to the deserted Greek naval camp (Her VIII.23) and subsequently proceeded by land (their marines) and sea westwards. They ravaged the north Euboean coast into submission (Her VIII.23; Diod XI.13,5), dashing the hopes of their informer for some goodwill, as this was too belated a token of reconciliation, bringing no tangible result. Most importantly, after three days and many casualties, the fleet had no other feat of war – a victorious one, at least – to show.

The Imperial fleet made contact with Xerxes at the shore of the plain of Malis (Her VIII.24). The important detail is that a messenger from Xerxes found them at the western tip of north Euboea. How did Xerxes know that the Greeks (stationed squarely in the path of the messenger) had withdrawn their whole fleet and sent this messenger and how this latter crossed the sea? Probably the admirals sent a message once they saw the Greek naval camp deserted and knew that they were to proceed westwards. Then came the messenger, who invited the crews to an excursion to witness the battlefield at Thermopylae. The scenery was set up by Xerxes' staff to bolster the waning morale of the fleet. At the same time, logistics were coming into place and up to pace.

There is an interesting issue, regarding the size of the Persian fleet. The total number of the ships-of-the-line was 1,207 at Doriscus (Her VII.184) but swelled by 120 more as the Persians subjugated the entire coast to Thessaly (Her VII.185).

The Egyptian connection

The Hoplite marines kept Persian boarders at bay; the Egyptian feat of capturing five Greek ships (Her VIII.17) means the other contingents of the fleet fared worse, implying 20 or less Greek casualties. Herodotus speaks of 'other Egyptian feats' as well, but reports none; had the Egyptians sunk any Greek vessel outright, they would have been bragging to the present day.

It must be noted that this achievement is often attributed to the Egyptian boarders and their heavy weaponry, suitable for boarding action. It is implied moreover that this performance led Mardonius to disembark and keep them for the next campaigning season (Her IX.32,1) – when they featured nowhere. But this is only one possible reading of the events. The Imperial boarders were more numerous and must have had a lion's share in these victories. The heavily armed Egyptian marines were a small proportion, aboard their native vessels, as the majority were always Persians, Medes and Saka (Her VII.184), to be able to contain mutinies and enforce loyalty and discipline, especially to the Egyptians, who had recently rebelled (Her VII.1,3). Disembarking them after the defeat in Salamis was much more a precaution, than anything else: to keep hostages and not bring back to Egypt seasoned fighters serving as boarders after a resounding defeat (reminiscent of the opening stage of the Ionian Revolt, which started from the crews of an Imperial fleet).

On the contrary, Diodorus (XI.13,2) says that the best performers of the Imperial fleet were the Sidonians. This is easier to accept; the Egyptians were never renowned for ruling the waves. Their only seaworthy fleet is assigned to Necos II (Her II.159) whose cordial relations with the Carian and Ionian military settlers during his father's reign and with their metropolis Miletus (Her II.159) imply – but do not prove – a foreign hand in the planning and perhaps execution of such undertakings. It must be noted that no Egyptian fleet was available to defend Egypt against Cambyses in the late sixth century BC, despite a strong presence of Greek mercenaries.

Which District Naval Command incorporated these additions is not known, although intriguing. But after Artemisium, the Persians were almost 500 ships low, down to 800. With 300–400 wrecks at the first gale, 45 prizes taken by the Greeks and any number of vessels sunk in action or in the second tempest, this is a possible tally, despite modern scepticism (i.e. Shepherd 2010). There are many similar cases of oared fleets suffering massive casualties in antiquity and later (Rados 1915), while the prizes taken by the Greeks were accurately numbered and the capture of the whole command of Sandoces would have provided a rough estimation on the ships-of-the-line lost during the first storm. So, either in Salamis, the Persian fleet fought with its lowest ever strength, or it had made good (part of) its casualties.

This is not impossible: the 670-odd ships of the bridges of the Hellespont (Her VII.36) must have been mobilized, as had happened with the ships of the bridges of the Bosporus under Darius I and was to happen at Ister, against the Scythians. After all, many crews were saved from the wrecks, as the greater disaster happened near the shoreline, both in battle and during the first tempest. Thus, a number of casualties in hulls might have been replaced. The ships of the bridges were triremes, but pentekonters also (ibid). The latter were not included in the inventory of the capital ships of the Imperial navy (Tarn 1908); they were freight haulers and would have been assigned to replace some of the respective losses due to storm (Her VII.191; Diod XI.12,3). This line of thought presupposes that the vessels in the bridges were not tallied in the 1,217 at Doriscus, no matter whether new builds, under Xerxes' preparations, or of previous blocks, used by Darius' generals a decade or more ago.

Chapter 13

Bowing Out?

After visiting the battlefield of Thermopylae (Her VIII.25), the Imperial fleet reformed, replenished its supplies, made repairs to damaged vessels and possibly was brought up to strength (Her VIII.66), as mentioned above. A royal audience was held to allow debriefing and an update of the naval strategy (Her VII.235–7). Three days after the Greek retreat, the royal armada moved southwards through the Gulf of Euboea, mopping up resistance on both sides of the strait, ravaging Euboea and the shoreline of Attica at quite some depth (Her VIII.66–7; Diod XI.14,5). It took the fleet three more full days to cover the distance, probably due to the chokepoint of Euripus, and to negotiate Cape Sounion so as to turn into the Saronic Gulf and occupy the main sea facilities (ports, quays, storehouses) of deserted Athens, casting anchor at Phaleron, the main port and beach of Athens (Her VIII.66).

The Greeks had made good their escape by all accounts. Themistocles probably asked for the entire fleet to call at Salamis and assist the evacuation of Attica (Her VIII.40). The more ships, the faster and more efficiently the task would be completed and this would have been rather acceptable to the Allies, not only on ethical grounds, but also for profit. Herodotus clearly states that people who stayed behind and barricaded in Acropolis were not only rednecks who did not believe the interpretation of Themistocles for the renowned Delphic Oracle recommending trust only to the Wooden Walls. They were also poor people lacking the means to evacuate (Her VIII.51).

Not only the population of Athens had been in Salamis, evacuating Athens, in what has been a clearly projected and rather competently executed strategic plan as is obvious by the decree of Troezen (Jameson 1960). It was also the sum of its land army, with a core of more than 10,000 Hoplites (including the marines of the fleet). The Plataeans had been excused from fleet service during the trek southwards in order to evacuate their city, which would be levelled by vindictive Persians and Thebans and transport their folk to safety (Her VIII.44). They were replaced in fleet duty by the last human reserves of Athens.

A large Athenian, or worse still, the full Allied fleet in Salamis was NOT among the plans of the League representatives in Corinth; after Artemisium, the next sea battle would have been in Euripus, if the Persian army was kept at bay, as is obvious by Herodotus' interpretation of the early retirement of the Greek fleet from Artemisium (Her VIII.4). The other alternative, the last resort, was at Isthmus. The contingency with the evacuation of Athens developed, however, a new situation, which was initially acknowledged and sanctioned by the Allied leadership. The final naval battle would be *for* Isthmus, not necessarily *at* Isthmus. It is true, good spots near Isthmus, similar to the one in Artemisium, could be picked to avoid flanking by a superior force; it may have been picked in advance. But a broader interpretation was NOT out of the question, encouraged by the successful contribution to the defence of Thermopylae of a fleet based and fighting many kilometres away and out of view.

Thus, the sanctioning brought to Salamis more squadrons from the home fleets (Her VIII.42–46), although by no means all, as the various states kept some guard vessels (Her VIII.46), to provide for the contingency of Persian raiding campaigns against their home ports. It is highly likely that at least some non-Athenian Allied squadrons had been mustered intentionally at the south of the Saronic Gulf, at the port of Troezen (Her VIII.42). This state had extremely strong ties with Athens and was ideally situated to intercept any Imperial attempts to link with the medizing Argives (Waters 2014) or any other Imperial incursion nearby. This might, just might have been intended for the Imperial wide flanking move by the 200-ship task force (Hale 2009), dispatched east of Euboea and carrying a total of 8,000 marines. It is unsafe to deduce, since heavy sea traffic between Athens and Troezen had been established to implement the evacuation (Her VIII.41), whether the naval vessels found at Troezen and moved to Salamis were stationed there, or just happened to be calling, while assisting in an evacuation. It is more than a suspicion that the Decree of Troezen had been voted and sanctioned but some of its provisions were not implemented till the last moment, which means that heavy naval traffic was registered in Troezen as in Salamis and the vessels there were not an operational muster but helping with the evacuation, especially of women and children.

The total evacuation, an expensive, unpopular and vastly offensive measure, especially for the landed citizenry (not aristocracy) must have been postponed until the last minute. Many times, whole Greek cities were indeed transplanted in the face of danger (Her I.164 & 168) but this does not mean they liked it or were comfortable with it. They hated the prospect. Thus, the dispatch of the last 53 vessels in Artemisium (Her VIII.14), their last reserves, was an all-out, desperate effort by the Athenians to stop cold or, even better, destroy the Imperial fleet as far away as possible, knowing that this would stop the onslaught of the land force (Tarn 1908). Although hopes for a total victory were overambitious, these vessels were essential for the defensive victory; they allowed the Greek fleet to hold its position and emerge resilient.

Still, if our reading of Herodotus is even partly correct, the massive concentration of force, the call upon most of the last reserves of some states, shows a definite intention of the Greek high command to engage the Persians in Salamis. It was not a settled issue, a final deliberation; but it was a sanctioned possible scenario and the concentration of force made it probable. Whether it would develop or things would revert to the default, meaning falling back to Isthmus, was a matter of conditions and circumstances and up to the board of admirals for implementation.

The position of the Greek fleet at the shores of Salamis, after the experience at Artemisium, was a prominent one. It was within the last practicable straits, which was advantageous for the Greeks; it protected the states of the western Saronic Gulf (Her VIII.60); and it allowed some optimism for surprise attacks on the exposed Persian fleet, assumed to beach at different parts of the southern shore of Attica. But, most importantly, it was an advanced interception position allowing the Greeks to survey and contest any Persian notion of deep, strategic seaborne manoeuvres carrying masses of land troops. If Themistocles had a hidden agenda to keep at least a part of Attica free, so as not to subject the Athenian citizenry to the infamy of becoming refugees, Eurybiadas was very fast to understand the tactical advantages *and* the operational ones. With the Greek fleet in battle array at Salamis, and poised to do the exact thing it was designed for – at least the Athenian vessels – namely the interception of assault convoys, the Persian fleet at Phaleron would be unable to attempt any massive landings anywhere. This 'anywhere' is vague, but included the shores of the Argolid; Corinth, behind the Wall; or Sparta and its backyard Cythera. The latter was suggested to Xerxes by Demaratus, the former king, (Her VII.235), who was inevitably thinking much like the Lacedaimonian government. From Cythera Demaratus might be taking the field against Sparta himself, implementing revenge and also, if he had risen high in the esteem of Xerxes, acquiring leverage to save his townsmen from extermination.

To a considerable extent, this inability of the Imperial fleet (the staff of which somehow was not convinced by the arguments of Lazenby, 1993 to the opposite) to effect deep strategic moves was a result of the massive loss at Artemisium. The loss of merchantmen aggravated the commissariat of the army and compromised its own ability to launch convoys for amphibious assaults. The loss of warships in storm and battle, combined with the threat posed by the Greek presence at an advanced and well-chosen position, made the Imperial admiralty reluctant either to fully compromise the mobility of the triremes by loading them with large landing parties, intended for large-scale seaborne assaults (Fields 2007), or to any further division of forces (Green 1970), at least for operational manoeuvres (Her VII.236,1–2), contrary to its previous practice (Her VIII.7,1). Probably this is the true meaning of the celebrated verses of Pindar, which assigned to Artemisium the foundation of freedom by the Athenians.

Epilogue or Act Two?

Since Xerxes broke through Thermopylae or, to be precise, into Boeotia, his army could trap the Greek fleet by an archery barrage at Euripus. Thus, this line of naval defence was compromised by the deteriorating situation on land. Not *one* Allied voice proposed a naval stand there, after retiring from Artemisium, contrary to previous deliberations and actions, when the Thermopylae position was still holding (Her VII.182 & VIII.4). As the Allied fleet could offer battle to no other location, the Imperial land forces, overrunning the defenceless Euboea, could emerge anywhere and invade through the west, south-west and east coasts of Attica massively, with the assistance of their fleet, thus turning any position meant to defend Attica.

In expeditionary terms, advanced defence was impossible on land. Multiple entry routes were always available and the Persian army was numerous enough to proceed along different entry axes, while the fleet could launch massive landings. Although there are no such accounts, the Imperial staff, with the assistance of the Athenian exiles, must have become privy to the wishes of the landowners, which were to have their fortunes intact. Having once deliberated so, in Marathon, and being exhilarated due to their victory, it was only natural for them to press for such a verdict of valour. But Themistocles was unyielding. He always believed and wanted to decide the issue at sea and there is preciously little indication that the Athenian mass, enlisted and led by him, thought otherwise. Thus, the notion of Themistocles wishing a land campaign in defence of Attica could have never been true. If such nonsense ever existed as a proposal for pursuing the war, it should be attributed to some followers of Aristides, Hoplite landowners with laurels since Marathon.

The defence over the borders with Boeotia was utterly untenable, as no less than five itineraries are crossing to Attica. Thus, the reports of Herodotus of an Athenian instigation for the Allied forces to defend Attica falling on deaf ears (Her VIII.40; Plut Vit Them 9,3) are either later Athenian besmirching attempts against the Peloponnesians or mind-guilt games of Themistocles for later cashing in at any opportunity to extract concessions. The latter suits well the methods and ethics of the great general, but in this case, the verdict favours rather the former. The Decree of Troezen, the traumatic experience at Tempe (not to mention Thermopylae) with the secondary routes and trails and the lack of any reference to such deliberation from the League at Isthmus are all telling. With a massive Imperial fleet nearby and enemies at their rear (from Helots to Argives and Achaeans) the Spartans would have never agreed to considerable troop dispatches north of Isthmus if Thermopylae had fallen (Shimpson 1972). If the Peloponnesian army had already reached Boeotia, as it most probably should have, the fall of Thermopylae by no means meant it was to be automatically diverted to the defence of Attica. It would retreat back to Isthmus.

The Spartans were no naval nation. The Athenians had not been, until recently; at least not to any great extent, and the Persians never were. Still, as far-reaching superpowers at their respective spheres of influence, both the Spartans and the Persians understood the strategic context of the sea and the usefulness of sea power. The Persians had the means to develop and acquire it. The Spartans did not, but had an excellent grasp of tactical and operational issues, despite wanting in technicalities and experience (an exact prequel to the Roman attitude). This is why they had embarked on amphibious operations against Naxos (Plut De Her Mal 21; Grant 1987) and Samos (Her III.54) during the previous century and in amphibious manoeuvres in Argolid (494 BC) and Attica (511 BC) during the last three decades (Her VI.76,2 and V.63,3 respectively), with an overall success rate of 50 per cent in terms of grand strategy and of 100 per cent in terms of technical feasibility and execution. Even if the action at Artemisium is entirely attributed to Themistocles, which is the Athenian wish and notion but not necessarily the truth, the Spartans will prove their tactical and operational grasp of sea power in the battle of Mycale (Her IX.98–9), a year later, and most probably in Salamis too.

The final issue in the sphere of strategy at the time is western Greece. There was no Allied force either available or capable of forestalling a Persian venture there, aimed at gaining access to the back door of the Peloponnese. During the Great Peloponnesian War (431–404 BC), bitter fighting took place in the area (Thuc III.97 & III.114,1). The Spartans, as Dorians, who in centuries past invaded Peloponnese not through the heavily defended Isthmus but by a massive amphibious operation staged in western Greece, with vessels built on the spot (Paus V.3,6, & X.38,10), were too reluctant to allow a replay. The divine and tactical beatings to the Imperial fleet made improbable any large flanking moves to transport land elements across the Gulf of Corinth, especially at that time of the year, and with the reputation of Cape Caphereus in southern Euboea and Cape Maleus in the SE tip of Peloponnese.

Carthaginian fleets from the west were also rather difficult to co-ordinate with the Imperials at the time. But a considerable part of the Peloponnesian shore belonged to openly medizing states. And the northern shore, belonging to Locrians, defeated Phocians – and openly medizing – Boeotians may have had little naval might, but sported a flourishing local commerce with the southern shore across the Gulf of Corinth, and could thus provide a multitude of small craft – the very same used for the evacuation of the Phocian populace after Thermopylae. If a Persian land force was to emerge there, such means were suitable and perhaps enough for the transportation of Imperial divisions to the realm of prospective subjects in north-west Peloponnese, especially if the native, patriotic Peloponnesian land units had been pushed forward in Thermopylae or Boeotia. From the medizing Achaea to the simmering Messene there was only the realm of the unreliable Elis, whose forces did a great job in missing the decisive engagement at Plataea the following year (Her IX.77), despite its prolonged nature.

What then was stopping the Persian army from undertaking such an enterprise? The central routes, up the Spercheios' valley and leading to modern-day Karpenisi, and then south-west to Agrinio and south to Messologi and finally south-south-east to Naupactus or Antirio (**Map**), actually through ancient Aetolia, were difficult and ill-supplied to support large invasion forces and possibly tricky should any local resistance have been inspired by the action at Thermopylae. This option was taken by Brennus in 279 BC to unlock Thermopylae (Paus X.22,2–3) and succeeded in doing so; but with horrific losses. Once Thermopylae fell and the Persian army was fuelled up by the supplies carried by the fleet, a route easier to negotiate, towards the northern shore of the Gulf of Corinth, became accessible, either through Delphi or through Thebes, as discussed previously. A route miraculously shut by God and Man at Delphi.

Bibliography

Ancient (re)sources

Homer The Iliad

Homer Odyssey

Hesiod Ehoiai

Alcaeus fr 357 (Armory)

Alcaeus fr 350

Herodotus *Mousae*

Thucydides *Histories*

Andocides Orations

Aristophanes Birds

Xenophon *Anabasis*

Xenophon *Hellenika*

Xenophon *Cyropaedeia*

Xenophon *Lacedaimonion Politeia*

Xenophon *Agesilaus*

Xenophon *Hipparchikos*

Xenophon On Horsemanship

Plato Laws

Plato Dialogues (*Menexenus* & *Laches*)

Demosthenes Orations

Aeschines Orations

Aristotle *Athinaion Politeia*

Aristotle *Politika*

Hellenica Oxyrhynchia

Q Curtius Rufus *Historiae Alexandri Magni*

Hyginus Gromaticus De Munitionibus
    Castrorum

Diodorus Sicilus *Bibliotheke Historike*

Pausanias *Hellados Periegesis/Graecae descriptio*

Plutarch *Vitae*

Plutarch *De Gloria Atheniensium*

Plutarch *De Herodoti Malignitate*

Plutarch Moralia/*Apophthegmata Laconica*

Plutarch Moralia/ *Regum et Imperatorum
    Apophthegmata*

Pollux *Onomasticon*

Clement of Alexandria *Stromateis*

Justin *Epitome*

Nepos *De Viris Illustribus*

Frontinus *Strategemata*

Polyaenus *Strategemata*

Livy *Ab urbe condita libri*

Strabo *Geographica*

Dionysius of Halicarnassus *Antiquitates
    Romanae*

Polybius *Histories*

Tzetzes I *Chiliades*

Book of Ezra/ The Holy Bible/The Old
    Testament

Book of Esther/ The Holy Bible/The Old
    Testament

Modern Scholarship

Abdi K. 2007. The 'Daivā' Inscription Revisited. Nāme-ye Irān-e Bāstān 6(1&2): 45–74.

Adcock F.E. 1957. The Greek and Macedonian Art of War. University of California Press, Berkeley.

Anderson J.K. 1991. Hoplite weapons and offensive arms. In Hanson V.D. (Ed) Hoplites: The Classical Greek battle experience. Routledge NY 2003, pp 15–37.

Badian E. 1993. From Plataea to Potidaea. The Johns Hopkins University Press Charles Village.

Barkworth P.R. 1993. The organization of Xerxes' army. *Iranica antiqua* 27: 149–167.

Benaissa A. 2018. Donysius the epic Fragments, Cambridge University Press.

Berthold R.M. 1976. Which way to Marathon? *Revue des Etudes Anciennes* 78–79 (1–4): 84–95.

Blair C. 1996. Hitler's U-Boat War: The Hunters, 1939–1942. Modern Library, New York.

Bodzek J. 2014. Achaemenid Asia Minor: Coins of the Satraps and of the Great King", In: First International Congress of the Anatolian Monetary History and Numismatics 25–28 February 2013, Antalya, Proceedings, pp. 59–78.

Bonaparte N. 1830. Maximes de Guerre 104 Paris.

Bonner R.J. 1910. The Boeotian Federal Constitution. *Classical Philology* 5(4): 405–417.

Boteva D. 2011. Re-Reading Herodotus On The Persian Campaigns In Thrace. In: Rollinger R. Truschnegg B. Bichler R. (Eds) Herodotus and the Persian Empire. Wiesbaden, 735–759.

Boyce M. 1983. '*Aməša Spənta*', *Encyclopaedia Iranica, 1, Routledge New York*.

Bradford A.S. 2001. With arrow, sword and spear. Greenwood PG CT

Bradford E. 1980. Year Of Thermopylae. Macmillan New York.

Brown D. 1977. *WWII Fact Files: Aircraft Carriers*. Arco Publishing New York.

Bryan E. 2013. The Turtle Ship. *Military History Monthly* 34. Accessed 8 Jul 2020 from https://www.military-history.org/articles/wmd-the-turtle-ship.

Buck R.J. 1972. The Formation of the Boeotian League. *Classical Philology*, 67(2): 94–101.

Bugh G.R. 1988. The Horsemen of Athens. Princeton University Press Princeton.

Burn A.R. 1962. Persia and The Greeks the Defense of the West, c.546–478 B.C. St Martin's Press New York.

Campbell D.B. 2012. Spartan warrior 735–331 BC. Osprey Warrior 163 Oxford.

Carmichael C.M. 2009. Managing munificence. *Historical Methods* 42(3): 83–96.

Cartledge P. 2006. Thermopylae: the battle that changed the world. Macmillan New York.

Charles M.B. 2011. Immortals And Apple Bearers: Towards A Better Understanding Of Achaemenid Infantry Units. *The Classical Quarterly* 61(1): 114–33.

Charles M.B. 2012. Herodotus, Body Armour And Achaemenid Infantry. *Histroria* 61(3):257–69.

Charles M.B. 2015. Achaemenid elite cavalry: from Xerxes to Darius III. *The Classical Quarterly* 65(1): 14–34.

Cilliers L. 1991. Menelaus' 'Unnecessary Baseness Of Character' In Euripides' "Orestes". *Acta Classica* 34: 21–31.

Cole M. 2019. The Sparta Fetish Is a Cultural Cancer. The New Republic.

Connolly P. 1981. Greece and Rome at War. Greenhill Books London.

de la Graviere J. 1885. La Marine des Anciens: La Bataille de Salamine Et l'Expédition de Sicile. Plon & cie Paris.

Delbrück H. 1920. History of the Art of War. University of Nebraska Press 1990.

Deligiannis P. 2014. The battle of Cumae, Italy (524 BC) https://periklisdeligiannis.wordpress.com/2014/06/04/the-battle-of-cumae-italy-524-bc/

DeRosa C.S. 2006. Political Indoctrination in the U.S. Army from World War II to the Vietnam War. University of Nebraska Press.

de Souza P. 2003. The Greek and Persian Wars 499–386 BC. *Osprey Essential Histories* 36 Oxford.

Dezső T. 2012. The Assyrian Army Eotvos University Press, Budapest.

Dickins G. 1912. The Growth of Spartan Policy. JHS 32: 1–42.

Elliott-Bateman M. 1968. Defeat in the East: The Mark of Mae Tse-Tung on War. Oxford UP.

Emanuel J.P. 2012. Race in Armor, Race with Shields: The Origin and Devolution of the Hoplitodromos. In University of Pennsylvania Center for Ancient Studies Conference 'Crowned Victor: Competition and Games in the Ancient World'. Philadelphia.

Encyclopaedia Britannica https://www.britannica.com/biography/Peisistratus

Encyclopaedia Britannica Vol 13 Herodotus.

Encyclopaedia Britannica https://www.britannica.com/biography/Akhenaten

Engels D. 1985. The Length of Eratosthenes' Stade. *American Journal of Philology* 106 (3): 298–311.

Epps P.H. 1933. Fear in Spartan Character. Classical. *Philology* 28(1): 12–29.

Evangelista M.A. 1983. Stalin's postwar army reappraised. *International Security* 7: 110–38.

Evans J.A.S. 1968. Father of History or Father of Lies; The Reputation of Herodotus. *The Classical Journal* 64(1): 11–17.

Farahmand A. 2015. Darius the Great Zoroastrian versus Cyrus the Emperor. https://authenticgathazoroastrianism.org/2015/04/06/darius-the-great-zoroastrian-and-cyrus-the-emperor/

Ferrill A. 1966. Herodotus and the Strategy and Tactics of the Invasion of Xerxes. *The American Historical Review* 72(1): 102–115.

Fields N. 1994. The anatomy of a mercenary. PhD Dissertation, University of Newcastle-upon-Tyne.

Fields N. 2007. Thermopylae 480 BC Osprey Campaign 188 Oxford.

Fields N. 2007. Ancient Greek warships 500–322 BC. *Osprey New Vanguard* 132 Oxford.

Fields N. 2013. The Spartan way. Pen & Sword Military Barnsley.

Flower M.A. 1998. Simonides, Ephorus, and Herodotus on the Battle of Thermopylae, *The Classical Quarterly*, New Series, 48(2): 365–379.

Forrest W.G. 1968. A History of Sparta. Bloomsbury Publishing Pl, London 1995.

Gaebel R.E. 2004. Cavalry Operations in the Ancient Greek World. University of Oklahoma Press.

García-Sánchez M. 2014. The Second after the King and Achaemenid Bactria on Classical Sources. In: Antela-Bernárdez B. Vidal-Palomino J. (Eds) Central Asia in Antiquity. *Interdisciplinary Approaches*, BAR International Series 2665, Oxford, p. 53–63.

Garrison M.B. 2007. By the favor of Ahuramazda. In: Iossif P.P. Chankowski A.S. Lorber C.C. (Eds) More than men, less than Gods. Peeters Leuven.

Gertoux G. 2018. Dating the Reigns of Xerxes and Artaxerxes. Orbis Biblicus et Orientalis Series. *Archaeologica* 40:179–206.

Gertroux G. 2016. Queen Esther Wife Of Xerxes: Historical And Archaeological Evidence. lulu.com

Goldsworthy A.K. 1997. The 'Othismos', Myths and Heresies: The Nature of Hoplite Battle. *War in History* 4(1):1–26.

Grant P. 2012. From Minnow to Leviathan: Transformation of the Athenian Navy (499–480 BC). Drumspeak: *International Journal of Research in the Humanities*. NS 4: 267–298.

Green P. 1970. The year of Salamis 480–479 BC. Weidenfeld & Nicolson London.

Haas C.J. 1985. Athenian naval power before Themistocles. Historia 34(1): 29–46.

Hale J.R. 2009. Lords of the Sea: The Epic Story of the Athenian Navy and the Birth of Democracy. Penguin New York.

Hammond N.G.L. 1996. Sparta at Thermopylae. JSTOR *Historia* 45(1): 1–20.

Hammond N.G.L. 1968. The Campaign and the Battle of Marathon. *JHS* 88: 13–57.

Hanson V.D. 1983. Warfare and Agriculture in Classical Greece. University of California Press.

Hanson V.D. 1989. The Western Way of War. A.A. Knopf NY

Hanson V.D. 1999. The Wars of the Ancient Greeks. Cassell London.

Hanson V.D. 1991. Hoplite technology in phalanx battle. In Hanson V.D. (Ed) Hoplites: The Classical Greek Battle Experience. Routledge NY 2003, pp 63–85.

Haubold J. 2012. The Achaemenid empire and the sea. *Mediterranean Historical Review* 27(1): 4–23.

Heliopoulos G.Z. 2020. The Chimerae of War. Bartzoulianos Athens [In Greek].

Henkelman W. 2011a. Herodotus and the Persian Empire. In: Rollinger R. Truschnegg B. Bichler R. (Eds) Herodotus and the Persian Empire. Harrassowitz-Verlag Wiesbaden.

Henkelman W. 2011b. Herodotus and Babylon Reconsidered. In: Rollinger R. Truschnegg B. Bichler R. (Eds) Herodotus and the Persian Empire. Harrassowitz-Verlag Wiesbaden.

Herzfeld E. 1932. A New Inscription of Xerxes from Persepolis (Studies in Ancient Oriental Civilization 5). The University of Chicago Press Chicago.

Hignett C. 1963. Xerxes invasion of Greece. Clarendon Press, Wotton-under-Edge

Hodkinson S. 2006. Was classical Sparta a military society? In: Hodkinson S. Powell A. Christien J. (Eds) Sparta and War. Classical Press of Wales Swansea.

Holland T. 2005. Persian fire. Doubleday New York.

Holoka J.P. 1999. Marathon and the myth of the same-day march. GRBS 38:329–353

Humble R. 1980. Warfare in the Ancient World. Book Club Associates London

Hyland J. 2018. Hystaspes, Gobryas, and elite marriage politics in Teispid Persia. *DABJR* 5: 30–36.

Jameson M.H. 1960. A decree of Themistocles from Troezen. Hesperia 29: 198–223.

Kambouris M.E. 2022. The Rise of Persia. Pen & Sword Books.

Kambouris M.E. and Bakas S. 2017. Gaugamela 331 BC: the triumph of tactics. *Archaeology and Science* 13: 17–33.

Kambouris M.E. et al 2019. The Hypaspist Corps: Evolution and Status of the Elite Macedonian Infantry Unit. *Archaeology and Science* 15: 19–30.

Kambouris M.E. et al 2015a. Greco-Macedonian Influences in the Manipular Legion System. *Archaeology and Science* 11: 145–154.

Kambouris M.E. et al 2015b. Thermopylae Revisited. *Archaeology and Science* 11: 127–44.

Kambouris M.E. 2008. Warriors of Ancient Greece Vol I. Alkalio Athens [In Greek]

Kambouris M.E. 2000. Ancient Greek Warriors. Communications SA Athens [In Greek].

Karber P.A. and Combs J.A. 1998. The United States, NATO, and the Soviet Threat to Western Europe: Military Estimates and Policy Options, 1945–1963. *Diplomatic History* 22(3): 399–429.

Klotz D. 2015. Persian Period. In: Grajetzki W. and Wendrich W. (Eds) UCLA Encyclopedia of Egyptology, UCLA, Los Angeles.

Krentz P. 1985. The Nature of Hoplite Battle. *Classical Antiquity* 4(1): 50–61.

Krentz P. 2002. Fighting by the Rules: The Invention of the Hoplite Agôn. *Hesperia: The Journal of the American School of Classical Studies at Athens* 71(1): 23–39.

Kuhrt A. 1997. The Ancient Near East: c.3000–330 BC. Routledge New York.

Kuhrt A. 2001. The Achaemenid Persian empire (c. 550–330). In: Alcock S.E. D' Altroy T.N. Morrison K.D. and Sinopoli C.M. (Eds) *Empires*: Perspectives from Archaeology and History, Cambridge University Press.

Kuhrt A. 2007. The Problem of Achaemenid Religious Policy. In: Groneberg B. and Spieckermann H. (Eds) Die Welt der Götterbilder. De Gruyter Berlin.

Kuhrt A. 2014. State Communications in the Persian Empire. In: Radner K. (Ed) State Correspondence in the Ancient World. Oxford University Press.

Kuhrt A. 2015. Can we understand how the Persians perceived 'other' gods / 'the gods of others'? De Gruyter Berlin.

Lazaridis D. 1978. The interior of Aegean Thrace. *Ekistics* 45(271):279–282.

Lazenby J.F. 1987. The Diekplous. *Greece & Rome* 34(2): 169–77.

Lazenby J.F. 1989. Hoplite Warfare. In: Hackett J. (Ed) Warfare in the ancient world. Sidgwick & Jackson Ltd London.

Lazenby J.F. 1993. The defense of Greece. Aris & Phillips Oxford.

Lazenby J.F. and Whitehead D. 1996. The myth of the Hoplite's hoplon. *The Classical Quarterly* 46(1): 27–33.

Lewis D.M. 1980. Datis the Mede. *JHS* 100: 194–195.

Llewellyn-Jones L. 2012. King and court in ancient Persia 559–331 BCE. Edinburgh University Press.

Llewellyn-Jones L. 2017. The Achaemenid Empire. T. Daryaee (Ed) King Of The Seven Climes. Samuel Jordan Center of Persian Studies, UCI, Irvine.

Llewellyn-Jones L. and Robson J. 2009. Ctesias' 'History of Persia': Tales of the Orient. Routledge London.

Luginbill R.D. 1994. Othismos: The Importance of the Mass-Shove in Hoplite Warfare. *Phoenix* 48(1): 51–61.

Malye J. 2007. La veritable histoire de Sparte et la bataille des Thermopyles. Les Belles Lettres Paris.

Matthew C.A. 2012. A Storm of spears. Pen & Sword Military Barnsley.

Matthew C.A. 2013a. Towards the Hot Gates. In: Matthew C.A. and Trundle M. (Eds) After the gates of fire. Pen & Sword Military Barnsley.

Matthew C.A. 2013b Was the Greek Defence of Thermopylae in 480 BC a Suicide Mission? In: Matthew C.A . and Trundle M. (Eds) After the gates of fire. Pen & Sword Military Barnsley.

Maurice F. 1930. The Size of the Army of Xerxes in the Invasion of Greece 480 B.C. *JHS* 50(2): 210–235.

Meijer F. 1986. A History of Seafaring in the Classical World. Routledge Revivals New York 2014.

Miller M. 2004. Athens and Persia in the Fifth Century BC: A Study in Cultural Receptivity. Cambridge University Press, Cambridge.

Monerie J. 2019. Invading Mesopotamia, from Alexander the Great to Antiochus VII. In: Da Riva R, Lang M, Fink S (Eds) Routes and Travellers between East and West. Zaphon, Münster pp 155-86.

Montagu J.D. 2000. Battles of the Greek and Roman worlds. Greenhill Books London.

Montagu J.D. 2006. Greek and Roman warfare. Greenhill Books London.

Morris D.R. 1965. The Washing of the Spears: A History of the Rise of the Zulu Nation Under Shaka and Its Fall in the Zulu War of 1879. Simon and Schuster New York.

Morrison J.S. and Coates J.F. 2000. The Athenian trireme: Reconstruction of an ancient Greek warship. 2nd Ed. CUP Cambridge.

Mumford G. 2019. Lecture 28: Dynasty 27 Persian Empire in Egypt Anth. 310: Imperial and Post Imperial Egypt, ca. 1550–332 BCE, Department of Anthropology. Birmingham: The University of Alabama at Birmingham.

Munro J.A.R. 1902. Some observations on the Persian wars 2. The Campaign of Xerxes. *JHS* 22: 294–332.

Nefedkin A.K. 2014. Once More on the Origin of Scythed Chariot. *AHB* 28(3–4): 112–8.

Nelopoulos E.D. 1999. The Greek Trireme. Floros, Athens (In Greek).

Nilsson M.P. 1929. The Introduction of Hoplite Tactics at Rome: Its Date and Its Consequences. *Journal of Roman Studies* 19, 1–11.

Ossendrijver M. 2018. Babylonian scholarship and the calendar during the reign of Xerxes. In: C. Waerzeggers, M. Seire (Eds) Xerxes and Babylonia. The Cuneiform Evidence. *Peeters* Leuven.

Pagliaro A. 1943. Fortuna di parole iraniche in occidente. *Asiatica* 9: 36–42.

Pagliaro A. 1954. Riflessi di etimologie iraniche nella tradizione storiografica greca. Rendiconti dell'Accademia Nazionale dei Lincei. Classe di Scienze morali, storiche e filologiche, 8th series, 9: 133–53.

Potts D.T. 2005. Cyrus the Great and the Kingdom of Anshan, in: Sarkhosh Curtis V. and Stewart S. (Eds) Birth of the Persian Empire. I B Tauris London.

Potts S. 2008. The Athenian Navy. PhD Dissertation, Cardiff University ProQuest LLC.

Pritchett W.K. 1957. New Light on Plataia. *AJA* 61(1): 9–28.

Pritchett W.K. 1958. New Light on Thermopylae. *AJA* 62(2): 203–13.

Raaflaub K.A. 2013. Early Greek Infantry Fighting in a Mediterranean Context. In: Kagan D. Viggiano G.F. (Eds) Men of Bronze: Hoplite Warfare in Ancient Greece. Princeton University Press Princeton.

Rados C.N. 1915. La bataille de Salamine. Fontemoing Paris.

Rankov B. 2017. Ancient Naval Warfare, 700 BC–AD 600 In: Whitby M. Sidebottom H. (Eds) The encyclopedia of Ancient battles. John Wiley & Sons Ltd Hoboken.

Ray F.E. 2009. Land battles in 5th century B.C. Greece. McFarland & Company Inc Jefferson.

Recaldin J. 2011. What Was The Main Purpose Of The Ephebeia? MA Dissertation School of Archaeology and Ancient History University of Leicester.

Rey F.E. 2011. Taktike Techne: the neglected element in classical Hoplite battles. *Ancient Society* 41, 45–82.

Ridley R.T. 2007. The Hoplite as Citizen : Athenian military Institutions in their social context. In: Wheeler E.L. (Ed) The Armies of Classical Greece. Ashgate Farnham.

Roisman J. 2017. The Classical Art of Command. Oxford University Press.

Rollinger and Ulf (Eds) 2004. Commerce and Monetary Systems in the Ancient World, Franz Steiner Verlag.

Rookhuijzen J.Z. 2019. Herodotus and the Topography of Xerxes' Invasion. De Gruyter Berlin.

Rupp G. 2013. The Topography of the Pass at Thermopylae Circa 480 BC. In: Matthew C.A. and Trundle M. (Eds) After the gates of fire. Pen & Sword Military Barnsley.

Sage M.M. 1996. Warfare in ancient Greece: A sourcebook. Routledge London.

Samuels M. 1997. Alexander the Great and Manoeuvre War. Available at: https://www.academia.edu/15306853/Alexander_the_Great_and_Manoeuvre_War

Sarantis T.H. 1975. Alexander the Great. Alkyon Athens (in Greek).

Sealey R. 1976. A History of the Greek City States, 700–338 B.C. University California Press, Berkeley.

Sears M.A. 2019. Understanding Greek Warfare. Routledge, London.

Sears M.A. and Willekes C. 2016. Alexander's Cavalry Charge at Chaeronea, 338 BCE. *JMH* 80: 1017–1035.

Seevers B. 2013. Warfare in the Old Testament: The Organization, Weapons, and Tactics of Ancient Near Eastern Armies. Kregel Academic, Grand Rapids.

Sekunda N. and Chew S. 1992. The Persian Army 560–330 BC. Osprey Elite 42 Oxford.

Sekunda N. and Northwood S. 1995. Early Roman Armies. Osprey Men-at-Arms 283 Oxford.

Sekunda N. 1986. The Ancient Greeks. Osprey Elite 7 Oxford.

Sekunda N. 1989. The Persians. In: Hackett J. (Ed) Warfare in the ancient world. Sidgwick & Jackson Ltd London.

Sekunda N. 1998. The Spartan Army. Osprey Elite 66 Oxford.

Sekunda N. 2000. The Greek Hoplite. Osprey Warrior 27 Oxford.

Sekunda N. 2002. Marathon, 490 BC: The first Persian invasion of Greece. Osprey Campaign 108 Oxford.

Shepherd W. 2010. Salamis 480 BC. Osprey Campaign 222 Oxford.

Shepherd W. 2012 Plataea 479 BC. Osprey Campaign 239 Oxford.

Shimpson R.H. 1972. Leonidas' decision. *Phoenix* 26(1): 1–11.

Sidebotham S. 1982. Herodotus on Artemisium. *The Classical World*. 75(3): 177–186.

Snodgrass A.A. 1965. The Hoplite revolution and History. *JHS* 85: 110–22.

Snodgrass A.M. 1967. Arms and Armour of the Greeks. Cornell University Press (Ithaca, NY).

Soudavar A. 2012, Astyages, Cyrus And Zoroaster: solving a historical dilemma. *IRAN* 50:45–78.

Spence I.G. 1993. The Cavalry of Classical Greece. Clarendon Press, Wotton-under-Edge.

Stein G.J. 2014. Persians on the Euphrates? In: Kozuh M., Henkelman W.F.M., Jones C.E. and Woods C. (Eds) Extraction and Control. The Oriental Institute of the University of Chicago.

Sternberg E. 2005. Classical Precariousness vs. Modern Risk: Lessons in Prudence from the Battle of Salamis. *Humanitas* 18(1&2): 141–63.

Strauss B. 2017. War and Battle in the Greek World, 800–168 BC. In: Whitby M., Sidebottom H. (Eds) The encyclopedia of Ancient battles. John Wiley & Sons Ltd Hoboken.

Strauss B. 2008. Battle. In: Sabin P., van Wees H. and Whirby M. (Eds) The Cambridge History of Greek and Roman Warfare Vol I. Cambridge University Press, 2008, pp 223–47.

Suda Lexicon, Letter X, 10th Century AD.

Sweet W.E. 1987. Sport and Recreation in Ancient Greece: A Sourcebook with Translations. Oxford University Press.

Tarn W.W. 1908. The Fleet of Xerxes. *JHS* 28: 202–233

Tarn W.W. 1948. Alexander the Great, vol. 2, Sources and Studies. Cambridge University Press.

Trundle M. 2013. Thermopylae. In: Matthew C.A. and Trundle M. (Eds) After the gates of fire. Pen & Sword Military Barnsley.

Tuplin C. 2017. War and Peace in Achaemenid Imperial Ideology. *Electrum* 24: 31–54.

van der Spek R.J. 2014. Cyrus the Great exiles and foreign gods? In: Kozuh M., Henkelman W.F.M., Jones C.E. and Woods C. (Eds) Extraction and Control. The Oriental Institute of the University of Chicago.

van Wees H. 2004. Greek Warfare: Myths and Realities. Gerald Duckworth, London.

van Wees H. 2013. Ships and silver, taxes and tribute. I.B. Tauris, London

Waerzeggers C. 2018. Debating Xerxes' Rule In Babylonia. In: Waerzeggers C., Seire M. (Eds) Xerxes and Babylonia: The Cuneiform Evidence. *Peeters* Leuven.

Ward C. 2012. Building pharaoh's ships: Cedar, incense and sailing the Great Green. British Museum Studies in Ancient Egypt and Sudan 18: 217–32.

Warry J. 1980. Warfare in the classical world. Salamander London.

Waterfield R. 2006. Xenophon's Retreat: Greece, Persia, and the End of the Golden Age. Belknap Press of Harvard University Press Cambridge.

Waters M. 2011. Parsumas, Ansan and Cyris. In: Álvarez-Mon J. and Garrison M.B. (Eds) Elam and Persia. Eisenbrauns Winona Lake.

Waters M. 2014a. Darius the first, the ninth king. In: Daryaee T., Mushavi A. and Rehakhani K. (Eds) Excavating an Empire. Mazda Publishers, Costa Mesa.

Waters M.W. 2014b. Earth, water and friendship with the king. In: Kozuh M., Henkelman W., Jones W.C., Woods C. (Eds) Extraction & Control. The Oriental Institute of the University of Chicago.

Waters M. 2004. Cyrus And The Achaemenids. *Journal Of Persian Studies* 42: 91–102.

Waugh R.L. Jr 1995. The Eye and Man in Ancient Egypt. Kugler Publications Amsterdam.

Whitehead I. 1987. The Periplous. *Greece & Rome* 34(2): 178–85.

Wijnsma U.Z .2019. 'And in the fourth year Egypt rebelled …' The Chronology of and Sources for Egypt's Second Revolt (ca. 487–484 BC). *Journal of Ancient History* 7(1): 32–61.

Wilson A .2005. An Analysis of the Possible Routes of Xerxes and the Persian Army from Cappadocia to Phrygia in Herodotus' Histories 7.26. EES 24, Furman University Greenville.

Wood A.K. 2013. Warships of the ancient world, Osprey New Vanguard 196 Oxford.

Index